Studies in Celtic History II

CELTIC BRITAIN IN THE EARLY MIDDLE AGES

STUDIES IN CELTIC HISTORY
General editor David Dumville

Already published
I · THE SAINTS OF GWYNEDD
Molly Miller

In preparation
III · THE INSULAR LATIN GRAMMARIANS
Vivien Law
IV · GILDAS IN THE MIDDLE AGES
David Dumville
V · NAVIGATIO SANCTI BRENDANI
Giovanni Orlandi

CELTIC BRITAIN IN THE EARLY MIDDLE AGES

Studies in Scottish and Welsh sources

by

the late

KATHLEEN HUGHES

(edited by David Dumville)

THE BOYDELL PRESS · ROWMAN & LITTLEFIELD

26244

First published by
The Boydell Press
an imprint of Boydell & Brewer Ltd
PO Box 9, Woodbridge, Suffolk IP12 3DF
and
Rowman & Littlefield
81 Adams Drive, Totowa, New Jersey 07512, USA

British Library Cataloguing in Publication Data

Hughes, Kathleen
    Celtic Britain in the Early Middle Ages. –
    (Studies in Celtic history).
    1. Civilization, Celtic – Sources
    2. Great Britain – Civilization – To 1066 –
    Sources
    I. Title
    941'.004'916   DA140   80-49940

ISBN 0-85115-127-2

US ISBN 0 8476 6771 5

Photoset in Great Britain by
Rowland Phototypesetting Ltd,
Bury St Edmunds, Suffolk
and printed by St Edmundsbury Press
Bury St Edmunds, Suffolk

Contents

List of illustrations   *vi*
General Editor's Preface   *vii*
Foreword and acknowledgments   *viii*

SCOTLAND

I   Where are the writings of early Scotland?   1
II   The Book of Deer (Cambridge University Library MS. Ii.6.32)   22
III   Early christianity in Pictland   38

WALES

IV   British Library MS. Cotton Vespasian A.xiv (*Vitae Sanctorum*
      Wallensium): its purpose and provenance   53
V   The Welsh Latin chronicles: *Annales Cambriae* and
      related texts   67
VI   The A-text of *Annales Cambriae*   86
      Bibliography   101
      Index of manuscripts   113
      Index   115

List of Illustrations

Plates (between pp. 34 and 35)

    I   Book of Deer, fos 29ᵛ– 30ʳ (two-thirds actual size). Picture of Luke and opening of Gospel.

  II *Above:* Book of Deer, fo 41ᵛ (actual size but upper and lower margins reduced). Picture of John.
      Below: Last few lines of fo 51ᵛ (actual size) showing arabesque.

 III *Above:* Book of Deer, fo 4ᵛ (actual size but upper and lower margins reduced). Picture of Matthew. The later Gaelic *notitiae* are written into the space around the picture.
      Below: Lower margin of fo 54ᵛ.

 IV Cross of the Scriptures, Clonmacnoise, north side, panel 3.
      (Photograph by Professor D. H. Greene.)

Figures (pp. 29–34)

1.   Picture of St Mark from the Lichfield Gospels.
2.   Upright cross-slab in relief, Elgin, front face (after Allen and Anderson)
3.   Detail from carved stone at Aldbar (after Allen and Anderson)
      Below: Book of Deer, fo 84ᵛ (actual size).
4.   David and Goliath from the Cotton Psalter.

General Editor's Preface

Encouraged by the enthusiastic reception given to *Studies in Celtic History* and to its first volume we offer a book of a rather different character, though in content by no means wholly unrelated to its predecessor. Planning for future volumes is well advanced, and it is now hoped to maintain regular publication at the rate of two volumes each year.

From the response of individual scholars to the announcement of the series, our initial impression has been confirmed that there exists a clear need for publication-outlets for Celtic historical work of short monograph size. To date, three different types of volume are planned: straightforward monographs; collections of papers, usually by a single author, whose publication would consolidate or clearly advance a scholarly position and be of considerable assistance for teaching purposes; and revised translations of classic works whose original language has proved to be a bar to their dissemination and use.

The present volume represents a deliberate selection of six papers written by a scholar of major standing in the field of mediaeval Celtic history. Three of these are published here for the first time. The death in 1977 of Kathleen Hughes at the age of fifty was a considerable blow to a field of study which she had made her own, and a grievous personal loss to her colleagues and pupils (among whom the general editor is grateful to number himself). A collection of papers such as this bears witness to her closeness to primary sources, to her ability to make a compelling synthesis from a wide range of evidence or to execute a detailed and sensitive study of a manuscript or a text – in short, to her critical standards of scholarly enquiry.

The general editor takes considerable pride in being able to offer papers of this quality as a volume of *Studies in Celtic History*. In so doing he wishes to reaffirm his previous expression of the very greatest interest in publishing both studies of primary sources and investigations employing new methods of exploitation of sources in the service of historiography.

David Dumville
Girton College, Cambridge

Foreword and Acknowledgments

The papers in this volume were written over a period of twenty years. They are all studies of primary sources for the early mediaeval history of Britain, and in particular Celtic Britain. Three of these papers have been published before; three have not. They have diverse origins and a word of explanation is called for about the circumstances which bring them together here.

Chapters I and II were delivered as the Hunter Marshall Lectures for 1977 in the University of Glasgow, a short while before Dr Hughes's death. It proved impracticable for the University to publish these lectures as a separate volume, but they have found a happy dwelling within the present work. This book is published, however, with generous financial assistance from the University of Glasgow, funding which has helped especially in the reproduction of the illustrations which accompany chapter II. The editor and the publishers wish to thank the University of Glasgow, and in particular its David W. Hunter Marshall fund, which provides for the lectures given under that name, and its Edwards fund which supports the study of palaeography. In addition, the editor would like to acknowledge with gratitude the help of Professor A. A. M. Duncan, Dr R. D. McKitterick, Miss P. McNulty, Professor D. Whitelock, and Professor J. E. C. Williams.

Anticipating separate publication of these lectures, Dr Hughes had written a preface (dated 24 March, 1977) which I reproduce in full below. She had given to the work the title 'Two approaches to early Scottish history'.

> The first of these lectures takes a question of fundamental importance to Scottish historians and examines a wide range of evidence in an attempt to answer it. The second looks in detail at one manuscript to see what history it will give up.
>
> I am indebted to a number of scholars: to Dr David Dumville, who read and criticised both lectures; to Mrs Anderson, Professor Donaldson, and Professor Stones who provided helpful comments on the first lecture and to Mr Nicolas Allen who saved me time by giving me bibliography on the seventeenth and eighteenth centuries. I first thought of examining the Book of Deer in conversation with Dr Henry Mayr-Harting, and Professor Julian Brown very kindly examined the manuscript with me and read the draft of this second lecture. I have incorporated most of the suggestions I received from these scholars, but of course they are not responsible for errors, or for the views I have expressed.
>
> I reproduce the photographs of the Book of Deer with the permission of the Syndics of Cambridge University Library. I thank Professor David H. Greene of New York University for his photograph of the panel from the Cross of the Scriptures (Plate IV). Figures 1 and 3 were drawn by Miss Caroline Page.

Chapter III completes the Scottish half of the book. Like chapters I and II, it was first given as a lecture, at Jarrow in 1970. It is reproduced here with the consent of the Rector of Jarrow; I have lightly revised it to remove a few minor errors, some of which had been noted in Dr Hughes's own copy, and to bring references in the footnotes up to date.

Chapter IV, which appears here with the consent of the Syndics of the Cambridge University Press, is the oldest of these papers. It remains the only substantial study of this important collection of Welsh saints' Lives; here, my revision has of necessity been more thorough than in chapter III. Some additional notes for which I am responsible have been printed within square brackets.

Chapters V and VI deal with the mediaeval Welsh annals. The former was first given as a British Academy lecture in 1973, and is reproduced here with the consent of the President and Fellows of that body. That survey of the texts is in part based on a thorough study of the earliest surviving text of *Annales Cambriae* which was written up by Dr Hughes but never published; it was discovered among her papers in the summer of 1977. Where the footnotes of the British Academy lecture gave details which are embodied in the more specialist paper, I have deleted them from chapter V, substituting cross-references to the detailed discussions in chapter VI. Most footnotes in chapter VI are editorial, for Dr Hughes's manuscript lacked such documentation; their provision has, however, been a mechanical task, for the text leaves one in no doubt as to the items requiring to be recorded in the notes. Among the notes any occasional excursus which I have deemed necessary to help the reader is printed within square brackets.

In short, these six essays ask fundamental questions of the major source-materials for early mediaeval Scottish and Welsh history: they are important papers in respect of both source-criticism and historical analysis. That they do so clearly and straightforwardly, in Dr Hughes's characteristic fashion, adds considerably to their value.

This volume contains Kathleen Hughes's main writings on early mediaeval Celtic Britain. Two other, related volumes will be published in 1981 and 1982 by the Cambridge University Press: a collection (*Early Mediaeval Ireland*) of Dr Hughes's papers on Irish history, edited by me; and a memorial volume (*Ireland in Early Mediaeval Europe*), edited by a team led by Professor Dorothy Whitelock, which contains essays by sixteen scholars on another theme close to Dr Hughes's heart – the interaction of Irish and non-Irish cultures in the early middle ages.

D.N.D.

June 1980

I

Where are the writings of early Scotland?

The written materials from which we have to construct the early history of Scotland – I mean the history before the eleventh century – are very few. There are references in Irish and English sources: an Iona chronicle which was contemporary from the later seventh century and which went down to 741 has been incorporated into the Irish annals.[1] The Life of Columba written by Adomnán between 688 and 704 has survived;[2] so has a tract called *Senchus Fer nAlban* which deals with the genealogy of the kings of Dál Riata, its divisions and expeditionary strength on land and sea.[3] Scottish and Pictish king-lists exist in various recensions.[4] To these sources we must add the account of the Convention of Druim Cett (which discussed the position of Irish Dál Riata),[5] the eleventh-century poem on the kings of Scotland (*Duan Albanach*), and the Book of Deer. The questions immediately arise: 'Why have so few written sources of early Scottish history survived? What happened to them? What sources once existed?' I shall first discuss some theories put forward to explain their absence, and then offer some considerations of my own.

One theory proposed to explain why the sources are so few is that they were deliberately destroyed, and one of the most obvious candidates as a destroyer of manuscripts is the reforming group during the years 1559 and 1560; 'this promiscuous burning of religious houses, with the registers and libraries of churches' as Thomas Innes writing in 1729 called it,[6] a view which was repeated in a modified form by David McRoberts in 1959, who sums up the destruction of 'archives, manuscripts and printed books' which took place then.[7] Some of our best evidence for this claim comes from John Spottiswoode, in his *History of the Church of Scotland* published in 1655.[8] There is absolutely no doubt that the reformers attacked what they termed 'the monuments of idolatry', 'idolis and imagis and tabernaculis and . . . altaris', and it is very likely that liturgical books, especially those in the churches, came under the heading of 'popish stuff'. There are other references to the destruction of

---

[1] Bannerman, *Studies*, pp. 9–26; Anderson, *Kings and Kingship*, pp. 1–42.
[2] Anderson & Anderson, *Adomnan*; the Life was perhaps written between 688 and 692.
[3] Bannerman, *Studies*, pp. 27–156.
[4] Anderson, *Kings and Kingship*; cf. Miller, 'Disputed historical horizon'.
[5] Bannerman, *Studies*, pp. 157–70.
[6] Innes, *Critical Essay*, p. 313.
[7] McRoberts, 'Material destruction'.
[8] Pp. 121ff., 175.

mass-books, for example by the Earl of Arran and Lord James Stewart in 1560, by the Regent Morton at Haddington, of the burning of mass-books in 1559 at St Andrews, of the '.vi. mess buikis' of Queen Mary's which were burned.[9] If any of these books were several hundred years old and regarded with veneration they may have had important historical records written into them, which we shall never know.

The violence of the reforming mobs affected quite a small area, Perth, Crail, Anstruther, St Andrews, Scone, Stirling, Cambuskenneth, Linlithgow, Edinburgh and Glasgow,[10] but the Estates in 1560 passed an act 'for demolishing cloisters and abbey churches',[11] which Spottiswoode says was generally applied.

> Thereupon insued a pitifull vastation of Churches and Church buildings throughout all parts of the realm . . . No difference was made, but all the Churches either defaced or pulled to the ground. The holy vessells and whatsoever else men could make gain of as timber, lead and bells, were put to sale . . . The Registers of the Church and Bibliotheques cast into the fire. In a word all was ruined, and what had escaped in the time of the first tumult did now undergo the common calamity.[12]

How true is this claim? Manuscripts were destroyed in the passion of 1559–60, but the list of printed books published between 1470 and 1560 which have survived in Scottish libraries shows that Spottiswoode's description cannot possibly be taken literally. There are about 1,000 volumes, including classical texts, early christian Fathers, mediaeval writings some at least of which the reformers would undoubtedly have regarded as popish, civil and canon lawyers, devotional works and sixteenth-century authors, books which are now in the University Libraries of Aberdeen, St Andrews, Glasgow and Edinburgh, in Blairs College, Aberdeen, and in the National Library of Scotland. Many of these would come within the categories which Spottiswoode claims were generally burned. Neil Ker, in his pilot list of surviving books from the mediaeval libraries of Great Britain lists books from Scottish libraries including works of theology, philosophy, grammar and rhetoric, the Fathers, sermons, liturgical books and bibles, jurisprudence, martyrologies and kalendars, chronicles, histories and romance, but there are very few eleventh-century manuscripts, more from the twelfth and thirteenth, most of all from the fifteenth and sixteenth centuries.[13] McRoberts himself lists over two hundred liturgical books and fragments from mediaeval Scotland, three of which are from the eleventh century.[14] This evidence makes it perfectly clear

[9] Fleming, *Reformation*, p. 318.
[10] Spottiswoode, *History*, pp. 121ff.
[11] *Ibid.*, p. 175.
[12] *Ibid.* Keith, *History*, III.37, quotes a manuscript of Spottiswoode's *History* which is differently worded from the printed version: 'Bibliothecks destroied, the volumes of the Fathers, Councells and other books of humane learning, with the Registers of the Church, cast into the streets, afterwards gathered in heaps and consumed with fire'.
[13] Durkan & Ross, *Early Scottish Libraries*; Ker, *Medieval Libraries*.
[14] The Drummond Missal, the Edinburgh Psalter (see below, pp. 25–7), and the Gospel Book of St Margaret: see McRoberts, 'Catalogue'.

that a lot of books did survive the Reformation in Scotland;[15] but that they were *not early books*. If early books were deliberately destroyed we have therefore to look further back for a possible earlier destruction.

Innes sees Edward I as the villain who denuded Scotland of her early documents. 'There is no doubt but generally all our ancient histories were destroyed or carried off in King Edward I's time'.[16] He claims that 'the Scots had formerly good, ancient, authentic chronicles and annals',[17] but that by 1301, five years after Edward had removed the Scottish writings, the ignorance of learned Scotsmen concerning their past history 'alone might suffice to prove that the Scots at that time were generally destitute of all ancient monuments of true history'.[18] This view is being repeated by reputable modern scholars.

It is necessary at this point to make some distinctions and define terms. I shall speak of 'records' only when I mean documents produced for or by the royal or local administration, and for or by ecclesiastical authority; that is, royal and episcopal charters, cartularies, papal bulls, and the like. The mere enumeration of these suggests at once that 'records' in the technical sense are not likely to concern us much. Before about the year 1200 the survival of 'records' anywhere in Western Europe was very much a matter of chance. Even papal registers are not continuously preserved before the time of Innocent III (1198–1216), nor in general do episcopal registers appear before the thirteenth century. English charters and laws of pre-Conquest date have survived, but in ecclesiastical and not royal collections. It was fortunate for English historians that, at the Reformation, the Church in England kept her episcopal government and diocesan structure, so that rich collections of archives were handed down, for example the charters of Canterbury cathedral. In France many of the great monasteries lived on until the Revolutionary period, when their archives were taken into public custody.

We can really have no idea what 'records' were written in Scotland before

---

[15] It is also clear that some buildings damaged in the violence of 1559/60 were subsequently rebuilt or repaired, and that some buildings were in a very dilapidated condition before the Reformation.

[16] Innes, *Critical Essay*, p. 139; cf. his pp. 303–7.

[17] *Ibid.*, p. 126. His view seems to be based on the 'Coupar Chronicle' (cited below, p. 6) but there are other references to Pictish 'books' and 'chronicles'. In a declaration by the clergy in 1310 which is propaganda in favour of Robert there is a very general reference to 'the ancient glorious histories of the Scots': Donaldson, *Scottish Historical Documents*, pp. 48–50. Pictish King-List C seems to be acknowledging that the scribe copies from a list of Pictish kings when he says 'as in the books of the Cruithnig': Anderson, *Kings and Kingship*, p. 83. Fordun (*Chronica*, ed. Skene, p. 152) cites the 'catalogue' of the King of the Scots and 'other things found in the volumes of the ancients', and refers (*ibid.*, p. 167) to a conspiracy of the *Morauienses* against Malcolm who was killed at Ulrim after a reign of nine years and three months and was buried at Iona; both of these references would seem to come from a king-list of the kind we have. *De Situ Albanie* cites 'histories and chronicles of the ancient Britons, and *gesta* and ancient annals of the Scots and Picts', which seems to boil down to Geoffrey of Monmouth and more than one of the regnal lists and Scottish Chronicle: Anderson, *Kings and Kingship*, p. 241 and n.5. Mrs Anderson tells me that 'Chadwick, *Early Scotland*, pp. 28–9, was inclined to take references of this kind more seriously than I should care to do . . . I wonder whether the "Coupar Chronicle" writer had in mind regnal lists he had seen. He would probably imagine, as much later writers have done, that every such list is an independent authority, and that the loss of some would be a real loss to history.'

[18] Innes, *Critical Essay*, p. 124.

the eleventh century, but we do know the scope of the records which Edward took to London from Scotland on 17 September, 1296, because there is an inventory of documents, concerning Scotland, which the English held in 1323:

> Muniments of the Kings of Scotland, and of various other persons of that realm, such as royal charters made by various kings of that realm, and also charters and documents of various magnates and other persons of the same realm, with various other memoranda, of which a detailed inventory could not be given here because of the disorder of the writing, and because of their trifling value: they are contained, however, in two leather forcers bound with iron, in four hampers covered with black leather, in nine wooden forcers, in eighteen hampers of wicker, and in thirty-two boxes.[19]

These documents must be administrative and legal texts, mainly of the thirteenth century, and such records would do little to help us to reconstruct early Scottish history.

I shall be talking mainly about a different kind of document, mainly about chronicles and king-lists. What effect did the Anglo-Scottish controversy have on these? In March 1291, at the beginning of the debate held in 1291–2, on the Scottish Succession, which is known as 'The Great Cause', Edward sent out letters to monasteries asking for information 'touching the status of the realm and the *regimen* of Scotland'.[20] The response was rapid. On 10 May, the king held a meeting of magnates and clerics at Norham. The Chronicle of Walter of Guisborough[21] and the Bury Chronicle[22] both say that monks came with their chronicles, and John of Caen's Great Roll, drawn up subsequently, contains extracts from chronicles, beginning in the year 901, in justification of Edward's claims.[23] The king's speaker, Roger Brabazon, declared the king's wish to do justice 'by virtue of the over-lordship which belongs to him', and asked for recognition of Edward's overlordship that 'he might act with your advice' (*voet ovrer par voz conseils a droit faire et <par>former*).[24] The meeting was adjourned, and the magnates of Scotland soon afterwards replied that though they accepted Edward's good faith in making the claim to overlordship 'they have no knowledge of your right, nor did they ever see it claimed or used by you or your ancestors'.[25]

This was the beginning of a long dispute. In 1301, or thereabouts, the Scots were claiming that Edward had 'removed by force the muniments and writings and *chronicles* that they had in Scotland',[26] in order to deprive the Scots of evidence to refute him. It seems to me intrinsically unlikely that Edward should have been able to make a clean sweep of Scottish historical writings, but our best evidence will be to examine what was the conception of early

[19] Stones, *Anglo-Scottish Relations*, p. 76. For the context, see Palgrave, *Antient Kalendars*, I. 127–37, and Stones & Simpson, *Edward I and the Throne of Scotland*.
[20] Stones, 'Appeal to history'.
[21] Rothwell (ed.), p. 234.
[22] Gransden (ed. & tr.), p. 98.
[23] Stones, 'Appeal to history', p. 18.
[24] Stones, *Anglo-Scottish Relations*, p. 52.
[25] *Ibid.*, p. 54.
[26] *Ibid.*, p. 116.

Scottish history in the thirteenth century before the alleged removal. Here we are enormously assisted by Mrs Anderson's reconstruction of the stemma of the king-lists.[27] The term 'king-list' is perhaps misleading to people who have not consulted them, for from Kenneth mac Alpin onwards (the king who combined Dál Riata and Pictland in the mid-ninth century) there are brief entries of historical events which took place during the reigns: the king-list is in fact a very elementary chronicle.

Mrs Anderson lists thirty manuscripts of the Scottish king-list which either survive or are known to have existed or can be deduced.[28] In addition there is a list of Pictish kings to the mid-ninth century which is included in some of the Scottish king-lists. The common source of the early Pictish king-list was probably drawn up not long after 724, for the versions diverge after this. There must also have been early Scottish lists, but all the surviving versions are in four eleventh-century Irish lists and the descendants of a twelfth-century Latin list in Anglo-Norman orthography. What is of particular interest to us is that there was a lot of interest in previous Scottish kings in the thirteenth century, and that some of the lists look as if they may be responses to Edward's request for information in 1291. The Huntingdon return is one such;[29] another prefixed to the Chronicle of Lanercost (near Carlisle) may have this origin.[30] A list entered in a Tynemouth manuscript was completed after 1290. In the early fourteenth century a Peterborough scribe introduced extracts on Anglo-Scottish relations under the year 1291 because, he says, 'on the failure of the line of kings of Scotland, when Scots were claiming the right of inheritance and were trying to exclude entirely the lord King of England to whom belongs the *supremum jus* of that kingdom, they [i.e., the inserted pieces] were sought out in chronicles of the ancients in different parts of England'.[31] If some of the king-lists were inspired by the controversy it is notable that this king-list was the *best chronicle of the Scots available to these English houses in the thirteenth century*.

It was being used before and immediately after Edward's request. For example one recension was used by a Melrose writer between 1240 and 1264,[32] and the text continued to be the received version of Scottish history. One list[33] comes down to 1306, ending with Comyn's murder, and may be a piece of English propaganda, for it tells us that all the kings to Alpin in the mid-ninth century were killed, 'but they were not kings, because they did not rule by election or by lineage, but by treachery'.[34] In this list John Balliol is cited as the man 'whom Edward illustrious king of England raised to the kingdom of Scotland', and Robert Bruce as the man 'who had himself crowned as king of Scotland at Scone, and slew John Comyn'. There is in fact no shortage of

27 Anderson, *Kings and Kingship*, pp. 43–102.
28 *Ibid.*, p. 234, for stemma.
29 *Ibid.*, p. 72.
30 *Ibid.*, pp. 73–4.
31 *Ibid.*, p. 76.
32 A list of the Y-group: *ibid.*, p. 74.
33 List N: *ibid.*, p. 67.
34 *Ibid.*, pp. 290–1.

interest in early Scottish history in the thirteenth and early fourteenth centuries, and a lot of material arising from it has survived; but both English and anti-English sides could only produce an interpolated king-list to work from. I am driven to the conclusion that in the thirteenth century the historian's sources for early Scottish history were as scanty as ours.[35] The only chronicle they had was the known king-list.

Edward's action was remembered by later Scottish historians who blamed him, and continued to blame him, for the absence of early documents. The preface to the *Scotichronicon* in the National Library of Scotland MS. Adv. 35.1.7 gives the version of the events current in pro-Scottish circles in the mid-fifteenth century.[36] It says that Edward usurped by oppression the protection of the Scottish kingdom, and after he had pried into all the book-chests and taken the ancient and authentic chronicles into his own hands, he took some away with him to England and burned the rest. Afterwards Master John Fordun, priest, travelled on foot around Britain and Ireland, 'through cities and towns, universities and colleges, churches and monasteries' and collected the missing materials until he could fill five volumes with the deeds of the Scots.

John of Fordun wrote his chronicle between 1384 and 1387, the continuator began his work in 1441 and finished it in 1447, and the passage I have quoted is from an abridged version of the continuation.[37] The first two books of Fordun are mythological prehistory. The Scots, he says, are descended from Scota daughter of Pharaoh and Gaythelos prince of the Greeks, who left Egypt together three hundred and thirty years before the capture of Troy. Fordun accepts Geoffrey of Monmouth's account of the origin of Britain from Brutus, descended from Aeneas after his flight from Troy, but he gives Albanact son of Brutus a kingdom stretching from Humber and Trent in the south to 'the Scottish sea' in the north (which I take to be the Firth of Forth), though now, he says, the Scottish border is on the Tweed. Fordun is building up a narrative based on popular legend, materials from St Andrews and Glasgow, saints' lives (some now lost) and English sources, among them Bede, William of Malmesbury, the Chronicle of Huntingdon, Higden, Ailred, the Chronicle of Melrose, John of Hexham and of course Geoffrey of Monmouth.[38] The genuine materials of Scottish history become rather fuller from the mid-ninth century on. All the same, *if* Fordun's chronicle were based on sources which Edward removed, it would show that Scottish historical materials were much the same in the thirteenth century as later. He found no set of Scottish annals comparable to Irish annals which he could use, but had to piece together a

[35] The Chronicle of Melrose, one of the main sources of mediaeval Scottish history, begins to show original Scottish entries only in the twelfth century. Its early sections are based mainly on Bede and other Northumbrian sources. See Anderson *et al.*, *Chronicle of Melrose*.

[36] The text is given by Skene, *Johannis de Fordun Chronica*, I, pp. xlix-li.

[37] Skene (*ibid.*, pp. xli, xix) thinks it is also by the continuator, Walter Bower, who died in 1449. This abridged version is entitled *Liber Monasterii Beatae Mariae de Cupro*, and it is what Innes calls 'The Chronicle of Coupar'.

[38] This list is largely dependent on Skene's notes.

narrative. The main interest of his account rests in what, in the fourteenth century, people thought had happened in the eleventh and twelfth; it adds nothing to our knowledge of early Scottish history.[39]

Innes's argument that the Scottish view of history is so mistaken that it proves that the country had been denuded of ancient sources[40] is obviously faulty, for the argument put forward by the English when writing to Pope Boniface in 1301 is ultimately based on Geoffrey of Monmouth but this does not prove the disappearance of reliable English historical materials. The English argued[41] that Great Britain traced her origins back to the Trojan Brutus, who divided the land of Britain which he had taken from giants between his three sons, Albanact (to whom he gave Scotland), Camber (Wales) and Locrine, the eldest, who maintained suzerainty and took liege homage and oaths of fealty. Arthur, king of the Britons, subjected 'a rebellious Scotland', and succeeding kings of England have enjoyed monarchy and dominion in the island.

The Scots told a different story. Scotland, they said, had an origin independent of England, derived from Scota daughter of Pharaoh who went to Ireland and afterwards to Scotland, taking with her the royal seat which Edward had recently removed.[42] Arthur was born in adultery, and what he won he gained by violence. He did subdue Scotland for a time, but he was ultimately killed by Mordred son of Loth king of Scotland, and Scotland then returned to her independence. In any case the English king is not a descendant of the Britons but of a Norman, William the Bastard. The Scots were converted to christianity four hundred years before the English (there were thirty-six Catholic kings in Scotland before the English were converted). Scotland had never been held from England in fee and Edward had recently usurped the kingdom of Scotland when its throne was vacant.

The apologists in this dispute, on both sides, were providing the commonly accepted view of their origins; but stories of origins, whether Roman, Irish, English, Scottish (and no doubt of many other peoples), are notoriously mythological or legendary and prove absolutely nothing about the presence or absence of reliable historical records. It is however very significant that – given the fact that there was material from which to write a narrative history for thirteenth- and early fourteenth-century Scotland – all that the Scots could

---

[39] We badly need a study, now proposed by Dr Donald Watt, of Fordun's sources. Mrs Anderson says: 'If Fordun really travelled in Ireland he seems to have missed annals, or perhaps did not realise that they contained anything to his purpose. I wonder whether he could read an Irish hand with any ease? There is one detail in the Chronicle of Huntingdon and in Fordun, the date XIII Kal. Aug. for the death of Alpin, Kenneth's father, which looks as if it ought to come from an annal-source and which is not in any of the annals we have.'

[40] *Critical Essay*, p. 124. The implication is that Edward was responsible.

[41] In the letter sent to Pope Boniface in 1301 'concerning the king's rights in the realm of Scotland': Stones, *Anglo-Scottish Relations*, pp. 96–109.

[42] 'Processus Baldredi contra figmenta regis Anglie', edited by Skene, *Chronicles*, pp. 271–84. This is not what the Irish Nennius says: Van Hamel, *Lebor Bretnach*, pp. 25–7, or, with translation, Todd & Herbert, *Irish Version*. Nor is it what *Duan Albanach* says: see Jackson's text and translation. It is nearer to the version of *Lebor Gabála Érenn* (ed. & tr. Macalister).

produce for the early period was this very scanty king-list.[43] We have therefore to deduce that Edward did not destroy all the Scottish historical sources, and we must find some other reason for their absence.

We had better begin at the beginning and ask what indications there are of early Scottish and Pictish scriptoria. Let us start with Scottish Dál Riata. We know that Iona was a flourishing early scriptorium. Adomnán says that it already was so in the late sixth century; he describes Columba constantly writing, and comments on the checking of the text after the manuscript was finished. If the *Cathach* comes from Iona (which is by no means certain) it suggests practised scribes there in the earlier seventh century.[44] Cuimine, abbot from 657 to 669, wrote a Life of Columba which is now lost. By the 670s the Iona chronicle becomes a contemporary account, and Adomnán himself wrote *De Locis Sanctis*, probably before 686, and his *Life of Columba* probably after 688. The chronicle went on in Iona certainly until 736, probably until 741. There are few other houses which have so large a known output by the mid-eighth century.[45]

The position in sixth- and early seventh-century Pictland is very different. By the second half of the seventh century christianity seems to have been quite widely established, for Adomnán says that it is the Columban houses which have saved both Scottish Dál Riata and Pictland from the plague which had ravaged Ireland and Britain twice in his lifetime.[46] But our other evidence suggests that christianity was much more firmly established in the south than the north of Pictland. According to the *Amhra Choluim Chille*, perhaps written in the early seventh century, Columba had preached to the tribes of *Toi* (Tay); between 664 and 678 Cuthbert made a journey from Melrose with two companions by sea to the *Niuduera regio*, or, as Bede says, *ad terram Pictorum qui Niduari uocantur*.[47] The eighth-century *Miracula Nynie Episcopi* claims that the tribes of Picts called *Niduari* had been converted by Ninian,[48] an idea compar-

---

[43] Henry of Huntingdon (ed. Arnold, p. 12), writing *ca* 1125–30 (and therefore well before Edward I) says of the Picts, 'iam fabula uideatur quod in uererum scriptis eorum mentio inuenitur'. Professor Stones reminds me that Scottish 'records' too late to have been removed by Edward have subsequently disappeared, even when their value to Scottish interests was great (for example, the English quit claim of the homage in 1328); and, by analogy, chronicles have had equally good opportunities to disappear. If Edward I did damage to historical scholarship in Scotland, it was far more by beginning the Wars of Independence, and so damaging law and order and discouraging the care of archives and libraries, than by his supposed depredations upon chronicles.

[44] The date is that of Lowe, *Codices Latini Antiquiores*, II (2nd edn), no. 266. I have not seen the detailed palaeographical study by Schauman, 'Emergence and Progress of Irish Script', pp. 206–84: I owe this reference to David Dumville.

[45] There is a commentary on Vergil attributed to 'Adananus': Kenney, *Sources*, pp. 286–7; but, in a review of Anderson & Anderson, *Adomnan*, Denis Meehan, *Medium Ævum* 31 (1962) 205–7, denies that there is any good reason for the suggested attribution to Adomnán of Iona. The latter was also supposed to have been the leader in drawing up the so-called Law of Adomnán: see Ryan, 'The Cáin Adomnáin'.

[46] Adomnán, *Vita Columbae*, II.46. The plague occurred in 664–8 and 683–4.

[47] For the text of the *Amhra*, see below, p. 50, n. 63. See also Colgrave, *Two Lives*, pp. 82, 192, and Hunter Blair, 'Bernicians', pp. 165–8.

[48] For a translation, see MacQueen, 'Miracula Nynie Episcopi', p. 25.

able to the one (which Bede heard) of Ninian as apostle to the southern Picts.[49]
But although Bede says that Columba converted the northern Picts[50] Adomnán, writing a generation earlier and in a position to know more directly about
the saint, says very little of his activities in Pictland.[51] It is true that Adomnán
is writing of the saint's prophecies, miracles and visions; all the same he has a
lot to say about Ireland and Irishmen and it is surprising that he does not say
more of Pictland had Columba been very active there. He makes it clear that
Columba had established diplomatic contacts with King Bruide who lived
near the river Ness, but he does not say Bruide was converted. There are
several references to a journey, or perhaps journeys, to Pictland,[52] and a few
miracles were performed,[53] but there is no suggestion in Adomnán of any
widespread evangelisation.

Scribal activity comes in the wake of christianity, and in Pictland some of
our best evidence for christianity comes from the symbol-stones. Scholars do
not agree on their date of origin, but they are found almost entirely in the east
and north-west of Scotland, not in Dál Riata, so it seems likely that they belong
to the period after the Irish settlement of the south-west.[54] We do not know
what they indicate, but the symbolism is definitely not christian.[55] It is
interesting to note that the Class I stones are much more thinly scattered in
southern Pictland, where christianity probably began earlier and seems to
have been quite well known by 600.[56]

The Class II stones, on the contrary, are definitely christian and show a real
integration between secular and christian art, for the secular symbols appear
together with the cross and other christian iconography. Some of them also
show Anglo-Saxon influence in the ornament. They may belong to the later
seventh century, for between 669 and 685 Anglo-Saxon influence had penetrated into southern Pictland,[57] or to the early eighth century, when Nechton
sent to Ceolfrith, abbot of Jarrow, for advice on the Easter question and
received builders to erect a church of stone 'after the Roman fashion'. I am
inclined to think the latter date more likely, since the Class II stones are
centred in the heart of southern Pictland, not near the Forth where English

[49] Patrick's Letter to Coroticus describes them (§15) as 'apostate Picts'. In the *Gododdin* (see
below, p. 50, n. 58) Picts are part of Mynyddog's christian warband.
[50] *Historia Ecclesiastica*, III.4.
[51] Anderson, 'Columba and other Irish saints'.
[52] Anderson & Anderson, *Adomnan*, pp. 81ff., think he visited Bruide only once.
[53] Not many. In Book II (miracles) Adomnán relates fourteen miracles performed by Columba
in Ireland or which primarily concern Irishmen, but only seven in Pictland.
[54] The most up-to-date maps are in McNeill & Nicholson, *Historical Atlas*, nos 8–10. See
Anderson, *Kings and Kingship*, p. 129.
[55] See Allen & Anderson, *Early Christian Monuments*. If we take the bull and the eagle in their
context here it seems perverse to regard them as christian symbols.
[56] In chapter III, below, I have argued that christianity had a late start in northern Pictland.
But see Kirby, 'Bede and the Pictish Church'.
[57] Wilfrid was 'administering the see of the church of York and of all the Northumbrians and
Picts, as far as Oswiu's power extended' in 669 (*Historia Ecclesiastica*, IV.3), and the see of
Abercorn was created for the Picts in 681 but had to be abandoned after the English defeat at
Nechtanesmere in 685. See also Miller, 'Eanfrith's Pictish son'.

influence must have been strongest. It looks to me as if christianity, though it was known in Pictland before, became popular among the upper classes of society only in Nechton's time.

If so, you would expect some evidence of scribal activity in Pictland in the early eighth century, for there is absolutely none recognisable earlier. And this is exactly what we have. The source of the Pictish king-lists P and Q was in writing probably not long after 724:[58] this is the earliest distinguishable Pictish king-list.[59] Between 724 and 736 there is a burst of entries about Pictland in the Irish annals. These almost certainly came in via the Iona chronicle, which up to 724 had included the obits of Pictish kings, an occasional battle or siege and a very few other Pictish entries,[60] but had not shown the lively interest in internal Pictish affairs which begins now. One is tempted to see a Pictish source behind this, but the Pictish king-list remains as laconic as ever, naming the king, his father, the number of years he reigned, and the building of certain churches, Abernethy (at the beginning of the seventh century), Dunkeld and St Andrews (in the first few decades of the ninth),[61] entries which may have been put in by a later scribe. We really have little ground for supposing a contemporary Pictish chronicle in the 720s and 730s. Had one existed in the thirteenth century the later Scottish kingdom would have been proud to own it, for List I, transcribed between 1286 and 1292, notes the time of those who reigned before the Scots as one thousand two hundred and thirty-nine years and three months.[62]

Undoubtedly during the eighth century Northumbria and Pictland were in close contact. Columban monks were expelled from Pictland in 717, a year after Iona had adopted the Roman Easter. Presumably it implies that the Picts were welcoming Northumbrian clergy, or perhaps introducing something like English ecclesiastical administration. Round about 710 the 'reformed nation' of the Picts had placed itself under the guidance and direction of St Peter,[63] and Bede's words suggest that by the time he wrote in 731 Iona was no longer exercising supervision over Pictland.[64] In 721 a Pictish bishop attended the Council of Rome and signed the decrees. The lower part of the tower of Restenneth Priory shows signs of very early romanesque work, 'easily the most

[58] Anderson, *Kings and Kingship*, p. 88.

[59] It went back at least twenty-eight reigns before Bruide son of Maelchon; Bruide was a contemporary of St Columba and died in the 580s. Later, probably in the ninth century, it was extended even further backwards.

[60] 668: 'Itarnan et Corindu apud Pictores defuncti sunt'.
671: 'Expulsio Drosto de regno'.
675: 'Multi Pictores dimersi sunt i lLaind Abae'.
698: 'Tarain ad Hiberniam pergit'.
712: 'Tolargg filius Drostan ligatur apud fratrem suum Nectan regem'.
716: 'Expulsio familiae Iae trans dorsum Britanniae a Nectano rege'.

[61] I quote from List F, which was in the lost St Andrews Register.

[62] Anderson, *Kings and Kingship*, p. 281.

[63] *Historia Ecclesiastica*, V.21. The usually accepted date is *ca* 710.

[64] *Ibid.*, III.3: 'Hii . . . cuius monasterium in cunctis pene septentrionalium Scottorum et omnium Pictorum monasteriis non paruo tempore arcem tenebat, regendisque eorum populis praeerat'.

archaic thing of its kind in Scotland', which W. D. Simpson regarded as an eighth-century porticus built, *more Romanorum*, by masons from Wearmouth.[65] Occasional literary reference shows us contacts between Northumbria and Pictland in the later eighth and early ninth century, for three Pictish kings of that period figure in the Lindisfarne *Liber Vitae*[66] and two deposed Northumbrian rulers took refuge in Pictland, Alhred in 774 and Osbald in 796. But the Class II stones are our best evidence if, as Professor Julian Brown maintains, they show that the Picts had the same range of scripts as Northumbria[67] and were using Northumbrian designs.[68] The decoration of the St Ninian's Isle treasure also has parallels with Northumbrian motifs.[69] Though no manuscripts of this period can be distinguished with certainty, some must have been written, basic texts for church worship and for learning Latin at the very least.

Professor Brown has recently argued the possibility that the Book of Kells was written in Pictland.[70] Northumbria, Pictland, Iona and Ireland share so much of the same art that it is difficult to be sure on so highly controversial a question. But although the Book of Kells shows Northumbrian and Pictish features, what he cites as the non-Northumbrian but Pictish elements found in the Book of Kells and in Pictish sculpture are also found in Ireland.[71] I would prefer to look for the home of the Book of Kells in what we know to be a flourishing scriptorium, such as Iona if the date is as early as the 740s (and I think Professor Brown proves his case for an earlier date than the one previously generally accepted). But if we are to argue for the distinguished scriptorium in Pictland which the Book of Kells would imply I should like some supporting and less controversial evidence.

I do not see that outstanding stone-work necessarily presupposes outstanding scriptoria. But during the eighth century manuscripts and possibly scribes must have passed between Northumbria and Pictland and Dál Riata, and books must have been written in Pictland. If so, what happened to them? Do the vikings provide the answer? In the early ninth century the vikings were a very disturbing factor in the west. Most of our evidence is for secular sites, but when we have ecclesiastical evidence it suggests violence, not initially the 'peaceful co-settlement' for which Mrs Anna Ritchie has argued.[72] At Birsay there was an existing Celtic settlement in the eighth (or perhaps in the early

---

[65] Simpson, 'Early romanesque tower'.

[66] Oengus (*ob.* 761), Constantine (789–820), and Eoganan (*ob.* 839): Brown, 'Northumbria and the Book of Kells', p. 238.

[67] *Ibid.*, p. 241.

[68] The Hilton of Cadboll stone and the fragment from Tarbat especially.

[69] Small *et al.*, *St Ninian's Isle*.

[70] Brown, 'Northumbria and the Book of Kells'.

[71] *Ibid.*, p. 239: namely, naturalistic animal and human figures, human figures interlaced, and fantastic animals. However, I believe that both Professor Brown and Mrs Henderson have more to say about this; so it would be wise to keep an open mind on the Book of Kells until their work is published and can be properly considered.

[72] Ritchie, 'Pict and Norseman'. I do not think the secular sites show this either. The evidence on some is indeterminate, but at Udal the Norse reused existing structures and there was no sandblow or fill-in. Are we to suppose that the natives willingly handed over their homes to the invaders?

ninth) century, for one of the headstones in the cemetery dates from that period; the Norse settled here and built houses of early type on the slope above the church, and one assumes that the church was abandoned, for when the Norse church was built later the wall of the Pictish church had become a low heap of stones.[73] When the vikings arrived at St Ninian's Isle, there was a church there whose cemetery had been continuously used from pre-christian into christian times.[74] A hoard of treasure was buried here under the church-floor about the year 800 or slightly later. The earliest object in the treasure is a hanging bowl dating from *ca* 700. The eleven brooches all belong to the second half of the eighth century; the two inscriptions date from the eighth or early ninth century. We have here a hoard of miscellaneous silver. David McRoberts has argued that all the pieces have a liturgical use,[75] that the six bowls are chalices and the hemispherical bowl a hand-basin for use in the liturgy, that the hanging bowl is a votive offering with no utilitarian purpose, the brooches ornaments worn on liturgical vestments, the chapes stole-ends, the spoon and pricker for use in the eucharist, the pommel and cone-shaped objects fitting for a flabellum. But why should a church have six chalices all this unusual shape, and not one the usual shape with which we are familiar? Brooches were used on the clothes of anyone rich enough to possess them; David Wilson has pressed the case that the pommel and chapes must be sword-fittings, and argues strongly against their use as a flabellum. In all, the case for the hoard as liturgical in content seems unacceptable. Nor does it seem likely that this is the accumulated treasure-hoard of some viking marauder, since the hack-silver, ingots and coins which might then be expected are missing.[76] I should support a different solution. Irish churches had no coinage and they must have kept small banks of precious objects with which to conduct legal agreements and purchases; they may also have acted as banks for laymen. The most likely explanation is that treasure belonging to, and under the protection of, the church was buried during a troubled period of viking raids and settlement. If so, presumably everyone who knew where it was deposited either fled or was killed. The archaeological evidence suggests that the pre-viking church on St Ninian's Isle was abandoned and possibly sacked, for beneath the twelfth-century church are the ruins of an earlier church. The fragments of the pre-viking shrine, lying at a level below the twelfth-century church, show that it had been smashed and dispersed.

This is exactly what Walahfrid Strabo says happened at Iona in 825.[77] The monks had already lifted the shrine of Columba from its place and had put it in a hole in the ground under a thick layer of turf, foreseeing the raid.[78] Although

---

[73] Radford, *Early Christian and Norse Settlements*; Cruden, 'Excavations at Birsay'.
[74] Small *et al.*, *St Ninian's Isle*, I.5.
[75] McRoberts, 'Ecclesiastical significance', and 'Ecclesiastical character'.
[76] David Wilson says it is 'too homogeneous' to be a viking's collection.
[77] Duemmler, *Poetae Latini*, II.297–301. I find that McRoberts quotes this text in his 'Ecclesiastical character'.
[78] Walahfrid, lines 144–6: '. . . de sedibus arcam / tollentes tumulo terra posuere cauato / cespite sub denso gnari iam pestis iniquae'.

most of the Iona monks had already fled, a few, led by Blathmac, stayed behind and were killed; but the vikings, though they did some digging,[79] failed to find the shrine. Perhaps something comparable happened at St Ninian's Isle. If the vikings settled here it would have been impossible for the clerics to return and rescue the silver, and in time its whereabouts would cease to be known.

Iona is the only house on the western seaboard which the annals speak about in this period, but they record attacks on it by Scandinavians in 795 and 802, and again in 806 when sixty-eight monks were slain. Abbot Cellach left Iona and began to build the monastery at Kells in the following year, though he returned after seven years to end his life on Iona. Thus the little written and archaeological evidence we have suggests that houses on the western seaboard were badly disrupted in the first half of the ninth century, and that considerable damage was sustained. This does not mean that scribal activity would have ceased, for it did not do so in Ireland or the Frankish kingdoms. But the centre of the Columban *paruchia* probably moved to Ireland.

We have therefore to envisage disturbed scriptoria in the earlier ninth century in the west. In the second half of the ninth and in the early tenth century there was sporadic fighting also in the south-east.[80] It seems likely that viking activity in the western seas would at first reduce communications between the churches in Ireland and Scotland, but in 874, after King Constantine had fallen in battle against the Scandinavians, the shrine of Columba and all his insignia arrived in Ireland 'to escape the *Gall*', and a century later, in 989, the *paruchia* of Columba was still seen as extending throughout Ireland and Scotland, for Dub-da-leithe, abbot of Armagh, then assumed the coarbship of Columba 'with the consent of the men of Ireland and Scotland'.[81] There are comparatively few references in the Irish annals for this period to the Church in Scotland, but we hear of a learned man (*saoi*) at Iona in 935 and a scribe and bishop of the Islands of Scotland in 961.[82]

There is very little evidence with which to reconstruct the effect on the Church of the union of Dál Riata and Pictland in about 841. Kenneth mac Alpin took Columba's relics to a church he had built (the implication is that it was in Pictland),[83] and for a time Dunkeld seems to be the chief church, for Tuathal is described as *prímepscop Fortrenn* (chief bishop of Fortriu) and abbot of Dunkeld.[84] This is not the place to discuss the vexed question of Scottish

---

[79] Walahfrid, lines 158–9: 'Quodque ferox miles censu pensare nequibat / rimari in gelidis coepit per uulnera fibris'.

[80] Smyth, *Scandinavian York and Dublin*, I. In 864 Óláfr devastated the south-east, fighting went on in Constantine's reign, and for one year the Scandinavians stayed in Pictland. They devastated it again in Donald II's reign (889–900) and in 903, and were fighting the Scots in 918. See Anderson, *Kings and Kingship*, pp. 250–1, and the Annals of Ulster (edd. & tr. Hennessy and MacCarthy), s. aa. 866, 871, 874, 918.

[81] Annals of Ulster, s. a. 988. In 927 Mael Brigte had been 'successor of Patrick and Columba' (Annals of Ulster, s. a. 926). In 936, according to the Annals of the Four Masters (ed. & tr. O'Donovan), Dubthach was successor of Columba and Adomnán 'in Ireland and Alba'.

[82] I draw both notices from the Annals of the Four Masters.

[83] Anderson, *Kings and Kingship*, p. 250.

[84] Annals of Ulster, s. a. 864; cf. Donaldson, 'Scottish bishops' sees'.

13

church-organisation in the ninth, tenth and eleventh centuries.[85] King-lists DFIK say that Giric (who ruled 879–89) was the first to give 'liberty (*libertas*) to the Scottish Church which was under servitude up to that time after the custom and fashion of the Picts',[86] and whatever this means it is a clear statement of change from Pictish to Scottish practice.[87] We find abbots fighting and marrying in Scotland as they do in Ireland: one distinguished marriage is recorded in the annals, when the daughter of King Malcolm early in the eleventh century was married to Crinan, abbot of Dunkeld; her son was King Duncan, killed by Macbeth.

Scanty as this evidence is, it shows that the Pictish Church was to some extent hibernicised. If so, we should conclude that some at least of the manuscripts of the Picto-Scottish Kingdom were written in Irish. There is a little evidence to support this assumption. A Pictish king-list seems to have been put together in Irish during the reign of Constantine, who died about 877.[88] There are two versions of an Irish legend of the origin of the Picts dating from the ninth century.[89] All the extant versions of the *Senchus Fer nAlban* derive from a compilation made in the tenth century.[90] The manuscript-tradition of this text is solely Irish, and it seems likely that the tenth-century original was Irish. The seventeenth-century manuscripts of the *Duan Albanach*, a poem on the rulers of Scotland which dates from the end of the eleventh century, are also Irish.[91] The native language of the scribe of the Book of Deer was Irish, for the colophon is in that language, and the directions to the priest in the mass for the sick are also in Irish. There was a manuscript written in Irish in the monastery of Loch Leven before 1150.[92] Professor Thomson points out the close connexion between Gaelic Scotland and Ireland, and that 'Gaelic Scotland leaned heavily on Irish initiative'.[93] When we look at the Gaelic manuscripts which have survived[94] the texts which they contain are mainly medical tracts,[95] genealogies, legends and stories; they show that in Scottish Gaelic culture 'history' meant genealogy and legend, not contemporary annals and historical narrative.

---

[85] Cowan, 'Post-Columban Church', pp. 252–5, argues that there is very little evidence for 'monastic communities' in this period; but in Ireland by this time monastic communities were also extensively secularised. See Hughes, *Church in Early Irish Society*, pp. 215–26. The assumption is that Cellach, abbot of Iona, who died in the country of the Picts in 864, was visiting his *paruchia*.

[86] Anderson, *Kings and Kingship*, p. 267. In the eleventh-century 'Fragmentary Annals of Ireland' (ed. & tr. Radner, pp. 168–71), it is Columba who helps the men of Alba in their battles.

[87] But, as Mrs Anderson points out to me, it may be a twelfth-century statement, invoking the name of Giric in support of current claims to the antique liberties of some church. She hopes to discuss this in a future article.

[88] Anderson, *Kings and Kingship*, p. 78.

[89] Mac Eoin, 'Irish legend', p. 153.

[90] Bannerman, *Studies*, pp. 27–156, who thinks that the material may go back to the seventh century. But see also the review by T. M. Charles-Edwards, *Studia Hibernica* 15 (1975) 194–6.

[91] See the introduction to Jackson's edition, 'The poem *A eolcha Alban uile*'.

[92] Anderson, *Kings and Kingship*, p. 58 and note. The *codiculus* which Jocelyn of Furness used *ca* 1180 in compiling his life of St Kentigern was *stilo scottico*, but the phrase *per totum soloecismis scatentem* suggests Latin: see Jackson, 'Sources for the Life of St Kentigern', esp. pp. 274–6.

[93] Thomson, 'Gaelic learned orders'.

[94] MacKinnon, *Descriptive Catalogue*.

[95] See Thomson, 'Gaelic learned orders', p. 61, on the reasons for their survival.

I think that we have to imagine manuscripts being written in the tenth and eleventh centuries, even if they were not many and not brilliantly executed. It is possible that some of these, now in Irish or English or Continental libraries, cannot be recognised.[96] Perhaps the clue to their fate lies partly in the history of the later eleventh and twelfth centuries. We have a lot of tenth- and eleventh-century texts concerning Ireland because they were copied into twelfth-century Irish manuscripts; Irish monks then transcribed much of the literature and history of early Ireland, for the twelfth-century renaissance arrived before the Anglo-Normans settled and it was centred not in new towns but in ancient monasteries which delighted in their past tradition. So in Ireland the renaissance is in many ways a backward-looking movement. Moreover the secular learned classes in Ireland survived the twelfth-century ecclesiastical reform, and their texts are copied into late mediaeval manuscripts.

In Scotland the position was different. What effect does this have on Scottish scriptoria? Anglo-French influence came in earlier. None of the children of Malcolm III (1057–93) and Queen Margaret had Celtic names. Their son David, by his marriage in 1113 or 1114, gained the earldom and honour of Huntingdon with lands in the eastern midlands of England, and a steady flow of Anglo-French and Flemings moved up to Scotland to be enfeoffed mainly in Lanarkshire, Fife, Clydesdale and Moray. Under William the Lion (1165–1214) feudalisation penetrated to the line of the Allan Water and the Tay Valley as far as Dunkeld.[97] In the Gaelic notes written into the Book of Deer in the first half of the twelfth century[98] the names are Celtic, but in 1196 a royal grant made at Elgin is attested not by Celtic mormaers and abbots but by clerics who have Anglo-French names and by seventeen lords of whom only two have Celtic names.[99]

Anglo-French influence spread through the Church. By the middle of the twelfth century we can scarcely doubt that the Scottish episcopate was Anglo-French instead of Celtic.[100] The names of bishops and cathedral chapters show that Celtic was being replaced by non-Celtic: in the mid-eleventh century at Glasgow Bishop Magsuen (1055–60) bears a Hiberno-Scandinavian name, in the eleventh century at St Andrews Maelduin, Tuadal and Fothad (?1028–1093) have Celtic names, a little farther north at Dunkeld Cormac was bishop in 1131–2, as was Nechtan at Aberdeen, and Macbeth

---

[96] For example, where did the 'Garland of Howth' originate? On this manuscript, see Lowe, *Codices Latini Antiquiores*, II (2nd edn), no. 272 and below, p. 31f. It does not fit easily into the Irish scene and Hiberno-Scandinavians could well have brought it from Scotland to Ireland's Eye.

[97] Duncan, *Scotland*, pp. 117–34, 176–80; Barrow, *Kingdom of the Scots*, pp. 279–336. Anderson, *Kings and Kingship*, p. 236, on the Poppleton manuscript. She tells me: 'One would like to know what prompted someone to make the collection of historical pieces that is preserved in the Poppleton manuscript; there is some reason to think that it was put together in the earlier part of William's reign'.

[98] Jackson, *Gaelic Notes*, p. 94.

[99] Barrow & Scott, *Regesta*, II.381: the number of Anglo-French clerical names in this volume (covering the reign of William I, 1165–124) provides incontrovertible evidence of the Anglo-French culture of the clergy. See Murison, 'Linguistic relationships', p. 73.

[100] I quote Duncan, *Scotland*, p. 265.

was bishop of Ross from 1127 to ?1131. They are followed by English and French names.[101] Many of these later bishops were Scotsmen, but Gaelic had gone out of fashion. The twelfth-century dioceses, however, were mostly in the old ecclesiastical centres, places such as St Andrews, Glasgow, Rosemarkie, Dunblane, Brechin, Dunkeld. Presumably this means that early manuscripts in those centres *could* have passed into mediaeval cathedral libraries. But very few of the bishops, chancellors, precentors and canons of those churches would have been interested in vernacular manuscripts, so any texts in Gaelic would have been likely to disappear through neglect. Houses of the new and reformed religious orders were founded in considerable numbers (though mainly in Lothian) from the time of King David onwards[102] – Tironensian, Cistercian and Augustinian, with the occasional Arrouasian and Premonstratensian house. These would not have been likely to favour vernacular works. In the west the clergy was a Gaelic-speaking class though its *lingua franca* was Latin,[103] but by the end of the twelfth century the clerics and important laity in some of the most influential areas of Scotland were primarily French- and English-speaking and the clergy wrote in Latin, so it is easy to see why Gaelic manuscripts would have disappeared from those areas.

The early church-sites of Dál Riata mentioned in the literary sources are mainly on the islands with a few on the western mainland, but in addition to these there are numbers of Celtic ecclesiastical names in the west[104] and sites which may be detected by their archaeological remains.[105] We know very little of what happened to such places in the western highlands and islands during the middle ages. Lismore became the cathedral site of the bishopric of Argyll,[106] Ardchattan nearby on the mainland was refounded as a house of Valliscaulian monks in 1230 or 1231, at Iona houses of Benedictine monks and Augustinian canons were founded by Reginald son of Somerled at the beginning of the thirteenth century, there were Augustinian canons at Oronsay and Cistercian monks at Saddell.[107] What of all the rest? By 1512 the cathedral of Lismore was said to be deserted and ruinous, with neither a bishop nor a resident chapter. Even if the early monasteries had had substantial libraries they would hardly have survived under such circumstances.

But although circumstances in the middle ages did not favour the survival of early manuscripts written in Irish, many manuscripts of the early Scottish Church must have been written in Latin. Only the Book of Deer survives of all these, though early legends were incorporated into the mediaeval material from

---

[101] Watt, *Fasti Ecclesiae.*

[102] Margaret had introduced Benedictine monks to a priory at Dunfermline, and Alexander I set up an Augustinian house at Scone, but the movement did not become popular until later. See Duncan, *Scotland*, p. 134.

[103] Thomson, 'Gaelic learned orders', p. 68.

[104] Watson, *Celtic Place-Names*, pp. 244–310. See also MacDonald, '"Annat" in Scotland'.

[105] Thomas, 'Early christian Church', p. 95, and his *Early Christian Archaeology.*

[106] But there seem to be gaps in the episcopal succession here in the thirteenth, fourteenth, and fifteenth centuries: see Watt, *Fasti Ecclesiae*, pp. 26–8.

[107] Cowan & Easson, *Medieval Religious Houses* (2nd edn); McNeill & Nicholson, *Historical Atlas*, maps 14–17 and 32, and texts 12 (by I. B. Cowan) and 22 (by D. E. R. Watt).

St Andrews.[108] In the late thirteenth century, as we have seen, there was a strong interest in Scottish history and kingship and no lack of legend. I am driven to conclude that there had been little written history and written literature in early Scotland, and that history and literature were mainly oral. King-lists and some genealogies were written, but they seem to have been sufficient.[109]

All the same, there were mediaeval ecclesiastical manuscripts in 1500 which are no longer extant. The late sixteenth and seventeenth centuries were the golden age of the private collector but conditions in Scotland in that period were not conducive to the preservation of manuscripts. In Ireland the seventeenth century was one of the most fertile periods in historical collection and production. Sir James Ware and Archbishop Ussher were assembling materials for their histories, some of them among the chief treasures of Irish history. Ware employed Duald MacFirbis to transcribe and translate Irish texts, Roderic O'Flaherty was making a study of Irish history and antiquities, Michael O'Clery collected saints' Lives in Irish and assembled Irish annals, John Colgan published two major volumes of hagiography, to mention only a few scholars. Some of their manuscripts were deposited in Trinity College Dublin, some collected at the Franciscan Houses in Louvain, Rome and elsewhere.[110]

Scotland offers a great contrast to this: Sir James Balfour and Sir Richard Sibbald were both major manuscript-collectors, and Sir George Mackenzie founded the Advocates' Library (now part of the National Library of Scotland) in 1682, where many of their manuscripts are now preserved. There are some seventeenth-century historians. But few Scottish historians of the seventeenth century deal with the history of Scotland before 1050, and those who do write legend not history. Balfour's *Annales* begin with Malcolm Canmore; William Drummond of Hawthornden wrote a *History of Scotland from 1423 until 1542*.[111] Spottiswoode's *History of the Church of Scotland*[112] begins at the dawn of the christian era, claiming the Scots as among 'the first fruits of the gentiles', but his first book is almost wholly legendary in content. David Calderwood's *True History of the Church of Scotland* is more typical of Scottish seventeenth-century writing in that it deals with contemporary affairs. This comparative neglect of early Scottish historical records needs explanation.

---

[108] Anderson, 'St Andrews before Alexander I', thinks that version A of the St Andrews legend may belong to the eleventh or possibly to the tenth century.

[109] Fordun (ed. Skene, pp. 294–5) says that at the inauguration of Alexander III in 1250 a highland Scot knelt before the throne and read in Gaelic the king's genealogy back to Scota. See Legge, 'Inauguration'. Anderson, *Kings and Kingship*, p. 238, points out that Fordun seems to have copied the genealogy of Alexander III from a text of Diceto's *Ymagines*.

[110] Kenney, *Sources*, pp. 37–48; O'Sullivan, 'Irish manuscripts in case H'.

[111] Published in London in 1654. A considerable part of Drummond's library is now in the University of Edinburgh Library: see MacDonald, *Library*. Drummond is a supporter of monarchy, though the king should accept aristocratic counsel and consider responsible criticism: see Rae, 'Political attitudes'.

[112] See above, pp. 1–2.

John Pinkerton, writing in 1814, says it was caused by 'the strange spirit of fanaticism'[113] and this has some truth, for early historical records are often ecclesiastical records and to the reformers these might have smelled of popery. Spottiswoode, who was a member of the moderate episcopalian party, shows his attitude to hagiography when he speaks of St Patrick as 'doubtlesse a notable person and most worthy to be remembered', but says that 'some idle and ignorant Monks have pitifully wronged his memory with their Legends'.[114] We know that Fordun had access to two written saints' Lives which are no longer extant, a Legend of St Congal and a Legend of St Brandan,[115] though it is not very likely that either was early, and when Martin Martin made his tour of the Hebrides at the end of the seventeenth century he knew of copies of a Life of Columba in Irish on Barra and Benbecula, one of which may have survived.[116] The Scottish reformers' attitude to hagiography would not be likely to produce a Colgan or an O'Clery.

Indeed, the Scottish presbyterians were not generally interested in the early mediaeval Church. They saw their origin in the Church of the New Testament, they did not wish to be aware of a long process of development through the mediaeval Church. They did not lack the techniques of enquiry, for they numbered educated men;[117] as early as 1560 Knox laid down a plan for a schoolmaster in every parish to teach the catechism, grammar and Latin, colleges in the notable towns for 'Logick and Rhetorick with the Tongues' and universities which were to be maintained by the temporalities of bishoprics and collegiate churches.[118] But the concern was with morality; the reformers were revolting against their own ecclesiastical past, seeking their beginnings in scripture rather than in history.

A hostility to hagiology would not necessarily imply indifference to the sources of secular history, but here again current events militated against interest in early Scottish kingship. When king-lists were transcribed in the 1290s they were written to express a proud recognition of a long and unbroken line of Scottish kings. One, for instance, which belongs to the time of John Balliol, begins with Fergus, who 'estoit le primer qy se disoit roy Descoce' and finishes with 'la soum dez aunz de touz les Roys Picys et Escotes . . . tanque lencorounement Johan de Baillolf' which the writer reckons as one thousand four hundred and seventy-six years, nine months and eight days.[119] Fordun started his *Chronica gentis Scotorum* with an origin in the days of Moses as thirteenth-century apologists had done and Boece, a humanist writing in elegant Latin and aiming to show that the Scots were a nation of ancient culture, also provided them with seven hundred and fifty-five years of history

[113] Pinkerton, *Enquiry*.
[114] Spottiswoode, *History*, p. 8.
[115] Fordun, *Chronica* (ed. Skene, I. 9, 16, 23, 45).
[116] Martin, *Description of the Western Islands*, p. 292 (1934 edition); MacKinnon, *Descriptive Catalogue*, p. 92.
[117] Trevor-Roper, *Religion*, p. 437.
[118] Spottiswoode, *History*, pp. 152–64.
[119] Anderson, *Kings and Kingship*, pp. 286–9.

before Fergus mac Erc.[120] But the scholar's problem after 1567, when Mary Stewart had been forced to abdicate, was quite different. Buchanan did not wish to deny the Scots' ancient origins, but he had to demonstrate that kings had always owed their authority to election, and reigned only during the pleasure of the electors. 'For the nobilitie and people of Scotland, being a fre people, in the beginning of thare kingdom choysit thair king, adjoining to him ane counsall of the wisest . . . And sen evir the regiment of a king was admitted within the Ralm the nobilitie hes understand that it apperteyned to thame to correct the enormities of thair princes, and all kings has acknowlegit the same, except ayther quhen tyrannye mantenit them or flatterie sylit thair eis and indurit thair hartis'.[121]

With the accession of James VI the attitude to kingship must have become more cordial, but Boece and Buchanan remained the standard histories. Charles I alienated all sections of opinion in Scotland; the Covenant drawn up during his reign was in opposition to both his secular and his ecclesiastical policy, and Scotland made common cause with the Parliamentarians against him. The Cromwellian period was not presbyterian, but neither did it encourage the study of monarchy. Even with the Restoration the Scots seemed unable to shake off the consciousness of their immediate past, and with James VII the king once more became a representative of 'idolatry'. It was not until the eighteenth century, the establishment of a new line of kings, and the act of union in 1707 that Scottish historians were freed from the shackles of their mythological origins and that the writing of critical history began.

The collection of manuscripts requires a cultivated, rich and leisured class. The educated class in seventeenth-century Scotland consisted of the kirk and the law, and by 1640 the kirk was the most highly organised force in Scottish life, providing an alternative focus of loyalty to the kingship. In the seventeenth century good work was done on Scottish geography and cartography,[122] memoirs and contemporary history were written, but there was comparatively little interest in early Scottish history, either ecclesiastical or secular. A typical example of a learned man of the time is John Scott of Scotstarvet, a lawyer by profession and one of the more extreme covenanters. He helped Blaeu of Amsterdam to collect maps for his *Atlas* and translated Sir Thomas Craig's *Ius Feudale*. His work on the *Staggering State of the Scots Statesmen*[123] is a moral one, which argues the short-comings of Scottish politicians and the retribution they have received. It needed the growth of a class not

[120] Major, *Historia*, is more critical than Boece but had much less influence in shaping the received view. The early part of Holinshed's *Historie of Scotland* is mythological.

[121] Trevor-Roper, *George Buchanan*, p. 42. This quotation is not from Buchanan's *Rerum Scoticarum Historia*, published in 1582 (translation by William Bond published London 1722) but from the document presented to the Queen's Commissioners by the Earl of Morton: it is printed by Trevor-Roper, *George Buchanan*, pp. 40–50.

[122] Donaldson & Morpeth, *Who's Who in Scottish History*, is an excellent brief biographical introduction.

[123] Published in Edinburgh in 1754. It covers the period 1550 to 1650.

dominated by the kirk and the expansion of the economy as a result of the increasing links with England in the eighteenth century to provide a wider foundation for early historical writing.[124]

But by then the situation was irretrievable. Dalrymple, writing in 1705, says: 'If the curiosity of our countrymen were but a little more excited, it is probable more records and authentick deeds concerning bishoprights, abbacies, priories and other ecclesiastical benefices might be discovered in the hands of public and privat persons at home and abroad'.[125] But by his day major manuscripts had already disappeared: 'The *Registrum Prioratus Sancti Andreae* which contained the Names of Scottish and Pictish Kings and many parts of ancient History is a missing, and was last seen in the hands of Mr. James Nairn, Minister of the Abbacy of Holy rood house after the year 1660, as Mr. George Martin of Cameron lately deceased affirmed. All we have of it is some excerpts in the hands of Sir Robert Sibbald, who is Master of a greater number of Scottish manuscripts than any of his country-men.'[126] Sibbald's manuscript of the Register is now also lost, but a copy written apparently in or after 1708 is in the British Library.[127] Dalrymple's position was already much the same as our own.

I think we have to conclude that some mediaeval manuscripts were lost in the seventeenth century, some liturgical books destroyed by the reformers, that Edward removed (mainly administrative) records of the twelfth and thirteenth centuries, that the initial impact of the Scandinavians on the Church was destructive, that some Gaelic manuscripts disappeared through neglect in the later twelfth and thirteenth centuries; but when all this has been admitted my conclusion would still be that comparatively little history was written down in the early Scottish Church, that history and literature must have been largely oral and vernacular, and that the concept of history was quite different from our own. The Picts were strongly interested in their origins and the antiquity of their royal line; as early as the eighth century they had a fictitious king-list which went back some nine hundred and forty-three years before Bruide son of Maelchon, contemporary of St Columba.[128] But their attitude to history is one which we find hard to understand. They did not want contemporary history, a year-by-year chronicle recording a few events which actually happened; the technique of a historian like Bede who critically examined his sources was incomprehensible. Legend and history were indistinguishable. The Scots learned early how to keep a chronicle, presumably from the Continental examples which they saw, but if they continued it after 741 no one was interested enough to preserve it. When the Picts and Scots united in the ninth century it was the mythological and legendary conception

---

124 See Stevenson, *Scottish Revolution*, pp. 321ff., and Trevor-Roper, *Religion*, ch. 8.
125 Dalrymple, *Collections*, p. LVII.
126 *Ibid.*, p. 150.
127 London, British Library, MS. Harley 4628, fos 213–42. See Anderson, *Kings and Kingship*, p. 55.
128 The number of years is from List F.

of history which prevailed. The little early Scottish history which we have – I mean history which attempts to record what actually happened – has survived as the result of Irish[129] and English stimulus.

[129] As Dr Dumville points out to me, Roderic O'Flaherty, *Ogygia* (1793 translation, pp. 226–7), recognises that much of the history of early Scotland has to be 'extracted from Irish monuments'. At least one Scot disliked O'Flaherty's views: see MacKenzie, *Antiquity of the Royal Line.*

II

The Book of Deer

(Cambridge University Library MS. Ii.6.32)

Although Professor Kenneth Jackson has recently provided a detailed discussion of the Gaelic *notitiae* which were added to the Book of Deer in the eleventh and twelfth centuries,[1] there has been very little discussion of the original book, when and where it was written and the historical problems its construction poses. Since the edition by John Stuart in 1869[2] most of the work connected with the Book of Deer has been on the *notitiae*. Deer has been dismissed as artistically a very poor production and so has received little notice; it does not even appear in the index to Françoise Henry's history of Irish art,[3] and has only a footnote in Geneviève Micheli's *L'enluminure du Haut Moyen Age et les influences irlandaises*.[4] But an artistically poor book may afford us valuable historical evidence, so it has seemed worth while to make a detailed examination of the manuscript.

Let me start by describing the structure of the book.[5] It is a gospel-book belonging to the type known as 'pocket-gospels', due to the tiny size and minuscule hand. Patrick McGurk, who has made a study of the Irish pocket-gospels,[6] points out: 'The group as a whole is so obviously eccentric and Irish in its connection as to make certain that Ireland was the home of this particular tradition of book making'.[7] In these books each gospel is often on a separate quire or quires and it seems extremely likely that the gospels were often not bound (the subscription to the Book of Mulling refers to *haec uolumina*) but were kept together in a book-satchel. There are no prologues or chapter-lists, only the text of the gospels. Each gospel usually starts with a picture, usually on the verso of the first folio; then, opposite it, on the recto of the second folio the gospel begins with an illuminated initial. As in other Irish gospel-books the chi-rho page (the passage beginning *Christi autem generatio*, Matthew I.18) is important.

[1] Jackson, *Gaelic Notes*.

[2] Stuart, *Book of Deer*.

[3] Henry, *Irish Art during the Viking Invasions*.

[4] Micheli, *L'enluminure*, p. 7, n. 1.

[5] Dr Dumville has drawn my attention to Henry Bradshaw's description of the manuscript in Cambridge, University Library, MS. Add. 4602 B (towards the end of the file, fos 16r–18r).

[6] McGurk, 'Irish pocket gospel book'.

[7] McGurk, *Latin Gospel Books*, p. 11.

The Book of Deer shares all these characteristics. It is tiny, 154 mm x 107 mm. This is a little larger than the Book of Mulling (Dublin, Trinity College, MS. 60) and approximately the same size as the Book of Dimma (Dublin, Trinity College, MS. 59) and the Book of MacDurnan (London, Lambeth Palace, MS. 1370). It begins with a blank page; then on the verso there is a cruciform-structured picture with four human figures, representing the four evangelists, and opposite it on the recto of fo 2 a framed page with a decorative initial beginning the text of Matthew's gospel. The genealogy ends on fo 3r, half-way down the page, with the words *Finit prologus. Item incipit nunc euangelium secundum matheum*. This folio is the end of a gathering and the remainder of the recto and the verso were originally blank. The narrative of Matthew's gospel begins with the next gathering in the same way. The recto of the first folio of this gathering (fo 4) was originally blank, then on the verso is a full-page portrait of Matthew and opposite it another framed page with decorative initial beginning the text *Christi autem generatio*.[8] Matthew goes on to the end of the recto of fo 15, the end of a gathering, and fo 15v is blank. Then a new gathering starts for Mark with a blank recto, a full-page portrait of Mark on the verso, and opposite it a framed page with decorative initial starting the beginning of St Mark's gospel. The text of Mark ends at the bottom of fo 27v which is the end of a gathering. A folio (28) has here been later inserted. The Luke gathering begins on fo 29 where the recto was originally blank, the verso contains a portrait of Luke, and fo 30r is a framed page with decorative initial. The text of Luke ends nine lines down fo 40r, and the rest of that page and its verso were originally blank. Folio 41 begins a new gathering with a blank recto, a portrait on the verso and, opposite it, a framed page with decorative initial beginning the Gospel of John. John's text goes on into a third gathering, and ends seven lines down fo 84v. The remainder of this page is taken up with a picture. Then, still in the same hand, on fo 85r comes a *Credo* and a colophon in Irish which Jackson translates: 'May it be on the conscience of every one with whom the splendid little book shall be, that he should give his blessing on the soul of the poor wretch who has written it'.[9] There is no quire-signature. The verso of fo 85 is a page with four evangelist-portraits, and on the recto of fo 86 is another full-page design. The verso is blank. Thus the book, with certain exceptions which I shall note, conforms to the usual pattern.

It shares another of the characteristics of the pocket-gospels. As McGurk points out, the use of the space in one and the same manuscript varies considerably. In the Book of Deer, though this feature is not nearly so pronounced as in some other manuscripts, it still remains very unstandardised. The pages of text within the frames and opposite the pictures contain from thirteen to eighteen lines of script, the versos of these pages have an irregular number of lines, the remaining pages in the text vary from twenty to twenty-six lines. The frames differ somewhat in size and in their position on the page.

[8] Professor Julian Brown tells me: 'The arrangement of quires, texts, and miniature at the beginning of Matthew seems very unusual and also rather ingenious, in the way in which it produces two openings in which a miniature faces framed text'.
[9] *Gaelic Notes*, pp. 8–9.

Full-page pictures vary from 70 to 80 mm in breadth, 102 to 116 mm in length. Some of them appear to be placed to one side of the page, but this may be due to the binder: we can, however, see that one is as much as 29 mm from the outer margin, one as near as 20 mm. The scribe always writes straight across the page, but in the Gospel of John there are arabesques, animal and occasionally human figures in the margins. So in its varied and unstandardised use of space the Book of Deer follows the Irish pattern.

It has, however, some peculiar features which are immediately noticeable. It is later than the other pocket-gospel books. The Book of Mulling is dated by E. A. Lowe to the second half of the eighth century;[10] he dates the pages found in the same shrine, but which came from a separate book probably written in the same scriptorium, 'saec. VIII–IX'. Lowe also dates the Book of Dimma as 'saec. VIII²', and the copy of St John's Gospel now bound up with the Stowe Missal as eighth-to-ninth-century, while MacDurnan, the latest of the pocket-gospels discussed by McGurk, probably belongs to the second half of the ninth century.[11] As we shall see, our book is later than any of these. Does this mean that pocket-gospels remained in fashion and that it is merely chance that Deer is the latest to survive, or does it mean that Deer was produced in a provincial scriptorium which continued in the old style?

This is not the only unusual thing about Deer. McGurk points out the irregular gatherings of most pocket-gospels, whether in an early book like Mulling or a late book like MacDurnan. In Mulling, for instance, there was one gathering of 4, one of 22, one of 14 + 3, one of 26 + 2, one of 12 + 1, four odd leaves and a gathering of 3.[12] MacDurnan has one of 6, one of 18, three of 16, four of 10, five of 12, four of 14. Of the pocket-gospels which McGurk lists, only the Bern, Burgerbibliothek, codex 671 (which I have not seen but which he describes as 'Cornish Gospels') has all its quires in tens. Deer is here in contrast to the general practice. The first gathering is of four leaves (of which one leaf is wanting) and the last is of ten, but the six central gatherings are all of twelve. This is more regular than the usual pattern.[13] The scriptorium which made this book put it together in the usual order, but was probably used to composing its quires in a standard and not an irregular form.

The book is in an unfinished condition. The texts of Matthew, Mark and Luke each stop after one quire (at Matt. VII.22, Mark V.35, Luke IV.1). Mark goes on to the bottom of the folio and stops at the end of a story (of the healing of the woman with the issue of blood), but Matthew stops with a blank verso on which the scribe could have written, the Luke stops nine lines down the recto of fo 40, leaving a page and a half blank. So at least two, and most probably three, of the gospels were deliberately unfinished. Only John is

[10] *Codices Latini Antiquiores*, II (2nd edn), no. 276; he follows Henry, 'Irish manuscript', p. 164.
[11] Lowe, *Codices Latini Antiquiores*, II (2nd edn), nos. 277, 275, 267. On MacDurnan, see below, p. 25.
[12] I take these details from Lawlor, *Chapters on the Book of Mulling*. The leaves are now all separately mounted.
[13] The Southampton Psalter also has irregular quires: I¹², II¹², III¹⁰, IV¹⁴ (14 canc.), V¹², VI¹⁰ (9 canc.), VII¹², VIII¹⁰, IX⁸.

complete. There are in all twelve full-page frames in the manuscript. Five are completed, five have no pattern but are merely coloured, two are half-finished. All the initials are finished. We have here therefore a half-finished manuscript – not, of course, a very unusual occurrence, but one which requires notice.

There is no colophon in Deer which provides for accurate dating, so it can only be dated in sequence. The Book of Armagh, in a minuscule script, was being written in 807. The Book of MacDurnan belonged to a man who was abbot of Armagh between 888 and 927 as the colophon implies, for it says MacDurnan *uses* the text and that he teaches or preaches it (*istum textum . . . dogmatizat*);[14] it does not say he wrote it, though this is usually assumed. The script is in fact exceedingly like that of the Book of Armagh,[15] but the illumination is different, and the abbreviations include some late forms (like *g* with two commas above it for *gra-*, *f̄te* for *forte*; though it retains some earlier symbols like *ŝ* instead of the later *sic̄*). So the second half of the ninth century seems a suitable time for MacDurnan. Deer appears definitely later than MacDurnan.

The hand of Lambeth Palace MS. 1229 seems to belong to the same period as Deer. These fragments once served as the fly-leaves to a twelfth-century Llanthony manuscript. They are the remnants of a commentary, in Irish and Latin, on the Sermon on the Mount.[16] The hand is definitely not the same as Deer. The editors note that a feature of the Lambeth script is the pointed top of certain letters, whereas in Deer *f*, *s*, *p*, *m*, and *n* have usually a much flatter top than they have in the Lambeth Commentary. However, the two manuscripts have a rather similar appearance, and one unusual abbreviation is found in both, *m̊* for *mihi* instead of the *m̊* which W. M. Lindsay says is almost universal in Irish and Welsh manuscripts before 850.[17] Doris Bains, in her continuation of Lindsay's work, does not mention our abbreviation.[18] The editors of the Lambeth Commentary place the manuscript in the tenth century. The hand of the Book of Deer is markedly earlier than the hand of the Edinburgh Psalter,[19] and I should be inclined to put Deer in the first half of the tenth century.

The text of Deer is Vulgate, but with quite a lot of Old Latin admixture. (Though it is a mixed version, it is not the same mixed version as Kells.) It has Irish-type idiosyncratic spelling and an extraordinarily large number of mistakes. Some of the mistakes, such as omitted passages, could easily be due to

[14] Mael Brigte mac Tornáin died as abbot of Armagh in 927. His predecessor named in the annals died in 888. Thirty-nine years in the abbacy is an unusually long time, but it is not impossible, and his obituary-notice comments on his old age. (If he died at, say, seventy-five he must have become abbot at thirty-six.)

[15] Cf. Millar, 'Les principaux manuscrits': 'Une jolie minuscule irlandaise pointue, ressemblent étroitement à celle du Livre d'Armagh'.

[16] Published, with facsimiles, by Bieler & Carney, 'Lambeth commentary'.

[17] Lindsay, *Notae Latinae*, pp. 123–6. The fragment of the double psalter in Dublin, Trinity College, MS. 1337 (H.3.18) is tenth-century, closely related to the tenth-century Psalter of St Ouen, but the hand of the *Hebraicum*, though it is minuscule, is definitely different from the hand of Deer.

[18] Bains, *Supplement to 'Notae Latinae'*, pp. 21–2. Dr Dumville tells me that it is in a Welsh manuscript of *ca* 900 – Oxford, Bodleian Library, MS. Auct. F.4.32 (*S. C.* 2176), fo 37r, line 10.

[19] Finlayson, *Celtic Psalter*.

carelessness, but it seems to me that an expert latinist would not make senseless mistakes, and that an inexpert latinist would automatically construe as he wrote, so that some of the mistakes here could not be made by anyone with any understanding of the text. Let us take a page at random, fo 45v. John XI.13 reads 'And the pasc of the Jews was near', in the Vulgate *et prope erat pascha Iudaeorum*, but Deer (line 2) has *et properabat phasca Iudiorum*. Six lines from the bottom the Vulgate reads *dixerunt ergo Iudaei*, but Deer makes non-sense of this with *dixerunt ei ego Iudei*. The text goes on 'This temple was built in forty-six years, and you will raise it again in three days', in the Vulgate *Quadraginta et sex annis aedificatum est templum hoc, et tu tribus diebus excitabis illud*. In Deer this has become *Quadraginta et sex annis edificatum est hoc et tucribus diebus illut excitabis*. I think this sort of mistake, especially *tucribus* which is not a word at all, suggests someone whose understanding of Latin was very slight. Examples could be repeated at length.

While the text is exceptionally bad, the hand in which the gospels are written is fluent and competent.[20] The lines are not always exactly parallel, though some of the folios are ruled with a hard point on the recto and there are double bounding lines at each side to accommodate the initials; the letters sometimes lean a little to the left, sometimes to the right. All the same, the general appearance of the book is neat and compact. The scribe often fills the available space at the end of a paragraph by running over the next line. I think the pages have been ruled with a stylus in groups. The rulings cannot always be seen, but where they can the letters hang from the line. The competence of the script is emphasised by the inserted page (fo 28v, where the text is continued on the first blank recto of the next quire, fo 29r), probably eleventh-century in date, written in a very crude and uneven hand.

The initials show little originality, but they are neatly drawn in rather wiry black lines, often double lines which knot, and end in animal-heads.[21] This is all very typical of Irish tenth- and eleventh-century manuscripts, and is found in the Psalter of St Ouen, in BL Cotton Vitellius F.xi, in the Southampton Psalter and the Edinburgh Psalter and, though looking rather different, in the Welsh Psalter of Rhigyfarch.[22] Sometimes the letters have a contour of dots, again a common feature. I think these initials in the Book of Deer compare quite favourably in conception with the similar wiry initials in the other more or less contemporary manuscripts.

In the Gospel of John some passages are emphasised with arabesques, some of which are topped with animal-heads.[23] Arabesques appear in a very simple form in one instance in the Codex Amiatinus (fo 972v), more frequently in Lindisfarne, and they become common in Kells and later manuscripts.[24] The frilled triangular motif used as an arabesque in Deer is frequently employed in

[20] See Plate I.
[21] See Plate I.
[22] Lawlor, *Psalter and Martyrology of Ricemarch*.
[23] See Plate II.
[24] R. L. S. Bruce-Mitford, *apud* Kendrick *et al.*, *Codex Lindisfarnensis*, II.260, and 'Art of the Codex Amiatinus', p. 20.

the decoration of the Edinburgh Psalter. In the lower margins of the Deer Gospel of John there are naturalistic animals and animal-patterns,[25] and in one case a human figure, all simply drawn but spirited, even comic, little creatures, more elegant than the dogs in the right-hand margin of p. 227 of the Ouen Psalter.[26] They are humble descendants of the Kells cocks and dogs. The Edinburgh Psalter has long leaping dogs in the lower margins of several folios,[27] but the Deer dogs have more humour.

When one turns to the illumination one is immediately struck by the contrast which the crude illumination presents to the practised script. The motifs of the borders are few and simple. There is a four-cord plait here which is found all over Scotland from Shetland and the Isle of Barra to Perthshire and Wigtown.[28] Unfortunately there is no Irish analysis of motifs comparable to Allen and Anderson's for Scotland, but the pattern is found in Ireland. The diagonal key pattern, frequent in Deer but very irregularly executed, is found in Monifieth, Dupplin and Lindisfarne[29] and elsewhere in a slightly different form. There is also a rectangular key-pattern in Deer found in the border of the Matthew portrait and occasionally elsewhere in the manuscript, which is already present in the Book of Durrow. These motifs are traditional patterns still in use in the tenth century, and they give little help in locating the book.

The full-page drawings belong to the same tradition as the Echternach Matthew and the Dimma Mark. Early Insular illumination shows both a naturalistic kind of figure-drawing, and also a style where the human figure is represented as a series of patterns. For the early mediaeval man art could be the opening on to another world, the world of the supernatural. In Irish culture the visual objects which moved the observer most were patterns and balanced design. Human figures expressed in patterns are superbly achieved in an Insular book like the Lichfield Gospels:[30] the Book of Deer belongs to the same tradition in a very degenerate form. Dr Werckmeister[31] argues that the petal-shapes which appear so markedly in the evangelist's robes in the Echternach Gospels, the Book of Dimma and the Book of Deer were originally adopted from patterns on the belt-buckles of southern Spain, which must have been transmitted in manuscript-art to Ireland. This is possible, but it requires a good deal of faith. If we look at a picture like the MacDurnan St Mark[32] we can see something mid-way in the transformation of a realistic prototype to a figure composed of non-realistic ornament. Here is the ovoid shape made by the shoulders, the arms hold up the cloak in front, and the sleeves loop over the arms and fall into wide folds. The Dimma St Luke shows the sleeves swinging

[25] See Plate III.
[26] Henry, 'Remarks'.
[27] Fos 59r, 60v, 69r, 77v, 86r.
[28] Allen & Anderson, *Early Christian Monuments*, p. 202 (no. 503).
[29] *Ibid.*, p. 359 (no. 1004). There is a superficially similar key-pattern in the Southampton Psalter, but it is not the same. Something similar is under the arms of the Market Cross at Kells and of Muiredach's Cross at Monasterboice.
[30] See Figure 1.
[31] Werckmeister, 'Three problems', pp. 176–80.
[32] Henry, *Irish Art during the Viking Invasions*, pl. 42, for Luke.

out in the petal-pattern, but in the Dimma St Matthew[33] much of the realism has been lost: this is the Book of Deer's nearest predecessor. The progress from reality to ornamental system in the small cartoon-like figures on fo iv and elsewhere in the Book of Deer can be seen if we look at a stone at Kirriemuir in Angus, where there is an evangelist with a triangular head and a cloak arranged in a triangular pattern.[34] In his treatment of the evangelists' robes our artist is following a long-established tradition of pattern and ornament, though his execution of it is very degenerate.

Just how far he has strayed from his prototypes can be seen in his treatment of the chair, now represented only by the horizontal lines behind the figures in Matthew, Luke and John,[35] though there are the vestigial remains of a chair in the Mark-portrait. If we look back at earlier decoration it is apparent that these lines are the remains of a chair. The front-faced seated evangelist is seen clearly in the St Mark[36] or St Luke of the Lichfield Gospels or the Luke and Matthew portraits in MS. 51 of the Abbey Library of St Gall.[37] Even the non-realistic Echternach Matthew and the Dimma Mark have the chair clearly in place. In the MacDurnan portrait of St Mark[38] the upright sides of the chair are clearly visible, though its function is completely ignored. By the time we get to the Book of Deer the vertical posts of the chair have disappeared altogether and the artist seems to have no conception of what the horizontal lines are meant to represent. In the Matthew portrait they are not even level on either side of the evangelist, and one wonders what sort of sketch the scribe is following.

In many evangelist-portraits the evangelist holds a book. In Deer it looks as if the book is in a satchel of tooled leather hanging from his neck, as it most probably would have been in the cleric's own experience. It has been suggested that a house-shaped shrine is represented, and this is certainly possible. Analogies may be found on the symbol-stones, in the satchels which hang from clerics' necks on the Class III stone at Bressay.[39] On Pictish stones human figures are nearly always shown in profile, but the clerics' arms here are not put through the strap and the satchels appear to be hanging round their necks on short strings much as in the Deer pictures. There is however a much closer comparison to Deer on a Class II stone in Elgin Cathedral showing four figures in the arms of a cross, and front-face, which is rather unusual on a Pictish monument.[40] The bottom figure on the left has an angel beside him, that on the right has an eagle, so these are clearly the four evangelists, and suspended round their necks are Gospels on short straps, as in the Book of Deer. It is rather interesting that this unusual representation which antedates the manuscript is only some fifty to sixty miles from Deer.

---

[33] Henry, *Irish Art in the Early Christian Period*, pl. G, opposite p. 182, shows Mark, where the treatment of the sleeves is similar to Matthew.
[34] Allen & Anderson, *Early Christian Monuments*, III, facing p. 227 (slab 1, bottom left).
[35] See Plates I–III.
[36] See Figure 1.
[37] Duft & Meyer, *Irish Portraits*, pll. I and VII.
[38] Henry, *Irish Art during the Viking Invasions*, pl. 42.
[39] Allen & Anderson, *Early Christian Monuments*, III.7.
[40] See Figure 2.

Figure 1. Picture of St Mark from the Lichfield Gospels.

One of the oddities in our manuscript is the picture which occurs at the end of St John's Gospel, after the story of the commission to Peter and the testimony of John, so the two figures seated side by side here are presumably Peter and John. In composition this picture is rather like the pair of enthroned ecclesiastics on the Class III stone at Aldbar.[41]

A most unusual feature in Deer is the portrait of Matthew, for it shows him seated, with an elaborate forked beard and holding a long sword between his

[41] See Figure 3.

29

Figure 2. Upright cross-slab in relief, Elgin, front face. (After Allen and Anderson.)

knees, while two little figures, presumably angels, perch on the back of the chair. The only Insular gospel-book I know which has any possible parallel to this is Codex Usserianus II, 'The Garland of Howth'.[42] It is a very puzzling

[42] Todd, 'Remarks', pl. XLV. The text is printed by Hoskier, *The Text of Codex Usserianus 2*. For the date, see Lowe, *Codices Latini Antiquiores*, II (2nd edn), no. 272.

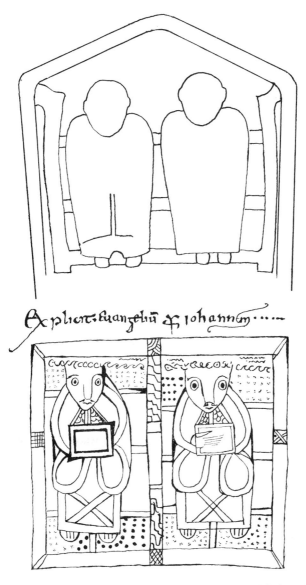

Figure 3. Above: Details from carved stone at Aldbar. (After Allen and Anderson.)
Below: Book of Deer fo 84v. (Actual size.)

manuscript. The text is based on an Old-Latin version. The hand is rather ugly, written across the page with a thick pen. There are two illuminated pages, one the *Christi autem gene(ratio)* page of Matthew (the beginning of the Gospel has been lost), the other the *Initium eua(ngelii)* page of Mark. In the decoration there are reminiscences of Kells but the uncontrolled broad-ribbon interlace looks considerably later. Lowe dates the manuscript *ca* 800.

One of the greatest difficulties is in the illuminated page for Matthew. It is

31

divided vertically into two, each half containing a figure with an angel above. Facing the reader on the left is a figure with his right hand raised in blessing, the left hand holding a book up (not in the conventional attitude), his legs crossed; on the right the figure holds what seems to be a short Irish sword (not a viking sword) over his shoulder, and in his left hand a book. Neither figure has a halo. The left-hand figure must be Matthew. The iconography and the text of the manuscript are both most peculiar. If the figure holding the sword is Matthew, then we have here a picture of Matthew holding a sword before the date of Deer. One wonders what sort of scriptorium this manuscript came from, and where it was located. Until Ussher's day the manuscript was on Ireland's Eye, but this does not of course mean that it was produced there.

Were it not for this picture of Matthew I should be inclined to say that the Deer scribe had misunderstood a design very similar to his own. The Deer Matthew is definitely sitting and holding what is clearly a sword between his knees.[43] There is a similar carving on the Cross of the Scriptures at Clonmacnoise.[44] It shows a seated cleric with another figure behind him. The stone is weathered, but round his neck hangs what I take to be a book-satchel. Between his knees is a tau-headed crozier. This tau-headed crozier could easily become a sword in the hands of a painter who did not understand the iconography and had an unclear sketch to copy.

Another peculiarity of the figures is the upraised or outstretched arms, of some of the evangelists, protruding through the frames of the pictures.[45] The human figure in the lower margin of fo 71v also has both his hands raised. This is the traditional attitude of prayer or blessing, found constantly in classical paintings. It is found on Irish slabs,[46] on Welsh[47] and on Scottish[48] stones. The angels in the Crucifixion-scene of the Southampton Psalter have their hands stretched out. So this must have been a posture quite frequently to be seen in art, though it is exceptional to find it in evangelist-portraits.

We can also see a figure with outstretched arms on the lower knop of the Lismore crozier, made for an abbot of Lismore between 1090 and 1113.[49] Thus though an evangelist-figure in this attitude is not the norm in gospel-book portrait-pages it has a respectable ancestry and was in use again in Scotland, Ireland and Wales about the time when Deer was written.

It seems quite clear that this artist was working in a scriptorium without well-established iconographical patterns. He was definitely using his own initiative by portraying the evangelists with suspended books instead of hold-

---

[43] See Plate III.

[44] See Plate IV. Henry, *Irish Art during the Viking Invasions*, says that the figure is St Matthew but I cannot see any wings on the figure behind the cleric: cf. her pl. 91.

[45] See Plate I.

[46] Roe, 'The orans'.

[47] On the ninth- or tenth-century figures at Seven Sisters and at Pontardawe, both in Glamorgan: see Nash-Williams, *Early Christian Monuments*, nos 269 and 265, and his pl. LIX.

[48] A figure on the front of St Martin's Cross, Iona, has both arms raised in blessing.

[49] For the dating, I quote Henry, *Irish Art in the Romanesque Period*, p. 77 (cf. pl. 26).

ing them, he may have been misunderstanding his prototype or copying a very unusual prototype by showing Matthew with sword instead of with crozier, and he was following an unusual manuscript-form by drawing figures with raised or outstretched arms. These features all give the book a very odd look. He has forgotten the evangelist's seat, yet the facts that the horizontal lines are still there and that he has put in an end-paper[50] show that he has some recollection, however ill-understood, of an ancient tradition.

I wondered at first if the very crude painting could be by a different man from the expert script, but I think not because the illuminations are the first page in the quire, not separate pages, as they might have been had they been executed separately. Moreover, the scribe certainly did the arabesques and the animals in the margins of the Gospel of John, and beneath the frame of the portrait of John[51] is an arabesque and a dog with raised paw. These were certainly done by the scribe. One must assume that he was practised in writing, but very unsophisticated in drawing pictures. Does this tell us anything further about the scriptorium? We have no comparative material of any kind about the productions of tenth-century Scottish scriptoria. Although there is much less Irish evidence about tenth-century drawing than about eighth-century illumination, what evidence there is suggests that the old sophistication had gone. The seventh and eighth centuries saw the development of a Hiberno-Saxon tradition from which Irish art profited enormously. Ireland, Scotland, Pictland and Northumbria all contributed to each other's art, and the discussion about the origin of the Book of Kells, a great masterpiece of this Insular art, shows how much was shared and exchanged. MacDurnan lay in that tradition. It is a beautiful book with splendid figures of the evangelists and splendid initial pages. It is written with a very fine pen, with big margins, and though the book is small the effect is sumptuous. The two tenth-century Psalters, the Southampton Psalter (St John's College, Cambridge, MS. C.9) and the Cotton Psalter (BL Cotton Vitellius F.xi), are in a very different style. The Southampton Psalter, 260 mm x 180 mm, looks like a service-book intended for the altar, a Gallican Psalter divided into three fifties with canticles, with a full-page picture at the beginning of each fifty and an illuminated initial opposite. There is comparatively little abbreviation and it is in the usual forms. Françoise Henry dates the manuscript 'in the second half of the tenth or the beginning of the eleventh century'.[52] It was glossed, probably in the early eleventh century.[53] The Cotton Psalter (Vitellius. F.xi) is probably rather earlier in the tenth century, for it appears once to have had at the end a verse asking a blessing for Muiredach, scholar and abbot.[54] Muiredach is a common name, but one of the illuminated pages has a

[50] There is an end-paper as the last page in the Book of Durrow, and Durham, Cathedral Library, MS. A.2.17 has the drawing of the crucifixion after the end of Matthew.

[51] See Plate II.

[52] Henry, 'Remarks'.

[53] This is Mrs O'Daly's view, quoted by Henry, 'Remarks', p. 34, n. 4, and it rests on the verbal forms of the Irish glosses, though some earlier elements are retained.

[54] The inscription comes from one of Archbishop Ussher's notebooks; the original manuscript was badly damaged in the 1731 Cotton fire. See O'Sullivan, 'The colophon'.

Figure 4. David and Goliath from the Cotton Psalter.

design strikingly similar to a panel on Muiredach's Cross at Monasterboice, so it seems probable that the book should be connected with Muiredach, the famous abbot of Monasterboice who died on 27 November, 924. The Cotton Psalter is a smaller book than the Southampton Psalter (approximately 168 mm × 122 mm), but it is similar in kind. The Psalters must both have been intended as splendid books, but they have the same cartoon-like quality as Deer, in which almost all trace of the humanity of the figures and the realism of the objects has disappeared. In the Cotton picture of David and Goliath, the treatment of David's eye, ear and chin is fantastic, though there is expressive feeling about the stricken Goliath.[55] The Southampton David-and-Goliath

[55] Figure 4. For the other pictures in the Cotton and Southampton Psalters, see the plates in Henry, 'Remarks'.

34

I Book of Deer, fos 29ʳ–30ᵛ (two-thirds actual size). Picture of Luke and opening of Gospel.

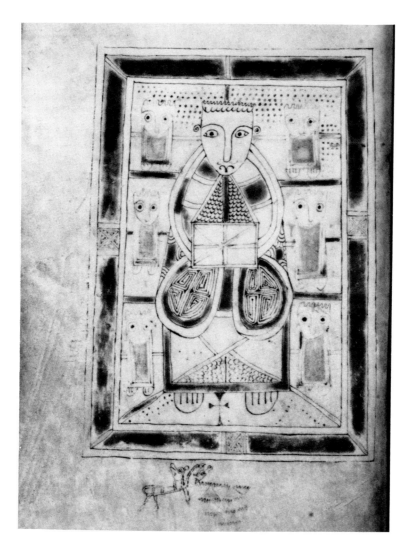

II Above: *Book of Deer, fo 41ᵛ (actual size but upper and lower margins reduced).*
Picture of John.
Below: *Last few lines of fo 51ᵛ (actual size) showing arabesque.*

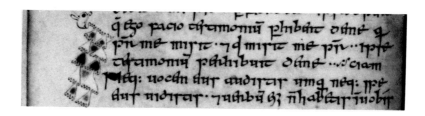

III Above: *Book of Deer, fo̅ 4ᵛ (actual size but upper and lower margins reduced).*
Picture of Matthew. The later Gaelic notitiae *are written into the space around the*
picture.
Below: *Lower margin of fo 54ᵛ.*

IV Cross of the Scriptures, Clonmacnoise, north side, panel 3. (Photograph by Professor D. H. Greene).

page is equally fantastic though less dramatic, and in the scene of David and the Lion the figures seem to be put on the page without any sense of structural composition, rather as if they were Pictish Class I symbols. The Southampton Crucifixion is the traditional scene, with angels, lance- and sponge-bearer, but it lacks emotional impact. These pictures do much to explain the ineffectiveness of the Deer illuminations: Deer is merely a very poor relation of Southampton and Cotton. The paint of the Cotton Psalter has been so badly damaged that it is difficult to imagine what it would have looked like, but in the Southampton Psalter the paint is lavishly applied to give an enamelled effect in yellow, purple, violet, pink, orange-red and brown. The scriptorium which produced Deer presumably had very little paint and was not used to mixing colours, for the only colours used are yellow and a pinky-brown. The vellum of Deer varies in quality, but is on the whole competently produced. So taking into account the hand, the vellum and the quiring, it looks as if our scriptorium was turning out some books, but that scribes were not used to illuminating them with anything more than quite small initials.

I should say one more thing about the manuscript before I try to sum up. The only gospel which the scribe copied in full was the Gospel of John, and scholars have pointed out how the early Church had a special affection for John, whom St Augustine calls 'the most eminent of the four evangelists'.[56] Bede relates that Boisil of Melrose, knowing his death was imminent, wanted to teach his disciple Cuthbert as much as lay in his power. Boisil says: '"Not more than seven days remain in which I shall have sufficient health of body and strength of tongue to teach you." Cuthbert, never doubting the truth of his words, answered, "And what, I ask, is it best for me to read, which I can yet finish in one week?" Boisil replied: "The evangelist John. I have a book consisting of seven gatherings of which we can go through one every day, with the Lord's help, reading and discussing it between ourselves so far as is necessary."'[57] The Stonyhurst Gospel, of the late seventh or early eighth century, is a Gospel of John, the eighth- to ninth-century single Gospel enshrined with the Stowe Missal is a series of selections from the Gospel of John, the eighth- to ninth-century Irish single gospel which constitutes St Gall MS. 60 is a Gospel of John in four quires. The Deer scribe has elaborated his portrait of John[58] with six angels and a cross beneath the evangelist; he has emphasised important passages in the text with arabesques, decorated some of the lower margins, and put a half-page drawing at the end. He obviously felt John was especially important.

The twelfth-century writer John of Salisbury says that St Cuthbert used the Gospel of John in healing[59] and this seems to be also what the Book of Deer was used for, because there is part of a mass for the sick on an inserted page in a hand which antedates the twelfth-century *notitiae*. This mass is very like the

[56] Brown, *Stonyhurst Gospel*, pp. 29ff.
[57] Colgrave, *Two Lives*, p. 182.
[58] See Plate II.
[59] *Policraticus*, II.1 (ed. Migne, *Patrologia Latina*, t. 199, cols 415–16), quoted by Brown, *Stonyhurst Gospel*.

Missa de infirmis in the Book of Mulling and the Book of Dimma and has the same 'Ephesine' non-Roman origins.[60] After the note *Hi sund du-beir sacorfaic dau*,[61] 'Here he gives him the sacrifice', there are almost the same words of administration as in the Book of Mulling: 'The body with the blood of our Lord Jesus Christ be health to you for perpetual life and salvation', *Corpus cum sanguine Domini nostri Iesu Christi sanitas sit tibi in uitam perpetua et salutem* (though there is a grammatical mistake in Deer).[62] It is interesting that all these three pocket-gospels have a mass for the sick, and it looks as if the gospel may have been used as a sacred object to help effect the cure just like any other relic.[63]

Can we reach any conclusions about the origins of Deer? It was a book in the tradition of Irish pocket-gospels, by a scribe with a competent hand, but whose illuminations were very crude and unsophisticated. Perhaps it might be argued that this fits what we know of tenth-century Irish books, but the more I look at the Cotton and Southampton Psalters the more it seems to me that these are splendid books. Irish scriptoria in the tenth century were not idle, though so few of their productions survive, for original writings were being composed, some in Latin but more often in Irish. However, if the Book of Deer was written in Ireland it could easily have passed to eastern Scotland via the Great Glen, following the route of the *cell*-names which demonstrate Irish penetration to the east coast of Scotland.[64]

But the book has real peculiarities in an Irish context. We have no Irish gospel-books of the tenth century, but it looks markedly different in its designs from either MacDurnan which comes a little before, or the two gospel books from the beginning of the twelfth century, one written by Mael Brigte Ua Maeluanaig (BL Harley 1802) at Armagh in 1138, the other (BL Harley 1023) probably also at Armagh rather earlier.[65] The earlier one, Harley 1023, begins towards the end of Matthew's gospel and has fairly simple initials at the beginning of Mark, Luke and John, both in frames empty of decoration but executed with great skill and spirit. Other than this the book is devoid of ornament, but it gives an impression of fluency and confidence. The manuscript written in 1138, Harley 1802, is smaller but more elaborately illuminated, with two coloured symbols (of the lion and the bull), each in decorated frames, with elaborate initials to begin Matthew and Luke and rather simpler ones (but still painted) for Mark and John, and initials blocked in with colour throughout the manuscript. The scribe Mael Brigte was clearly used to writing

---

[60] Warren, *Liturgy and Ritual*, pp. 163–73.

[61] Jackson, *Gaelic Notes*, p. 9.

[62] The Book of Mulling reads 'Corpus cum sanguine Domini nostri Iesu Christi sanitas sit tibi in uitam eternam': Warren, *Liturgy and Ritual*, thinks this means that both elements were administered at once. The Book of Dimma says 'Corpus et sanguis . . .' and the Stowe Missal has 'Refecti Christi corpore et sanguine . . .'.

[63] See the references for this practice quoted by Brown, *Stonyhurst Gospel*, p. 36, n. 1, who says, 'I think the pocket-gospel books were token books, part portable furniture for the mass and part amulets; and no doubt oaths could be taken as well'.

[64] McNeill & Nicholson, *Historical Atlas*, map 4b.

[65] Henry, *Irish Art in the Romanesque Period*, pll. 6–7, D and F.

and illumination. Both these manuscripts clearly belong to the Irish tradition, but they are at the heart of it, whereas Deer is on the fringes.

The peculiarities of Deer seem to me to make it likely that it was written in some provincial scriptorium, quite possibly in Scotland, and it is remarkable that the Elgin stone provides so close an analogy to the Deer evangelists with their books. If you are inclined to argue that so badly illuminated a book could not have been produced in a society with a fine monumental art, then the same might equally well be said of Ireland. You would expect a Scottish scribe of the tenth century to be producing an Irish-style book with peculiar features. This is what Deer is.

The scribe of Deer was used to writing, though he had been very badly trained in Latin, for the text is extraordinarily bad; he was fluent at executing initials and drawing little animals and marginal arabesques. He knew quite well how gospel-books were put together. But I doubt very much that he was copying an illuminated book. He seems to have had sketches which were not at all clear: this would explain why St Matthew's tau-headed crozier turns into a sword, why the uprights of the chairs have disappeared and why in one case the seat and back are not level. He clearly did not understand what he was copying. If he had had a sketch-book and not an illuminated manuscript to copy it would also explain the unconventionality of some of the pictures, the evangelists' hands stretched upward or outward through frames, the gospels suspended round their necks instead of held in front of them, all designs found on contemporary stones but not the norm in gospel-books either earlier or later. I would suggest that the Book of Deer was written by an experienced scribe who had seen an illuminated gospel-book and was familiar with carved stones, but that the models for drawings which were circulating in his monastery and which he used were certainly not finished manuscript-illuminations but possibly sketch-books. The scriptorium he worked in was a provincial one, not one which already had a finely illuminated book for him to copy. It was not used to illuminating, and had little paint for the pictures.

You may be thinking that these deductions about the scriptorium are untenable, that the manuscript is the work of an incompetent scribe and it is mere chance that this one survived. But the writing is good, the initials are competent, the arabesques and animals are spirited, and the vellum is on the whole quite well prepared. Monasteries did not throw away valuable vellum. Moreover, it was not only the scribe (and almost certainly his contemporaries) who thought this was a 'splendid little book', as he says. In the eleventh and twelfth century it must still have seemed so to the monks of Deer, for when they sought out their most valuable book in which to record their title-deeds, this was the most precious book they could find, probably the oldest one and the one with the holiest associations. This fact tells us something about at least one Scottish centre in the eleventh and twelfth centuries.

III

Early christianity in Pictland[1]

Bede was interested in the Picts. They were his neighbours on his northern frontier. During his childhood the English had penetrated deeply into the land of the southern Picts, and in his youth his own king, Ecgfrith, had been decisively beaten by them in a great battle at Nechtanesmere. When King Nechton consulted Bede's abbot, Ceolfrith, about Roman customs Bede must have known of the reply and he must almost certainly have met the Picts who came with Nechton's message. His reporting of Pictish events is brief but sympathetic: he tells us that Bishop Cuthbert advised Ecgfrith against the disastrous attack of 685, and this tone is in marked contrast to a contemporary description of 'the bestial tribes of the Picts'.[2]

The information which Bede gives us about the Picts is basic to our knowledge of them, so we shall begin by summarising it. He tells us that they spoke a language different from that of the Britons and Irish[3] and that they were divided into northern and southern groups, separated by 'steep and rugged mountains'. It is generally agreed that this is the Mounth, the range running roughly east-west, south of Aberdeen, which separates Mar and Buchan from Angus and the Mearns. When Bede wrote, the southern boundary of Pictland was clearly on the Forth, though he claims that King Oswald (634–42) had brought the Picts under his dominion.[4] Certainly during Ecgfrith's reign (670–85) the English must have penetrated far into southern Pictland,[5] and St Wilfrid's biographer asserts that this territory was part of the 'ecclesiastical kingdom of St Wilfrid'.[6] The monastery of Abercorn on the Forth was founded, and Trumwine was made bishop over the Picts. But Nechtanesmere, fought north of the Tay in 685, changed the situation, the Picts recovered control of their territory, and Abercorn had to be abandoned. In telling us of the events of Ecgfrith's reign Bede speaks of his own lifetime and from his own experience.

---

[1] The Jarrow Lecture for 1970. I owe the idea of this lecture to an undergraduate of my own, Mrs Siân Victory. I am most grateful to Mrs Isabel Henderson for reading the typescript and allowing me to incorporate her criticisms, and to Professor Kenneth Jackson for discussion.

[2] Colgrave, *Life of Bishop Wilfrid*, § 19.

[3] See the definitive study by Jackson, 'The Pictish language'.

[4] *Historia Ecclesiastica*, III.6.

[5] *Ibid.*, IV.26; cf. Colgrave, *Life of Bishop Wilfrid*, § 19.

[6] *Ibid.*, § 21.

He also gives us an account of the original conversion of the Picts. The southern Picts had been converted by Nynias (Ninian), a British bishop 'who had been regularly instructed at Rome'. The northern Picts had been converted by St Columba, who came to Britain in the ninth year of Bruide son of Maelchon 'to preach the word of God to the northern Picts'. The Picts gave the island of Iona to the saint to found a monastery.[7] It is worth noting that Bede expressly says that Columba came to evangelise the Picts, for this is very unusual. Irish pilgrims usually went out, like Fursey, 'seeking salvation and solitude' and, though they soon found themselves preaching and teaching, evangelisation seems to have been something which happened as a result of pilgrimage rather than its motivation. Either Columba was quite different from other Irish 'exiles for Christ', or Bede's informants were reading history backwards from a Pictish standpoint.

Who were Bede's informants? He really tells us very little about early Pictish christianity and he had not himself been in Pictland. He may have heard of Ninian from Pehthelm, who was the recently appointed bishop of Whithorn which Bede believed to have been Ninian's own see. But surely the most likely people to give him his account of Columba's settlement at Iona on land given by a Pictish king were the messengers sent by King Nechton to Ceolfrith of Jarrow?[8] Nechton had become aware that Easter was kept in his land at a time different from the time the English kept it. He himself, so he said, was well informed about Easter and the Roman tonsure, but he asked Ceolfrith for arguments with which to confute his opponents. He also wanted architects to build a church for him 'in the Roman manner' which he promised to dedicate to St Peter; and he declared that he and his people would follow Roman custom 'as far as their remoteness from the Roman language and nation would allow'. Ceolfrith's long reply was interpreted for Nechton who 'it is said' (*perhibetur*) received it gladly and declared that it was to be accepted 'by all my clergy in my kingdom'. Bede tells us that he had the new Easter-cycles 'sent throughout all the provinces of the Picts to be transcribed, learned and observed', and ordered that all monks and clerics should receive the Petrine tonsure.[9]

This has become the received view of early Pictish christianity. Nevertheless, it raises some difficulties. Pictish historians are aware of them. They are implied in Mrs Anderson's admirable paper on 'Columba and other Irish saints in Scotland'.[10] In recent years archaeologists have underlined the significance of material remains as evidence for the progress of conversion. But the only recent scholars who have openly rejected Bede's account of the christianisation of the Picts have done so by means and reached conclusions which are unacceptable. I therefore thought it would be worth while to face the

---

[7] *Historia Ecclesiastica*, III.4. Bede also says that Columba converted the Pictish people (*gens*).

[8] The forms of the names of Bruide (*Bridio*, as a Latin ablative) and Nechton (*Naiton*) which he gives are Pictish.

[9] *Historia Ecclesiastica*, V.21.

[10] Cf. Henderson, *The Picts*, p. 76.

problems raised by Bede, reexamine the evidence, and see if we can find a solution which will accommodate it all.

I shall take the bull by the horns and deal first with what is usually regarded as the 'negative' evidence. With one exception, which I shall discuss in a moment, we have not a single surviving Pictish text. If Pictish vernacular literature was ever written down it might well not have been copied after the language had been superseded by Irish. But Pictish clerics must have written in Latin. The lacuna is the more surprising if we consider what was happening in seventh-century Ireland, for among the Irish this is a period of intense activity. There the *sapientes* were getting to work on the study of the Bible, writing commentaries which approached the subject in various ways. We know the names of various exegetes, and have the tracts of some. One of the most famous was Manchán, whose name is still found as an authority in tenth- and twelfth-century manuscripts.[11] Lismore seems to have been a centre of exegetical studies.[12] Churchmen of both the 'Roman' and the 'Irish' party were holding synods and drawing up canons, a great many of which survive in manuscripts copied outside Ireland. This was the period when the 'Irish' party was trying very hard to bring the Church into line with the native law.[13] Individual churches were drawing up their claims to ecclesiastical jurisdiction.[14] Penitentials and monastic rules were being compiled. The earliest Irish hagiography was written then, Lives of Brigit and Patrick and Columba. Hymns were composed for singing in church – we have several of these – and one service-book of this period has come down to us, a book written at Bangor, taken to Bobbio and now in the Ambrosian Library at Milan. Letters were written.[15] The standard of calligraphy was sometimes high: the *Cathach* of Columba was written in an Irish scriptorium and the Book of Durrow, though it may have been written in Northumbria, was produced in a scriptorium with Irish associations. If the Columban Church was firmly established in Pictland, why were Pictish monasteries not joining in these varied activities?

Let us suppose that they were. Then why has nothing of all this survived? The usual explanation of the troubled state of Scotland, during the viking age and towards the end of the middle ages, is no answer, for the Irish kingdom of Dál Riata in south-western Scotland suffered similar disturbances, but texts written there are extant. The fact is that Iona was an active scribal centre. A chronicle was kept there in the seventh century and it got incorporated into the Irish annals *ca* 740.[16] The seventh- or eighth-century 'History of the Men of

---

[11] I owe this information to the kindness of Robert McNally, who showed me photographs; the text has been partially edited as 'Catéchèses celtiques' by Wilmart, *Analecta*, pp. 29–112. See further Bischoff, 'Turning-points', pp. 145–9.

[12] Grosjean, 'Sur quelques exégètes'.

[13] Hughes, *Church in Early Irish Society*, pp. 123–33.

[14] *Ibid.*, pp. 84–90, 111–20.

[15] Cummean's on the Easter question and the collection of Columbanus's have survived. For another, see Hughes, *Church in Early Irish Society*, p. 93.

[16] Bannerman, *Studies*, pp. 9–26. Incidentally, it may be worth noting that the Annals of Ulster, which incorporate the most entries from this chronicle, use the word *Picti*, not *Cruithni*, for the Picts. This is also Adomnán's usage. See Bullough, 'Columba, Adomnan', p. 25, and Anderson & Anderson, *Adomnan*, p. 63.

Scotland', which contains the genealogies of Dalriadic kings and an account of the households and naval forces in each area, survives in Ireland in fourteenth-, fifteenth-, and seventeenth-century manuscripts and still later copies.[17] The earliest manuscript of Adomnán's Life of Columba was written by Dorbbéne in the early eighth century and taken to the Continent perhaps before 800, certainly not later than the ninth century.[18] One of the compilers of the *Collectio Canonum Hibernensis* at the beginning of the eighth century, a collection which is in many Continental libraries, was Cú Chumine of Iona. Not one of these manuscripts survives in Scotland. Irish monks were great travellers and they took their manuscripts with them. We hear of one Pict who went to Ireland, presumably from Iona, carrying a book of hymns written by St Columba.[19] Where are all the other Pictish pilgrims, with their books? Bede constantly mentions Irish monks, and even British clerics, but never a Pict. If the Columban Church was securely established in seventh-century Pictland with active scribes, why have all their recognisable works perished?

If we argue that Pictish monastic scriptoria were active like their Irish counterparts in the seventh century then much the best explanation to account for the loss of their work is given by Nechton's expulsion of the Columban monks in 717. A closure of monasteries might have resulted in a dispersion of manuscripts and an interruption of scribal tradition. Some manuscripts from such Columban houses, presumably written in an Irish script, may survive unrecognised. Even this explanation is hardly adequate to explain the lacuna. It is surprising that more texts recognisably Pictish from their contents did not enter Irish Columban libraries. Pictish scribes who could copy Easter-tables certainly existed in 710, but the lack of sources suggests that the monastic scriptoria were not very active, that there was no Pictish Adomnán, no Pictish Lindisfarne.

There is one early Pictish text, a list of kings. The best version of it (A) is in a manuscript (now in Paris) written in the fourteenth century at York. Three other manuscripts (B, C, and H) are in the hands of fifteenth-century Irish scribes. The remaining four manuscripts (D, F, I, K), all of the later mediaeval or modern period, were written in Scotland or written from Scottish originals, though only one is now in Scotland.[20] This is exactly what one would expect, and it once more compels the question why, if mediaeval scribes were prepared to copy a list of names, they would not have copied an early chronicle or the Life of an early Pictish saint if such a text had been known to them.

There is no satisfactory edition of the Pictish king-lists in their variant versions, and I am most grateful to Mrs Isabel Henderson for allowing me to use the transcripts she has given in an appendix to her Cambridge doctoral thesis, where she sets out, in parallel columns, the readings of these eight

[17] Bannerman, *Studies*, pp. 27–156.

[18] Anderson & Anderson, *Adomnan*, p. 3.

[19] Adomnán, *Vita Columbae*, II.9.

[20] Mrs Henderson tells me that these four manuscripts ultimately go back to the same text. The other four manuscripts also represent one text; in other words, there are two archetypal lists, the transcriptions of List II being textually very corrupt.

manuscripts.[21] I shall not discuss the purely legendary material at the beginning of the lists, which Mrs Marjorie Anderson and Mrs Henderson both believe to be late (a view with which no one is likely to disagree). The main part of the lists consists of the names of kings with the names of their fathers, followed by a number indicating their regnal years. I want first to consider the kings from Bruide son of Maelchon, who was reigning when Columba came to Iona, up to Nechton son of Derile who, in Bede's day, brought the Picts over to Roman observance. All the lists for this period are nearly unanimous about the names and sequence of the kings (though the spelling is often very different), [22] but there is often substantial divergence about the regnal years. Usually, A, B, C, and the Book of Í Mhaine are in agreement, and since these seem to be the best manuscripts I am following their readings.

The first and most remarkable thing to note is that every single one of these fourteen kings between Bruide and Nechton is mentioned in the Irish annals, and except one each has his obit recorded there. In a most illuminating article John Bannerman has followed up the suggestions of Eoin Mac Neill and T. F. O'Rahilly and has argued that an annalistic record was kept at Iona from the time of Columba until ca 740, primarily noting events concerning Scottish Dál Riata, but including Pictish, British and some English happenings.[23] The obituary notices of the Pictish kings must have been copied into an Irish chronicle ca 740 in Ireland from the Iona text, and the one obit not in our late copies of the Irish annals has probably been dropped in manuscript-transmission. The seventh century is still an early period in the development of Irish annalistic writing, and the fact that all these fourteen kings of the Pictish lists are here in the Iona chronicle with (save in one case) their regnal years calls for comment.

The first possibility to be examined is that one of the texts may be derived from the other. It is impossible that the annals could be derived from the king-lists. The Iona chronicle becomes much fuller in the second half of the seventh century, and from the reign of Drust son of Domnall (663–78) to 740 when the chronicle was transcribed in Ireland, there is a number of entries about Pictish affairs other than the obits. Indeed, it would be possible to write a fairly detailed political history of Pictland during this period. Since the king-lists are regnal lists without further information[24] the annals were not derived from them. It also seems extremely unlikely that the king-lists copied the chronicle.

There is a considerable degree of similarity between the chronology of the

[21] Henderson, 'Critical Examination', and Anderson, Kings and Kingship, are now the starting-points for any enquiry.

[22] List A seems to preserve the Pictish forms best.

[23] Bannerman, Studies, pp. 9–26; cf. his 'Critical Edition'. I think that the first half of this chronicle may go back to entries made in the margins of Easter-tables, for it is fairly sparse, but it becomes much fuller ca 670 and from this time on it must imply a proper chronicle with a year-by-year entry.

[24] Other than the fact that Bruide was baptised by Columba in the eighth year of his reign, which the annals do not mention. The notes in the king-lists belong to the earlier part of the lists and are almost certainly scribal annotations.

king-lists and the Iona chronicle between 631 and 761, but not identity. This is seen most clearly in the form of a table.

Names from A	Chronicle dates	King-list regnal years
Garnard f. Uuid	631–5	4 (A), 5 (BCH), 8 (DK)
Breidei f. Uuid	635–41	5 all versions
Talore frater eorum	641–53	12 (ABCH), 11 (DFI)
Talorcen f. Enfret	653–7	4 all versions
Gartnait f. Donuel	657–63	6½ (ABCH), 5 (DF), 6 (I)
Drest frater eius	663–72	7 (ABC), 6 (DFHIK)
Bredei f. Bili	672–93	21 (ABFI), 20 (CDHK)
Taran f. Entifidich	693–7	4 (ABCHK), 14 (DFI)
Bredei f. Derelei	697–706	11 (ABCH), 18 (D), 31 (FIK)
Necthon f. Derelei	706–24/26, 728–9 died 732	15 (ABCH), 31 (D), 18 (FIK)
Drust et Elpin	724/6–8	5 (ABCH), 24 (DFIK)
Onuist f. Urguist	729–761	30 (ABCH), ½ (D), 16 (FIK)

It looks, therefore, as if the two sets of calculations were made independently. There is one variant reading which supports the view that the king-lists did not copy the chronicle. The chronicle gives the death of Nechton son of Cano in 621 (his predecessor had died in 598). This seems to be the *Nechton nepos Uirb* of the king-list. The lists normally give the king's patronymic, not his family name. If the list had been copied from the chronicle it seems almost certain that the patronymic, as in other cases, would have been given.[25]

Both Mrs Anderson and Mrs Henderson believe lists and chronicle to be independent, and I am driven to the same conclusion. Nevertheless, the correspondence needs explaining. Mrs Henderson, in the all too brief appendix to her book on the Picts, says that 'only the position of Iona as head of the church in Pictland can account for a non-Pictish source being sufficiently interested in the Pictish succession' to enter all these kings.[26] This, I am sure, is right but can we take the explanation further? I have toyed with what seemed, at first, an attractive hypothesis. Have we here a list of donors? Bede, you will remember, says that Bruide gave the site of Iona, and Irish law was interested in the heirs of the founder and, secondly, in the heirs of the donor. The Irish chronicler was not so much concerned with Pictish as with Dalriadic events, yet he gives us a list of the heirs of Bruide which is only paralleled in its detail by his list of the heirs of Columba. Yet this hypothesis raises difficulties. These kings are all overlords of Pictland, but are they all strictly the kin of Bruide? For some seem to have their family-lands in northern, others in southern, Pictland. And if the Irish sources (Adomnán and the annals) see these kings as the donor's heirs why do they not say that Bruide granted Iona

---

[25] Even if the identification is wrong, a compiler without an independent source would have been deceived by it.

[26] *The Picts*, p. 167.

to Colum Cille? Moreover there are ten kings ranging back before Bruide to Drust son of Erp (who reigned a hundred years and belongs to the semi-legendary past). They need only represent a century or so in time, for the average length of a Pictish king's reign during the seventh century, calculated from the annals, is just under ten years.[27] But if this list was a list of donor's heirs for whom the Columban monks prayed at mass the kings before Bruide would not be remembered. I am reluctantly compelled to reject this explanation and with it my supporting evidence for Bede's account of the donation. Bede's story thus has to rest on his authority alone, and we have to remember that his source was most probably Pictish-orientated.

I thus return to the explanation of a king-list kept in a Columban monastery. Why was it kept? It is worth noting that it was the fashion to keep king-lists with regnal years in Northumbrian scriptoria (where scribes were prepared to omit the names of kings whose rule had not accorded with their notions of propriety).[28][29] Did they learn this habit from the Irish?[29] Did the Picts learn it from their Irish or from their Northumbrian teachers? Mrs Anderson believes that the king-lists were carelessly deduced from native annals.[30] Mrs Henderson thinks that when the new Easter-tables were drawn up about 710, the annotations in the margins of the old tables might have been separately assembled.[31] This hypothesis seems extremely likely.

The chronology of the king-lists and of the chronicle cannot both be correct. Here it seems to me likely that the Iona chronicle will provide a more accurate chronology than a king-list. The chronicle has entries from Columba's time onwards, entries which become much fuller in the second half of the century. It would not have been kept with any *anno Domini* dating, but, at least as the entries become fuller, the separate years would have been clearly indicated. The calculations for the king-lists, on the other hand, were probably based either on the occasional marginal entry or on synchronisation, and in this way errors would be much more likely. The discrepancies between the different versions of the lists are sometimes so great that one wonders if the scribe merely guessed.[32] Our only reasonably reliable dating for the Pictish kings is from the Iona chronicle.

It looks as if the compilers of the king-lists from Bruide to Nechton extended the list backwards, drawing on legend and providing a chronology. The narrative art of the later symbol-stones suggests that the Picts had a lively oral

---

[27] According to version A of the Pictish king-list these ten kings reigned 102 years.

[28] Bede, *Historia Ecclesiastica*, III.1. Those who compute the dates of kings omitted the names of Æthilfrith's sons who apostasised during the disastrous year between Cadwallon's defeat of Edwin and Oswald's victory. Cf. Dumville, 'Kingship'.

[29] The northern section of the *Historia Brittonum*, interested in north British affairs, used as its chronological framework a list of Northumbrian kings: see Dumville, 'North British section'. This seems to suggest that British scribes were not computing British king-lists; cf. Miller, 'Geoffrey's early royal synchronisms'.

[30] 'Lists of the kings', p. 20.

[31] *The Picts*, pp. 164–5.

[32] For example, for Gartnait son of Domelch the Annals of Ulster record a reign of 584–98, while texts of the king-list give *xi* (ABCH), *xx* (DFI), and *xxx* (K).

literature, and we know that the vernacular heroic poetry of their neighbours the North Britons was flourishing in the sixth century. Sources such as these provide the means for taking the list back a century with a reasonably accurate sequence of names. After Nechton the different recensions of the king-list seem to have been continued independently.[33] The annals continue with a fairly full account of Pictish affairs until about 740, when the Iona chronicle was taken to Ireland and used in compiling the Irish annals to which all extant versions go back. Pictish entries continue thereafter, but they are comparatively few and very laconic. Mrs Henderson has proposed that the chronicle was continued, possibly at Applecross on the mainland opposite Skye, a monastery founded from Bangor by Maelrubai in 673.[34] This seems likely. Applecross had a scriptorium which kept a record of its founder's heirs and it stayed in touch with Bangor, for a cleric from Applecross died as abbot of Bangor in 802. Certainly the entries suggest that the chronicle was kept somewhere on the western seaboard. Wherever it was kept, the transmission of the chronicle changed. Whereas a scribe in Ireland, possibly at Bangor *ca* 740, drew up his Irish annals with an Iona chronicle before him, using it as one of his basic sources, the later Scottish entries were most probably inserted into an already existing Irish chronicle. This would make for abbreviation and substantial cutting.

This long discussion of the absence of early texts and the possible origin of the king-lists leads me to take a sceptical view about the condition of latinity in the early Pictish Church. There were clerics who could keep lists of kings, say the services and copy Easter-tables; there were some at Nechton's court who could translate Ceolfrith's Latin, but I would take Bede quite literally when he reports that Nechton promised to accept Roman usages for his people 'in so far as their remoteness from the Roman language would allow'. Latin was equally a foreign tongue to the Anglo-Saxons, yet one cannot imagine Bede using this phrase of the Northumbrian Church. I think Nechton knew that the practice of Latin among the Picts was much more limited than it was among the Irish or among the English.

Now let us turn to the positive evidence of the symbol-stones and, first of all, to the Class I stones. These show a series of stereotyped designs in various combinations, incised on stone slabs.[35] The largest group bears two symbols, but there are sometimes three or four symbols on a single slab. They are usually expertly executed and must imply aristocratic patronage and specialist execution. The designs themselves are artistically sophisticated. Scholars disagree about the purpose of these stones. Were they funerary or commemorative in character, did they register ownership or obligation as has been recently suggested? Yet in spite of varying interpretations it is universally

---

[33] Mrs Henderson thinks that the compilers of both versions of the king-list used the same source for their entire lists, but drew them up independently. Mrs Anderson thinks that up to Nechton the lists depended on a common source, but that they are thereafter independent.

[34] *The Picts*, pp. 167–8.

[35] Stevenson, 'Pictish Art', p. 98, or Henderson, *The Picts*, p. 105, set out some of the most common Class I symbols.

agreed that these stones had a specific meaning for the Picts, for the combination of symbols is not haphazard but deliberate.[36]

Now the normal way to convey a message in a society which possesses a literate class is by an inscription. The British put up their inscribed memorial stones; the Irish recorded some names in ogom, an 'alphabet' which is based on Latin. The Picts evolved a different method: does its evolution and general practice not belong to a pagan society?[37] This is not as conclusive an argument as I should like it to be because we do not know what was the purpose or context of the symbol-stones and no significant number of the Class I stones appears to be associated with ecclesiastical sites. Thus it is impossible to draw any strict analogy between the symbol-stones and early British memorials. Nevertheless I still think that the most obvious way in which an early christian society on the fringes of the Roman world would record a message would be by an artistic design accompanied, at least sometimes, by a few words.

There is nothing specifically christian about the Class I symbols, and there is considerable disagreement among archaeologists and art historians about their date. Professor Thomas thinks that they originated between the first and third centuries A.D., Dr Stevenson and Mrs Henderson connect the evolution of the symbols with Anglo-Saxon jewellery and Hiberno-Saxon manuscripts of the seventh century. There is general agreement among modern scholars that they first appeared on the field-monuments between about 500 and 750.[38] I am not qualified to enter this discussion and merely reiterate that their evolution seems to belong to a non-literate society, on which christianity had had little, if any, influence.

The Class I stones are scattered throughout Pictland, but by far their heaviest area of concentration is north of the Mounth, on the shores of the Moray and Dornoch Firths, down the Spey corridor and up the Don-Urie valley.[39] As Professor Thomas points out in his thought-provoking article on North British christianity, it is probably significant that the Class I stones are much less heavily represented in the territory of the southern Picts,[40] for conversion to christianity began in the south earlier than it did in the north. The Class II stones, on the other hand, are concentrated in southern Pictland, with a much lighter scatter north of the Mounth.[41] These stones clearly point to a society which had accepted christianity and was fusing pre-christian symbols and christian imagery. They bear a cross decorated with interlace ornament carved in relief on a dressed slab, accompanied by symbols usually

[36] This remains the view of the most recent writers on the subject: Henderson, 'Meaning'; Anthony Jackson, 'Pictish social structure'.

[37] We may leave the Pictish ogom-inscriptions out of account here, for they are a late import, probably of the eighth or ninth century and showing Gaelic influence.

[38] [But Duncan, *Scotland*, pp. 35–6, is prepared to date a Class I stone to *ca* 400.]

[39] Henderson, *The Picts*, p. 110. See her distribution-map, p. 109. She argues that the stones round the Moray and Dornoch Firths are of specially high quality, and that the monuments therefore originated in this region.

[40] Thomas, 'Evidence', pp. 106–7. Mrs Henderson's map (*The Picts*, p. 109) shows twenty-one sites between the Forth and the Mounth.

[41] Mrs Henderson's map (*ibid.*, p. 111) gives eighteen sites.

on the other side of the slab. Although some of the Class I and Class II stones may overlap in date, scholars agree that Class I must precede Class II in type.

The influence of Hiberno-Saxon art on the Class II stones has frequently been noted. Mrs Henderson regards 'the beginning of Class II as one of the effects of the Pictish-Northumbrian rapprochement brought about by Nechton around 710'; Professor Thomas dates them from the late seventh century onwards.[42] As we have already seen, Bede claims that English influence was penetrating into Pictland before the death of Oswald in 642, and it was indisputably present from the beginning of Ecgfrith's reign in 670. Nevertheless there seems to me to be a real difficulty about the earlier date. The area of deepest English penetration must have been immediately to the north of the Forth. It was beside the Forth that they founded their bishopric for the Picts. Nechtanesmere is considerably to the north of the Firth of Tay, but Bede makes it clear that Ecgfrith made an attack on Pictish territory, leading his army into Pictland to raid, and that he pursued the Picts farther into their own country when they appeared to flee. Thus the battle was fought well beyond the anglicised area, which may have extended only to Strathearn and the southern shore of the Firth of Tay. The Class II stones are concentrated in quite a small area. With the exception of two outliers on the northern shore of the Firth of Forth they are all north of the Earn and the Firth of Tay, with the main concentration in Strathmore and Angus. This could not have been the chief area of English influence. The Iona chronicle describes Bruide as 'king of Fortriu' when it gives his obit, and this, the land immediately north of the Forth, was the area which the Picts recovered after their victory and Ecgfrith's death. *Yet in this area there is not a single Class II stone.*

Though the Class II stones show Hiberno-Saxon influence, it is transmuted into something distinctively Pictish. Strathmore and Angus, the centre of the Class II stones, also have quite a number of Class I stones, whereas Fortriu has only one, though there are four in Fife. This suggests that the Class II stones did not evolve until Hiberno-Saxon influence had penetrated north and west of the Tay, that is, not before Nechton's reign. The comparatively light scatter of Class II stones in northern Pictland may suggest that a Roman-type Church established under English influence was much less apparent in the north.[43]

Before we can draw any conclusion about early Pictish christianity we must look carefully at the evidence of Adomnán. Adomnán was not Bede, and he was writing hagiography to glorify his patron; nevertheless he is an honest man who is trying to be accurate. Like Bede, he often tells us who his informants were, and sometimes gives us the transmission of the story he reports.[44] He writes an orderly account, in three books, of the saint's prophecies, miracles and visions. He is not, like his contemporary Tírechán (who

---

[42] Henderson, *The Picts*, p. 132; Thomas, 'Interpretation', p. 33.

[43] Mrs Henderson points out to me that, although these stones are fewer in number, they include some of the most ambitious and distinguished monuments.

[44] For example, that he had oral information from his predecessor, Abbot Faílbe, who had it from Ségéne, the fifth abbot. Other instances are cited by Hughes, *Church in Early Irish Society*, p. 61, n. 1.

wrote of Patrick in Ireland) attempting to make claims to ecclesiastical property, so when we hear of monastic houses which were part of the saint's *paruchia* it is only because they are connected in some way with the narrative. He wrote almost certainly between 688 and 692 (in any case before his death in 704), so his account is a generation earlier than Bede's.[45] And if Columba really had come, as Bede's informants told him, in order to preach to the Pictish people, no one was in a better position to know it than Adomnán, who would surely have recorded his successes under the heading 'miracles wrought by his saintly powers'.[46]

Adomnán does not seem to know very much about Columba in Pictland. There are several references to journeys 'across the ridge of Britain'. Most of his stories centre on the court of King Bruide (son of Maelchon) and the river Ness. Outside Bruide's court only one miracle is located in a definite place, at *Airchartdan* beside Loch Ness, now Urquhart.[47] The other miracles, unlocated, concern a malignant well and the resurrection of a dead boy.[48] There is also an occasion when Columba rescues one of his own monks from a sea-monster in Loch Ness, to the wonder of the 'pagan barbarians'.[49] These stories are all in the book on Columba's miracles, but it is surprisingly little for one who was supposed to have converted the northern Picts.

What Adomnán does and does not say about Columba's relations with King Bruide is worth nothing. Bruide, like his people, was pagan. At his court was a *magus*, Broichan, who was the king's fosterer. There were contests between Columba and Broichan, in which Broichan was worsted. But there is absolutely no suggestion by Adomnán that the king was converted and baptised. It is astonishing that Adomnán omitted to say this in winding up his account of miracles at Bruide's court if it actually happened. Bruide regarded Columba 'with high esteem' touched with fear; he received him at court and listened to his request for protection for Irish pilgrims who might land in the Orkneys. But the implication of Adomnán's account is that he never formally accepted christianity. There are reports of the conversion and baptism of two Pictish households.[50] These households were obviously headed by men of substance, but there is no suggestion that Columba succeeded in making widespread conversions among the pagan Pictish aristocracy.[51]

By Adomnán's time there were Columban foundations among the Picts, whom he regards as separated from the Irish by the spine of Britain.[52] During his own lifetime, he tells us, the world had twice been ravaged by pestilences, but on both occasions the Picts and the Irish in Britain had escaped. This was

---

[45] For the dating see Anderson & Anderson, *Adomnan*, p. 96.

[46] As Professor Bullough translates in his excellent paper, 'Columba, Adomnan'.

[47] Watson, *Celtic Place-Names*, p. 271. See also Anderson, 'Columba and other Irish saints', p. 33. In the sixteenth century there was a 'Croft of St Adampnan' here and Mrs Anderson suggests that the land was granted to Adomnán.

[48] *Vita Columbae*, II.11 and 32.

[49] *Ibid.*, II.27.

[50] *Ibid.*, II.32; III.14.

[51] Cf. Anderson, 'Columba and other Irish saints', pp. 32–3.

[52] *Vita Columbae*, II.46.

due to the merits of St Columba, whose monasteries, 'placed within the boundaries of both peoples, are down to the present time held in great honour by them both'. The inescapable inference is that Columban monasticism spread in Pictland during the seventh century.[53]

Now let us put together our evidence and see what picture we obtain of early christianity in Pictland. Bede tells us that Ninian, the British bishop of *Ad Candidam Casam* (presumably Whithorn in Galloway), was the first mission-ary. The verse *Miracula Nynie Episcopi*, written in the last quarter of the eighth century, repeats this, saying that Ninian on his return from Rome converted the pagan Picts.[54] The eighth century is a long time after the event, but there is good reason to think that there were christians at Whithorn as early as the fifth century. Barrovadus set up a stone, probably soon after 500, to his grandfather Latinus, who must have been alive in the second half of the fifth century. At Kirkmadrine, on the next peninsula, there is a late fifth-century stone bearing the Latin name Florentius, and a sixth-century inscription which reads *Hic iacent sancti et praecipui sacerdotes, id est Viventius et Mavorius*, indicating a church of some importance.[55] Professor Thomas has traced a christian cemetery and shrine on Ardwall Island (nine miles across the bay from Whithorn) to about 500 and a timber oratory to the seventh century.[56] It is not impossible that a British bishop should have conducted a mission to the Picts from this area. Where among the southern Picts Ninian worked we do not know, for there is no early evidence to show that the commemorations to Ninian in Pictland are early, and since the form of his name in such commemorations is either latinised or in a Gaelic form derived through Scots vernacular the commem-orations may go back only to a later development of his cult.[57]

Ninian was not the only contact between British christians and pagan Picts. The Picts spoke a P-Celtic language akin to British and we have evidence in a British heroic poem composed *ca* 600 that the two peoples were sometimes not enemies but allies. The poem is a series of panegyrics on heroes who had fallen in a battle against the English. The British prince Mynyddog the Wealthy had collected a troop of aristocratic warriors and feasted them in his hall at Eidyn for a year preparatory to their attack. There was at least one Pictish warrior in Mynyddog's war-band, 'the foreign horseman, the young only son of Cian from beyond Bannog', and probably three others may be identified. The North Britons were christian, giving gold to the altar, doing penance before battle,

---

[53] Anderson, 'Columba and other Irish saints', p. 33. It is interesting that the church in Banffshire which is said, in the Arbroath Register, to have been granted 'to God, St Columba and the Brecc Bennach', is in fact dedicated to Adomnán: Anderson & Anderson, *Adomnan*, p. 95.

[54] For a translation of this work, see W. MacQueen, 'Miracula Nynie Episcopi'. John MacQueen, *St Nynia*, p. 5, postulates a pre-Anglian Life, possibly of Irish provenance. For Ninian's Pictish activities, see *ibid.*, pp. 22–3.

[55] I have followed Professor Jackson's dating and readings of these stones (in a private communication, in which he observes that their assignment to earlier dates requires an excess of wishful thinking).

[56] For a general discussion of early christianity in Galloway, see the conclusion of Thomas, 'Early christian cemetery'.

[57] See Watson, *Celtic Place-Names*, pp. 295–6; MacQueen, *St Nynia*, pp. 80–5.

and it is likely that Pictish warriors who spent a year with them were christian also.[58]

Once christianity had been established among the North Britons it would almost inevitably spread into Pictland. Professor Thomas sees its progress in a series of long-cist burials across the Firth of Forth, round the coast of Fife and across to the northern coast of the Firth of Tay. These long-cist burials are densely distributed in the Lothians, and those north of the Firth of Forth have all the appearance of being outliers of the group.[59] Professor Thomas dates these to the late fifth and early sixth centuries, and sees them as evidence of the spread of christianity from Britain into Pictland. This is a very attractive hypothesis. The historian has to note that archaeologists find it difficult to date the burials with any accuracy; they are not even positive that the graves are christian.[60] Nevertheless the interpretation of the long-cist burials put forward by Professor Thomas makes sense, and fits well with the known evidence.

The Church introduced by Britons into Pictland must have been the Church of the late Empire. Patrick, writing in the fifth century a letter of protest to the soldiers of the Briton Coroticus cannot bring himself to address them as his fellow citizens or 'fellow citizens of the holy Romans' as he should have been able to do. Instead 'like our enemies they live in death, allies of the Scots and the iniquitous Picts'.[61] This does not suggest that christianity had fared well among the Picts up to Patrick's time.[62] We can, however, safely assume that it was filtering in from Celtic Britain during the sixth century.

Meanwhile Columba had arrived in Scotland and had received Iona, according to Bede, from King Bruide. Yet the king, if we follow the account of Adomnán, was not baptised. Although Columba travelled to Pictland and attended Bruide's court, he had little success in converting the Pictish aristocracy. Columba may have also preached to the southern Picts. There is a very obscure Irish panegyric on the saint, saying that he preached to the tribes of *Toi*, a name which the later glossator understood as meaning the Tay.[63] This is an Irish tradition independent of Adomnán or Bede and not inconsistent with either.[64] Between Columba's lifetime and the 680s or 690s, when Adomnán

---

[58] This poem can now be read in English translation by Jackson, *Gododdin*. See B.13 (p. 103): Bannog is the mountain massif which blocks the narrow neck of land between Stirling and Dumbarton. See also B.3 (p. 99), B.27 (p. 108), and A.34 (p. 130).

[59] Thomas, 'Evidence', pp. 107–8: see his map on p. 107, or the more detailed one by Henshall, 'A long cist cemetery', p. 266.

[60] Henshall, 'A long cist cemetery'; Stevenson, 'Long cist burials'.

[61] *Pictorum apostatarum*: the interpretation, 'unrighteous' / 'immoral', was put forward by Grosjean, 'Les Pictes apostats', p. 374.

[62] Cf. Thomas, 'Evidence', p. 111: 'Christianity did not apparently travel fast or far during the fifth century'.

[63] Strachan, 'Date of the *Amra*', assigns the work to *ca* 800, but modern scholars are inclined to date this *ca* 600: see, for example, Greene & O'Connor, *Golden Treasury*, p. 2. The text may be consulted in Bernard & Atkinson, *Irish Liber Hymnorum*, I.169 ('Ar ni forcetlaid forcanad tuatha toi') and I.179 ('Cluidsi-us borbb beolu bendacht batar ic toi tolrig'). Professor Jackson says of the glossator: 'I am sure he was right. But the Irish poet could easily have been using "the tribes of Tay" in a very broad sense.'

[64] Adomnán says he made journeys across the ridge of Britain, and Bede says he preached to the Pictish nation.

wrote, the cult of Columba had spread. Adomnán suggests that the chief saint of the Picts was Columba; Bede implies that Iona was the chief of all the Pictish churches.[65] We know on good authority of one other Pictish non-Columban foundation, that of Applecross, founded by Maelrubai on the western seaboard in 673[66] but it is unlikely that his influence would rival Columba's in so short a time.

The conclusion based on literary and archaeological evidence must surely be that the seventh-century Columban foundations of Pictland other than Iona were minor cells, established without royal patronage, exercising little influence on society. What little evidence we have suggests that the state of the Pictish kingdom in the seventh century *could* have been conducive to the rapid spread of christianity. The *rex Pictorum* was a powerful overlord.[67] Bruide son of Maelchon had a *regulus* from the Orkneys in attendance at his court;[68] a century later Bruide son of Bile was able to devastate the Orkneys in 682 and drive the English Ecgfrith back to the Forth in 685. The kingdom seems to have been on the whole more powerful than Scottish Dál Riata and was producing art of a high order. If the Pictish overkings had given their support to christianity, if Irish monks trained at Iona had moved into Pictland in considerable numbers and had gained the backing of the Pictish aristocracy, then we would expect to see some evidence of their literature and a different kind of art from that of the Class I stones. There were undoubtedly christians and some christian communities in seventh-century Pictland, but our first evidence that christianity was exercising major influence on society comes with the reign of King Nechton and the Class II symbol-stones. It is quite possible that the Irish mission to Northumbria drew off manpower which might otherwise have found its way to Pictland.

Under Nechton royal patronage was effectively exercised: indeed, Bede says that the impetus came entirely from the king. The Columban clergy were subsequently expelled,[69] for Nechton preferred a Church under the protection of St Peter. This seems to be the date to which the prototype of the king-lists can be traced back. Nechton asked for architects to build a church 'after the Roman manner'. Dr Simpson believed that he could see traces of such a church in the tower of Restenneth Priory in Angus,[70] an area where the Class II stones are heavily concentrated. It looks, also, as if St Andrews may

---

[65] *Historia Ecclesiastica*, III.3.

[66] Anderson, 'Columba and other Irish saints', surveys the evidence for sixth-century saints in Scotland and comes to the conclusion that 'there is hardly an Irish saint associated with Scotland in the sixth century for whom the evidence is more than barely admissible'.

[67] I toyed with the idea that the 'Kings of the Picts' reported in the Iona chronicle and the king-lists were just the particular dynasty in which Iona was interested; but this will not hold water. The kings of the Picts seem to have been exercising more authority than Irish overlords at the same period. The kings of Gwynedd in the early seventh century seem to provide a better comparison.

[68] Adomnán, *Vita Columbae*, II.42.

[69] Annals of Ulster (ed. & tr. Hennessy), s. a. 716 (=717); for the context, see Bede, *Historia Ecclesiastica*, V.21 (cf. III.3).

[70] Simpson, 'Early romanesque tower'.

have been founded or revived about this time, since the annals first mention it in 747, with the death of its abbot Tuathalán. The St Andrews Sarcophagus, one of the finest examples of Pictish art, was probably carved in the half-century or so following.[71] Experienced Pictish sculptors were now turning their art to a christian medium, an art which, as Mrs Henderson says, is not a late or provincial reflection of Hiberno-Saxon developments, but 'the creation of artists freely participating in the evolution of that style and contributing to it some of its most daring and magnificent monuments'.[72] I think it is probable that, even in the eighth century, the chief contribution made by the Pictish Church to the arts was in ornament rather than in literature. Their stone sculpture already showed a highly developed expertise which needed only to be given a new direction, whereas in the field of Latin written literature they seem to have been beginning more or less from the start.

Thus our study of the problems raised by Bede's evidence reaffirms his minute accuracy on Nechton's recognition of the scarcity of Latin learning in Pictland. But, contrary to Bede's report, it requires us to understand that Ninian and Columba only started the work of evangelisation,[73] and that it proceeded slowly. This is historically likely. Christianity was introduced into Ireland probably early in the fifth century, but a set of canons drawn up *ca* 550 shows us that christians were still in a predominantly pagan environment, holding themselves aloof from secular courts, their clergy not automatically incorporated into the noble grades of society.[74] It was not until the late sixth or the seventh century that ecclesiastical lawyers succeeded in adjusting the Irish Church to the secular law.[75] Among the Picts east of the spine of Britain we should not think of a king and aristocracy giving christianity their active support, nor of a Church commanding artistic patronage, until the beginning of the eighth century.

[71] There is not complete unanimity on this dating.

[72] *The Picts*, p. 157. Mrs Henderson believes that artistic contacts are evident between the Picts, Irish, and English from the time of the Book of Durrow onwards.

[73] Bede, *Historia Ecclesiastica*, III.4, says that the southern Picts 'embraced the faith' preached by Ninian, and that Columba 'converted [the northern Picts] to the faith of Christ'.

[74] For the dating of these cannons see Hughes, *Church in Early Irish Society*, pp. 42–52; cf. Binchy, 'St Patrick's "First Synod"'.

[75] Hughes, *Church in Early Irish Society*, pp. 123–33.

IV

British Library MS. Cotton Vespasian A. XIV
(*Vitae Sanctorum Wallensium*): its purpose and provenance[1]

The first manuscript (fos 1–105) bound up in Cotton Vespasian A. xiv is a collection consisting of *Lives* of Celtic saints and extracts from monastic cartularies, preceded by a document described as a kalendar, a glossary, a short tract *De Situ Brecheniauc* and a list of contents. The manuscript has been described by Robin Flower as written in a number of Anglo-Norman hands of about 1200 'all of the same general type and period, but of varying accomplishment'.[2] Its importance for a study of the Welsh Church has long been recognised. Just over a century ago W. J. Rees printed some of the *Lives* for the Welsh Manuscripts Society. This is an execrable though amusing edition. There are hundreds of mistakes in the transcription of proper names. Rees occasionally creates exciting new names – out of the manuscript-reading *uoce in audientia* he produces *nomine Snaudrentia* – or raises the hopes of his readers with words such as *antiqui* for the more prosaic *antequam* of the manuscript. Kuno Meyer in 1900[3] gave twenty pages of corrigenda, but never completed his arduous task. Charles Plummer used the Vespasian manuscript for his excellent critical edition of the *Life of Maedóc* published in 1910;[4] and A. W. Wade-Evans reedited most of the Vespasian *Lives* in 1944.[5] The peculiarities of the *Vita Cadoci* have recently been noted by H. D. Emanuel.[6] Though most of the texts are well known, there is no satisfactory study of the problems raised by the manuscript as a whole. Silas Harris has cleared much of the ground

---

[1] First published in *Studies in the Early British Church*, ed. Nora K. Chadwick (Cambridge 1958), pp. 183–200.

[2] Description in Wade-Evans, *Vitae Sanctorum Britanniae*, pp. viii-xi.

[3] Meyer, 'Collation'.

[4] *Vitae Sanctorum Hiberniae*, II.295–311.

[5] *Vitae Sanctorum Britanniae*; see the review by Thomas Jones, *Transactions of the Honourable Society of Cymmrodorion* (1943/4) 157–65. Wade-Evans omits the kalendar (fos 1r–6v), the Old Cornish glossary (fos 7r–10r), a Life of St Teilo by Galfridus (fos 52r–55v), *De primo statu Landauensis ecclesiae* (fos 56r–58v), two Lives of St Dyfrig (fos 58v–61r, 71r–77r), a Life of St Clydog (fos 84v–86r), a Life of St Maedóc (*Aiduus*) (fos 96v–104v), and the Navigation of St Brendan (fos 104v–105v, ending incomplete).

[6] Emanuel, 'Analysis'; cf. his 'Latin Life'.

with an enlightening and provocative study of the kalendar.[7] He provides an introductory discussion of the kalendar, notes on individual entries and an edition of the text, and reaches three conclusions which have not before been publicly stated. He claims an eighth-century origin for the 'basic framework' of the kalendar, argues that kalendar and *Lives* from the first belonged together and that the whole compilation was put together by the monks of Monmouth. We shall return later to these theories.

In the century before Vesp. was written the Anglo-Normans had pushed their conquest across South and Central Wales. The Welsh Church assumed a new look; the old *clas*-system was disintegrating, ecclesiastical lands were redistributed and new religious communities were set up. Where Anglo-Norman and Celtic influences met, there was sometimes inquiry into the historical or pseudo-historical past. It was both profitable and interesting for the monks to know of the origin and development of the traditions into which they had entered. So they pursued their studies and speculations, and wrote up the results, or employed someone to do it for them. Outside Wales, at Glastonbury, William of Malmesbury was invited to write *Concerning the Antiquity of Glastonbury*. Caradog of Llancarfan and other hagiographers were busy compiling or composing the *Lives* of Celtic saints. The clerics of the newly created see of Llandaf forged the brief for their claims to diocesan boundaries, rewriting charters and including *Lives* of saints. Geoffrey of Monmouth, concentrating on secular rather than ecclesiastical romance, created a *History of the Kings of Britain*. It is against this background of pseudo-historical research and literary activity that Vesp. must be considered.

The question of its provenance and origin immediately arises. Robin Flower, in his excellent description cited above, suggested that it was written at Brecon, about twenty miles north-west of Monmouth. The contents to some considerable extent show a Brecknock interest. A tract *De Situ Brecheniauc*[8] precedes the *Vitae* which form the bulk of the manuscript. Brecon was in the diocese of St David's, and the collection contains a number of saints from West and South-West Wales. In the sixteenth century the manuscript belonged to Sir John Prise, in whose hand it is annotated, and Sir John held a lease of Brecon priory.[9] Flower had therefore strong grounds of general probability for suggesting Brecon as its original home. But the arguments are not decisive. Sir John Prise was one of the visitors to the monasteries at the time of the Dissolution and could have picked up the manuscript at some house other than Brecon, and the Brecknock association of the contents can find another explanation.

The contents of the manuscript suggest three great influences on its compilation – the peculiar connections of Monmouth, the wide authority of Gloucester, and the interests of the hagiographical school of Llandaf. Mr Harris argues that certain independent clues point to the monks of Monmouth

---

[7] Harris, 'The kalendar'.

[8] Now edited by Bartrum, *Genealogical Tracts*, pp. 14–16.

[9] On Prise, see Ker, 'Sir John Prise', and Huws, 'Gildas Prisei'.

as the compilers of the manuscript. The kalendar contains the feast of a very rare saint, Dochelinus, the patron of Allonnes and Varrains, two villages near Saumur. Both these places were connected with the great Benedictine house of Saint-Florent de Saumur. Allonnes was one of the ancient priories of Saint-Florent. The church at Varrains was built after the destruction of the chapel in the château of Saumur – a chapel which had housed the relics of St Dochelinus and had been used by the monks of Saint-Florent before their new church was built after the fire of 1025. The cult of St Dochelinus comes from the neighbourhood of Saumur, and the monks of Saint-Florent would have retained an interest in it after their new church was built in the eleventh century. But the Vespasian kalendar is clearly the production of a Welsh scriptorium. It requires special circumstances to account for the familiarity of a Welsh house with Dochelinus, so Mr Harris looks for a Welsh house connected with Saumur. He finds it in Monmouth, the one Welsh priory of Saint-Florent. Monmouth was founded about 1080 by the Breton Gwethenoc, who became a monk of Saint-Florent and gave lands in the neighbourhood of Monmouth to found a dependent priory of twelve monks and a prior.

The presence of St Dochelinus is obviously of vital importance in any discussion of the provenance of the Vespasian kalendar. Mr Harris finds support for a Monmouth origin in two other entries. One of these is the obit of *Hathulfus de Aura*. Nothing is known of Hathulfus, but the church and manor of Awre belonged to Monmouth. Cuthman of Steyning (Sussex) is a rather surprising entry, but may be explained by the position of Steyning, a mile from St Peter of Sele, a sister house of Monmouth and a cell of Saint-Florent.

There is a number of very odd features in the kalendar which this explanation leaves unaccounted for. Dochelinus is the only Saint-Florent saint here; Florentinus himself is absent and his day is a blank. Nevertheless there are so many peculiar gaps in this kalendar that it is very dangerous indeed to base an argument on omissions. Dochelinus is here, extremely rare and unusual, and must be accounted for. Of the other four rather unexpected Continental saints, Bar[ba]cianus on January 2, Ludger on March 26, Sigismund on May 1, Teuderius on October 29, three at least were known at this date in south-west England, the area from which the Old Cornish glossary in Vesp. presumably ultimately comes.[10] Ludger and Sigismund are in the twelfth-century manuscript of the Exeter Martyrology, and although the period containing the dates January 2 and October 29 is lost from this Exeter manuscript, Barbacian is in an inferior fourteenth-century copy.[11] Dochelinus, on the other hand, shows knowledge which in Wales could only come via Monmouth, and forms a very strong argument for a Monmouth origin for Vesp..

To argue the provenance of the kalendar along orthodox lines of liturgical criticism, seeking in its omissions as much as in its entries evidence of the type of community, religious or secular, to which it was attached, or trying to find in

[10] The Old Cornish glossary was made *ca* 1100 from Ælfric's Latin-Old English glossary (of *ca* A.D. 1000): Jackson, *Language and History*, pp. 60–1; Williams, 'Vocabularium Cornicum'.
[11] Both manuscripts are used by Dalton *et al.*, *Ordinale Exon*, esp. IV. 1–43.

its local feasts the liturgical interests of one particular house, implies a fundamental misconception about the nature and purpose of the kalendar. For it is
not a liturgical document. Mr Harris accepts without question the liturgical
purpose of the kalendar and of the *Lives* which follow.[12] So too does Robin
Flower, who suggests that the manuscript was intended as a 'supplementary
legendary of Welsh saints for use in one of the new Benedictine monasteries of
the Anglo-Norman foundation, in addition to the ordinary legendaries'.[13]
Some of the *Lives* are homiletic in type,[14] but the document which precedes
them does not appear to have any liturgical intention. There is no colour or
grading which would point definitely to a liturgical purpose. The Roman
element is unusually thin, and Mr Harris explains this by saying that the
original framework of the kalendar goes back to a type antedating the Caro-
lingian reforms. But the complete absence of octaves, some of which go back to
the ninth century or earlier, and of other important Roman feasts gives the
document, as a liturgical kalendar, an impossibly peculiar look.

What then is the purpose of this document, which it is convenient to call a
kalendar? It can hardly be regarded as a supplementary martyrology. Such an
explanation would account for the absence of St Florentinus, who would
already be in the monastery's main martyrology; but it does not fit all the facts,
for the Roman feasts and one or two of the Welsh saints, such as Cadog and
Dyfrig, would already be well known to the monks of Monmouth. Nor is the
kalendar merely an index of the *Lives* which follow, since it contains a number
of saints of whom the *Lives* make no mention, and it omits other saints who
occur in the *Lives*. It looks as if the kalendar was intended as a means of
identification and record. Someone entered the major Roman feasts to act as a
framework and added a number of rather haphazardly selected saints, whose
particulars happened to be accessible. Its purpose is historical, not liturgical,
and the manuscript should probably be regarded as an example of that activity
in pseudo-historical research which has already been mentioned. Mr Harris's
theory of a pre-Carolingian kalendar from Saint-Florent as the basic framework of the Vespasian document is too ingenious. The kalendar which the
monks of Monmouth presumably brought from Saint-Florent when they
settled in Wales in the late eleventh century must have been one embodying
their contemporary practices. To imagine them using an eighth-century
original for their twelfth-century compilation is strained and unnatural, and
leaves far too many peculiarities unnoticed.

It is essential to consider whose interests the compilation represents, and for
this purpose the kalendar must be considered with the *Lives*, for kalendar and
Lives are, as Mr Harris shows, complementary texts. He argues that the Welsh
entries in the kalendar were made by referring to the *capitula* (or list of contents

[12] 'The kalendar', p. 20.

[13] See above, p. 53, n. 2.

[14] For example, the Lives of Padarn, Brynach, Cybi, and Carannog; the Life of Tatheus has a
homiletic conclusion; the Passion of St Cadog could be used for lections (it is divided up for this
purpose in the copy in London, British Library, MS. Cotton Titus D.XXII) and other Lives could
be so adapted.

on fo 12v), and not directly to the *Vitae*. There are certain cases where the entries of kalendar and *capitula* agree together, and differ from the corresponding entry in the *Lives*. For Cybi and Carannog, dates are correctly given in the *Lives*, incorrectly in the *capitula* and kalendar. In six cases the titles of saints in *Vitae* and *capitula* are slightly different, and in all these the kalendar agrees with the *capitula*.[15] The palaeography of the manuscript supports Mr Harris's view. Kalendar and *capitula* are a part of two irregular gatherings at the beginning of the manuscript. The manuscript is written in a number of different hands, but the scribe who transcribed the last section of the *Vitae* (from Carannog onwards) also wrote the first two gatherings. It is probable that he finished transcribing the available *Lives*, and then turned to drawing up the *capitula* and kalendar. The *Lives* are faithful copies; the kalendar is an original production.

Vesp. is a peculiar collection both for what it brings in and for what it leaves out. The Welsh ingredients raise interesting problems. There is a number of saints from South-East Wales in kalendar and *Lives*, as might be expected in a manuscript put together in this area. But how did saints, in some cases extremely obscure saints, from the far west of Wales and from Ireland enter the compilation? St David's own cult was of course widespread, so he may be excluded from the discussion. Padarn was also, at any rate in the pre-Norman period, a most important saint.[16] But there seems to be no reason why Brynach, whose chief church was at Nevern, a few miles south of Cardigan,[17] should occur twice in the kalendar. He is the only Welsh saint for whom a feast of translation is given, and the date of his translation, which is not in his *Vita*, is recorded in no other source. Brynach, Carannog and Cybi are all saints of West Wales. Carannog's churches are to the north and west of Cardigan, at Llangrannog and St Dogmael's.[18] His festival is correctly given in his *Vita* at May 16 and his *Life* identifies him with the Irish Cairnech of Dulane.[19] Cybi also seems to belong to this group of West Welsh saints. He has dedications in south-east Cardiganshire, Anglesey and Monmouthshire. The two *Lives* of Cybi in Vesp. have a very strong Irish element, and are more likely to come originally from a West Welsh foundation than from Monmouthshire: if the *Life* came from Llangibby in southern Monmouthshire some mention of Llandaf might perhaps be expected. Another Irish *Life* is given in the collection – that of Maedóc of Ferns. This is no place to discuss whether the Irish Maedóc and the Welsh Madog are historically identical:[20] they were certainly identified in Welsh hagiography, where Maedóc (*Aidus*) of Ferns is represented as the

---

[15] Harris, 'The kalendar', pp. 18–19.

[16] Bowen, *Settlements*, pp. 53–6, shows that Padarn's dedications are ranged along the north-south routes in West Wales and in Radnorshire where the road ran from Brecon northwards.

[17] For the distribution of his cult, see Bowen, *Settlements*, pp. 28–9.

[18] He also has a dedication in the parish of Llandudoch (Pembrokeshire), and another near Newquay: Bowen, *Settlements*, p. 89.

[19] See Carney, *Studies*, pp. 407–12.

[20] In Irish kalendars Maedóc of Ferns is commemorated at January 31, but in Vesp. at February 28. This apparent disparity of dates may be a slip on the part of a scribe. It would be easy to confuse *Prid. kl. feb.* with *Prid. kl. mart.*.

disciple of St David at Cill Muine,[21] and the Irish *Life* was used for Welsh circulation. Madog has dedications in Gower and in Brecon, besides two churches on St Bride's Bay. There are other saints appearing in the Vespasian kalendar who have festivals localised in the diocese of St David's. A kalendar of the St David's diocese may be partially reconstructed from two sources – from the sixteenth-century Llanbadarn Fawr kalendar edited by Mr Harris[22] and from the sixteenth-century additions to an unpublished kalendar in BL MS. Additional 22720. The reconstruction is not very satisfactory because it does not provide a complete kalendar, and the entries are very late. But it does appear that David, Gistlian, Nonnita, Kieran and Caradog of St David's were commemorated in the diocese. On the evidence of dedications, three other saints may be added to the local festivals: Ishmael who has a cult confined with one exception to Pembrokeshire and who is attested in no other kalendar than Vesp., Decuman with his chief foundation at Rhoscrowther in southern Pembroke, and Justinian with dedications only in southern Pembroke. These saints (twelve in number if we exclude St David) have cults whose native source is in West Wales. Monmouth may have become acquainted with one or two of them through churches within her own geographical orbit – this applies to Cybi with a dedication in Monmouthshire and to Madog, patron of Llanvadog in Brecknock. But others of them, notably Gistlian, Nonnita, Kieran, Caradog, Ishmael and Justinian have no dedications in the east and their cults are confined to the south-west of Wales. The compilers of Vesp. must have had access to a Llanbadarn or St David's kalendar. What was their most likely source of information?

The influence of Gloucester constantly intrudes on the composition of Vesp.. The Benedictine house of St Peter's, Gloucester, had profited by the Anglo-Norman advance to secure extensive grants of properties in Central, South and West Wales, as her cartulary records. Llanbadarn Fawr was granted to Gloucester with its properties and appurtenances probably soon after 1115, and was clearly regarded as an important acquisition.[23] Padarn entered the Gloucester calendar,[24] and the monks probably had a short *Vita* for use at his festival. The Vespasian *Vita Sancti Paterni* seems to be a twelfth-century production and may have been compiled soon after Gloucester obtained the church.[25] Through Llanbadarn, Gloucester could have had access to some West Welsh legendary containing *Lives* of Padarn, his neighbour Brynach, Carannog, and Cybi (whose *Lives* have Irish elements), and the Irish *Lives* of Maedóc and Brendan. None of these shows any Llandaf influence. The

[21] Wade-Evans, *Vitae Sanctorum Britanniae*, pp. 159–60; Plummer, *Vitae Sanctorum Hiberniae*, II.297–300.

[22] Harris, 'A Llanbadarn Fawr calendar'.

[23] Brooke, 'St Peter of Gloucester'; Lloyd, *History of Wales*, II.432–3, n. 111, points out that, though the *Historia* of St Peter's, Gloucester, dates the foundation 1111, the foundation-charter is witnessed by Bishop Bernard and cannot therefore be earlier than September 1115.

[24] Wormald, *English Benedictine Kalendars*, II.47 and 41.

[25] It ends with an interesting *possessio agrorum sancti Paterni*, which must be derived from a much longer and more explicit source. In so far as the boundaries are defined they may be compared with the more particular account printed by Hart, *Historia et Cartularium*, II.76.

Lives of Maedóc and Brendan were certainly known to a West Welsh hagiographer about 1090.[26] Rhigyfarch, a member of the hereditary ecclesiastical house of Llanbadarn Fawr, used them in writing his *Life of St David*, and it is not without significance that these two Irish *Lives* appear at the end of Vesp., a manuscript with an undeniable Ceredigion element. Apart from Gloucester's direct connection with Llanbadarn Fawr, her abbots were on friendly terms with the bishops of St David's. Bishop Wilfred of St David's returns the pastoral staff which William of St Peter's has lent him, thanking him warmly for his support.[27] Bishop Bernard witnesses the charter granting St Padarn's to Gloucester.[28] St Peter's, Gloucester, held properties elsewhere in the diocese of St David's. She was in a most favourable position for providing information on the saints of West Wales.

It is probable also that Gloucester influence may account for some of the eastern saints in the kalendar and *Lives*. Ailwin almost certainly entered the Vespasian kalendar via Gloucester, which owned Coln Saint Aldwyn. His festival is attested only in Vesp. and in the kalendar of St Peter's, Gloucester, compiled before 1170. The presence of so rare a saint forcibly suggests Gloucester influence. Keneder is another obscure saint who appears in the Vespasian kalendar and whose main foundation at Glasbury was owned by Gloucester. St Peter's acquired Glasbury in 1088 during the time of Serlo. Bernard of Neufmarché, lord of Brecon, was the donor, and he granted St Keneder's church at Glasbury to Gloucester with certain rights in Brecknock:[29]

> Be it known both to those present and future, that I, Bernard of Neufmarché, have given to God and St Peter, and to Abbot Serlo and the monks of Gloucester: Glasbury, with all things pertaining to it, free and quit of all secular service and custom, for perpetual alms; and the church of St Keneder in the same village, with all things pertaining to it. I also grant to them, and confirm by my charter, an entire tenth of my whole lordship through all the land of Brecknock in woodland and meadow wherever my lordship is acknowledged, that is to say, in grain, herds, cheeses, venery and honey and in all other things of which tithes ought to be granted. . . .

It is possible, though the point cannot be pressed, that Gloucester's interest in Brecknock may account for the presence in Vesp. of the tract *De Situ Brecheniauc*. The note on Ecgwine in the kalendar is clearly inserted in order to connect him with Keneder and Cadog; it identifies the three saints as sons of Gwynllyw.

Cadog himself is clearly the most important saint in the collection. His *acta* are followed by a detailed account of the property of the canons of Llancarfan and by a group of charters, the whole of which section is from a different source. Where would these charters be kept? Llancarfan was granted to

---

[26] Davies, *Episcopal Acts*, II.500–1.
[27] *Ibid.*, I.236.
[28] *Ibid.*, I.249.
[29] Hart, *Historia et Cartularium*, I.314; confirmation, I.222.

Gloucester with fifteen hides of land some time between 1093 and 1104 during the abbacy of Serlo.[30] Gloucester leased it for some years to archdeacons of Llandaf, but her ownership was carefully safeguarded, and when Archdeacon William overstepped his rights, Gloucester successfully resumed seisin (1175–80).[31] It seems probable that the final section on Llancarfan properties was added with the cooperation of Gloucester.

Gloucester also owned the chief church of Cadog's father, Gwynllyw, whose *Life* is the first in the Vespasian collection. She was granted his foundation at Newport between 1094 and 1104.[32] In the middle years of the twelfth century Archbishop Theobald of Canterbury granted indulgences of fifteen days to those who visited and assisted the church.[33] Gwynllyw's *Life*, as we have it, was rewritten some time after 1120.[34] Gloucester would have been closely concerned in attempts to increase the revenues of Newport.

A connection with Gloucester is explicitly attested in one of the two *Lives* of Dyfrig (*Dubricius*) which appears in Vesp.. The author introduces himself, 'ego Benedictus habitu cenobii apostoli Petri Claudiocestrie monachus'. This explicit reference to Gloucester is particularly valuable, since otherwise Dubricius's presence in Vesp. would be attributed solely to the influence of either Monmouth or Llandaf. Monmouth would have been specially interested in both Cadog and Dyfrig. The monks had used the church of St Cadog for nearly twenty years before their new church dedicated to St Mary was built; they owned Dyfrig's foundation at Whitchurch, were interested in his chief church at Hentland, and were living in a part of the country where his dedications were thickly clustered.[35] And Llandaf's claim to Dyfrig as one of her three great patrons is too well known to need further comment here.

Gloucester influence on the Vespasian collection seems undeniable, though the manner in which it was exercised must be a matter of dispute. But it cannot be accidental that two very rare saints, Ailwin and Keneder, are connected with Gloucester and also appear in the Vespasian kalendar. Gwynllyw was patron of an important church owned by Gloucester, the second *Life of Dyfrig* was indubitably composed by a St Peter's monk, and the Vespasian compilers could most readily have copied their Llancarfan charters with the cooperation of Gloucester. Gloucester's ownership of Llanbadarn Fawr accounts not only for the *Life of Padarn*, but for the definition of his boundaries with which it concludes. Gloucester interests provide the essential link between the eastern and western elements in the Vespasian collection.

It seems therefore almost certain that, some time before Vesp. was com-

---

[30] *Ibid.*, I.93; confirmations, I.222 and 349.

[31] *Ibid.*, II.12–14; Davies, *Episcopal Acts*, II.660–1 and 664–5.

[32] Hart, *Historia et Cartularium*, II.51; for the date, see Davies, *Episcopal Acts*, II.612.

[33] Hart, *Historia et Cartularium*, II.62; Davies, *Episcopal Acts*, II.636 and 651.

[34] The Life implies recognition that Newport came within the diocese and under the jurisdiction of Llandaf and her Bishop Dyfrig. These conditions were not fulfilled before 1120. The title *episcopus Landauensis* is not found before 1119, and Dyfrig's body arrived at Llandaf in 1120.

[35] Bowen, *Settlements*, pp. 35–9.

piled, the acts of certain Welsh saints had been collected at Gloucester. It may be possible to venture a more precise statement on the date at which this material was accumulated. Llanbadarn Fawr was acquired by Gloucester soon after 1115, and became independent again after the Welsh rebellion of 1136. Gloucester would have had access to Llanbadarn and West Welsh sources most readily between these dates. Of the two *Lives* of Dyfrig in our manuscript, one, postdating the death of Bishop Urban in 1134, is the same as the version now found in the *Book of Llandaf*, a collection for which Christopher Brooke suggests a date in the 1130s.[36] The other, by Benedict of Gloucester, uses the Llandaf *Life* and Geoffrey of Monmouth's *History*, first published in 1138.[37] Geoffrey dedicated his work to Robert, earl of Gloucester, who was in charge of the temporalities of Llandaf during the vacancy of 1134–40,[38] and Robert's charge may have created considerable opportunities for exchange between Llandaf and Gloucester. It would appear that in the 1130s Gloucester, whose influence on Vesp. is evident, had particularly good opportunities for obtaining hagiographical material.

The peculiar selection of saints present in Vesp. is thus accounted for partly by the connexions of Monmouth, partly by the interests of Gloucester. It is clear that the compilers also drew on Llandaf material, though in a version which seems in some respects to be earlier than that of *Liber Landauensis*[39] itself. The *Life of Teilo* is certainly in the pre-*LL* version, though the rubric suggests that it may be a product of the Llandaf school.[40] The Vespasian *Life of Clydog* corresponds to the material in the *LL-Life*, but it is differently arranged, with the one long formal witnessed charter, obviously a Llandaf forgery, at the end of the collection and following the *Life* and miracles. This would appear to be a more logical order than that of *LL*.[41] In Vesp. the tract *De Primo Statu Landauensis*, the first *Life of Dyfrig* and the account of his translation are, with minor variations, each identical with the version in the *Book of Llandaf*.[42] Oudoceus, the third patron of Llandaf, does not appear in the Vespasian kalendar and his *Life* is not given.

This presentation of Llandaf material raises some problems, but it helps to solve others. Most important, it shows that it is very unlikely that the manuscript was compiled at Llandaf. Monmouth, Gloucester and Llandaf had the greatest influence on the contents of our manuscript, and if the theory of a Monmouth origin is rejected, Gloucester and Llandaf are the most obvious alternatives. But surely no Llandaf scribe writing after the composition of the *Book of Llandaf* would spend his energies copying the *Life of Teilo* in a version

---

[36] Brooke, 'Archbishops', pp. 201, 204 n. 3, and 205 n. 1; cf. Davies, *The Llandaff Charters*.
[37] Tatlock, *Legendary History*, p. 434. Griscom, *Historia*, p. 42, suggests 1136 as the date; cf. Brooke, 'Archbishops', p. 231, n. 2.
[38] Davies, *Episcopal Acts*, II.634.
[39] Henceforth '*LL*'.
[40] 'Incipit uita Teliaui episcopi a magistro Galfrido [*glossed* id est Stephano] fratre Urbani Landauensis ecclesie episcopi dictata.'
[41] Evans & Rhys, *Book of Llan Dâv*, p. 362, give the Vesp. variants of the Life of St Clydog.
[42] *Ibid.*, pp. 358–60, for the Vesp. variants.

which omits the Llandaf claims. A few comparisons will show the kind of propaganda which the *LL Life of Teilo* includes and Vesp. omits:[43]

> (i) St Teilo received the pastoral care of the church of Llandaf to which he was consecrated with the whole *paruchia* adjacent to it which had belonged to his predecessor Dyfrig.
> (ii) Both *LL* and Vesp. begin their accounts of his end: 'Now on the night of his death a great dispute arose between the three clergies of his three churches, with each claiming his own authority and privileges for possessing the body'. *LL only then enumerates the three churches, in particular pressing the claims of Llandaf, the see of Dyfrig.* Both versions then describe how, after a night of prayer, three bodies appeared, of equal splendour, and each cleric took one home for burial in his own church. *LL then alone continues: 'It was known to all the people both by the great number of miracles and the records of former persons in authority* (monimentis antiquorum seniorum) *that it was indubitably taken to Llandaf'.*
> (iii) *LL*. and Vesp. give a final account of his miracles: 'Wherefore celebrate the feast of so great a man with all zeal of mind' – *and LL continues: 'frequent his church, and each of you according to your ability bestow your substance on the poor'.*

The older *Life of Teilo*, as we have it preserved in Vesp., has been emended with considerable skill in the version contained in the *Book of Llandaf*. It is unreasonable to suppose that the Vespasian *Life* would have been copied by a Llandaf scribe writing in a centre where the *LL*-text was available.

Llandaf had some knowledge of the Llancarfan charters, and used them in forging her own title-deeds,[44] as we may see from the one charter in the *Life of Clydog*. Here two of the witnesses, Bishop *Berthguin* and *Saturn* of the church of *Docunn*, are identical with witnesses in a charter of Llancarfan, in which *Guoidnerth* makes a grant of *Lann Catgualader* to *Cadoc*.[45] Elsewhere in the *Book of Llandaf*, in a long forgery, the same man is made to grant the same church to Llandaf.[46] The contents of the Llancarfan charters are not in fact consistent with the Llandaf claims, and betray the sources of the Llandaf forgeries. After the publication of *LL* they would be best forgotten. Moreover, the *Life*, miracles and charters of Cadog, whose *Life* is the most important one in the Vespasian collection, have not been edited in the Llandaf interest and give no hint of a Llandaf interpretation, as they would surely have done had they come from a scriptorium which had earlier in the century produced the *Book of Llandaf*.[47]

It is mainly the date of Vesp. in relation to *Liber Landauensis* which makes Llandaf so unlikely a centre for its compilation. But Vesp. is certainly the *kind* of source-book which lies behind the *Book of Llandaf*. If we had any evidence that, at the end of the twelfth century, the authorities of Llandaf were planning a claim to metropolitan status and primacy in Wales, then Vesp. is just the

[43] *Ibid.*, pp. 107, 116–17, 117.
[44] Davies, *Episcopal Acts*, I.163 and 171; Davies, *The Llandaff Charters*.
[45] Wade-Evans, *Vitae Sanctorum Britanniae*, p. 134. The forms are those of the texts.
[46] Evans & Rhys, *Book of Llan Dâv*, pp. 180–3; cf. p. 196 for the *Life of Clydog*.
[47] Far from supporting the Llandaf brief, the Life of Cadog provides material which St David's was quoting to support her opposing claims. Cf. Wade-Evans, *Vitae Sanctorum Britanniae*, pp. 54 and 60, and Davies, *Episcopal Acts*, I.262. See also Brooke, 'Archbishops', p. 221.

kind of collection of sources which they would have needed. Geoffrey of Monmouth and the *Book of Llandaf* had made an archbishop of Dyfrig, but the papacy had not believed them. During the century metropolitan pretensions were being hotly debated for St David's. We know that St David's first put forward a claim to metropolitan status in the 1120s,[48] and that Bishop Bernard raised the case again in *ca* 1144.[49] The controversy was reopened by Giraldus Cambrensis, and pursued with skill and energy between 1199 and 1203. In the first half of the century Urban of Llandaf and his *familia* had provided, in the *Book of Llandaf*, a formidable counter-claim to the St David's propaganda. They failed to establish against St David's the boundaries which they asserted, but it was not for want of trying. Did they make any counter-moves *ca* 1200? It is tempting to speculate, but unless any evidence is forthcoming the arguments must be weighted against a Llandaf origin for Vesp..

There is a hint, no more, in Vesp. that the compilers borrowed a copy of some Llandaf material for transcription. The Vespasian *Life of Teilo* concludes, quite irrelevantly, with the world *valete*. The text or texts may have been received with a polite message and salutation; in copying, the scribe correctly omitted the opening greeting but inadvertently copied the concluding farewell. This is too slender a piece of evidence to bear much weight, but, if it does indicate that a copy of Llandaf material was borrowed, it might explain why Vesp., compiled after the *Book of Llandaf*, contains pre-*LL* matter. Llandaf would not be likely to let so precious an authority as the *Book of Llandaf* out of her keeping, but she might be persuaded to lend other copies of the *Lives* of her saints.

The Llandaf material in Vesp. also throws a little more light on the Gloucester connection. Benedict, a Gloucester monk, was sufficiently interested in Dyfrig to write his *Life*, using the Llandaf text which is in Vesp. and Geoffrey of Monmouth's *History*. Teilo, the second Llandaf patron, is entered as a later addition in the twelfth-century Gloucester kalendar,[50] so Gloucester may have possessed his *Life*.[51] Of all the Llandaf texts in Vesp., the *Life of Clydog* is the most difficult to account for in a book not of Llandaf origin, since Clydog is not a popular saint. His cult is confined to Merthyr Clydog in Ewias, three or four miles west of Ewias Harold. But Gloucester was interested in Ewias Harold. Harold of Ewias had granted certain churches and tithes to St Peter's. After a specification of certain properties his charter continues:[52]

> I also grant and confirm to the aforesaid monks of Gloucester all my churches of my whole honour, and the lands which belong to them, with all tithes which my men shall grant to that church, freely and quit of all secular service and exaction, to have as alms for ever.

[48] Davies, *Episcopal Acts*, I.249–50.
[49] *Ibid.*, I.260.
[50] Wormald, *English Benedictine Kalendars*, II.45.
[51] Did Gloucester borrow the pre-*LL* Life of St Teilo, ending *ualete*, when it obtained the Llandaf Life of St Dyfrig which Benedict of Gloucester needed for his *Vita Sancti Dubricii*?
[52] Hart, *Historia et Cartularium*, I.285–6.

Gloucester made no claim to the church of Clydog, but she had rights in neighbouring property, and this may have aroused her interest in Clydog and the boundaries which Llandaf claimed for him.

It is possible that the material in Vesp. which must come originally from Llandaf did not do so directly, but entered the compilation via Gloucester. There were plenty of opportunities for exchange between the churches. Conway Davies shows that the Benedictine Nicholas ap Gwrgan, bishop of Llandaf 1148–83, had previously been a monk of Gloucester;[53] and the litigation in which Gloucester was not infrequently involved brought her into contact with the bishop and his *familia*.

Our examination of the evidence suggests that, in the 1130s or later, material from the hagiographical schools of Llanbadarn Fawr in West Wales, and possibly from Llandaf, was gathered together at Gloucester.[54] These texts were copied about 1200 into Vesp.. The final compilers belonged to a scriptorium which had several competent scribes, one of whom glossed many of the Welsh names. After the *Lives* had been transcribed, the 'kalendar' was drawn up, by someone familiar with the feast of Dochelinus. Monmouth was a border monastery, in an anglicised area accessible to Welsh influences; her monks were the only people in Wales likely to know the date of Dochelinus's festival. Until further evidence is produced it seems likely that Mr Harris is right in claiming the Monmouth monks as the actual compilers of the manuscript.

Wherever the compilation was made it has odd omissions. Its purpose was to identify and record Welsh saints. Monmouth monks might therefore be expected to enter the native patrons of the churches which formed part of their own properties.[55] Cadog and Dyfrig are here, for Monmouth owned two churches of St Cadog and St Dyfrig's foundation at Whitchurch. But native patrons of other properties are absent. Guénolé,[56] Tudy,[57] Custennin,[58] comparatively well-known saints with local cults, all had churches in the immediate neighbourbood of Monmouth, and yet they are omitted. The absence of octaves, of the feast of the dedication of St Mary's, Monmouth,[59] of the feast of St Florentinus, need

---

[53] Davies, *Episcopal Acts*, II.655.

[54] Christopher Brooke has suggested to me that some of the diverse interests represented in the compilation may reflect the work of one or more professional hagiographers: Caradog of Llancarfan was working at this time, and someone of his type might account for elements as diverse as the Old Cornish glossary and the variety of the *Vitae*. This suggestion, though it is hypothetical, may explain some of the details discussed above. It does not affect my argument that, at a preliminary stage, materials were assembled at Gloucester.

[55] Cf. Wormald, 'Calendar of the Augustinian priory', pp. 4–5, on the custom of the canons of the Augustinian priory of Launceston of entering 'the patron saints of the churches appropriated to them, or over which they exercised some jurisdiction'.

[56] Marchegay, *Chartes anciennes*, p. 15, for *ecclesia sancti Wingaloei*. For his church at Wonnastow, near Monmouth, see Wade-Evans, 'Parochiale', p. 74. Some of his relics were at Glastonbury and at Exeter; he is in the Leofric Missal and in the litany from Salisbury, Cathedral Library, MS. 180. His Life must have been known to the Breton founder of Monmouth.

[57] Marchegay, *Chartes anciennes*, p. 18. He is patron of Dixton: Wade-Evans, 'Parochiale', p. 111. He is in the Exeter Martyrology at May 9.

[58] Marchegay, *Chartes anciennes*, pp. 15 and 28: *Ecclesia S. Custenin de Bicenouria* (Welsh Bicknor, near Ross).

[59] We know that this was being observed in 1398: Bliss, *Calendar*, V.257.

cause no surprise if it is accepted that the purpose of the kalendar is not liturgical but historical. But the absence of Oudoceus from the Llandaf material is illogical, for the legend of the three patrons was by this time fully developed. The collection of material is indeed so haphazard as to require comment. The palaeography of the manuscript provides some explanation of the way in which the monks went to work.

The gatherings of the manuscript are normally eights, though there are four exceptions: the kalendar, glossary and Brecknock-tract at the beginning of the manuscript are on two gatherings of ten and four, and of the twelve gatherings on which the *Lives* are transcribed one is of five and one of seven. The last gathering of the manuscript is lost. The standard of execution throughout the manuscript varies considerably. The beginning is carefully produced, but as the manuscript proceeds it acquires a less finished appearance. The first three *Lives* in the collection – Gwynllyw, Cadog and Illtud – have coloured capitals, paragraphs, and chapter-headings which were filled in afterwards. The next four have coloured capitals and paragraphs, but the spaces left for rubrics have not been filled in. The remainder, with the exception of Maedóc and Tatheus, have no coloured capitals, no paragraphs and no chapter-headings. After the first few gatherings little care is taken to secure uniformity – the hands vary in size and the ink and colours change. The amount of care taken over the appearance of the manuscript has declined. This is, in itself, a common enough occurrence; it must, however, be considered together with the extent of revision in the manuscript. The first three *Lives* – of Gwynllyw, Cadog and Illtud – have been intensively revised with marginal interpolations and interlinear glosses. In the *Life of Cadog*, two slips were inserted[60] with six extra chapters to be interpolated at different points in the text. In the next four *Lives* there is a little revision – the interpolator's hand appears occasionally in the margin of the Gloucester *Life of Dyfrig*, and in the other three of this group there are a few interlinear glosses. The Brecknock-tract at the beginning of the manuscript has also received one or two interlinear glosses, and a few additions have been made to the kalendar. Practically no revision occurs in the remaining ten *Lives*. How is this palaeographical evidence to be interpreted, and what light does it throw on the selection and omissions in the contents?

The scribes set to work first on the *Vitae*. The *Life of Gwynllyw*, the first in the collection, starts at gathering three, and this begins a series of regular gatherings of eight, with two exceptions. The first three *Vitae* were carefully written, and coloured capitals and rubrics were filled in. The life, passion, miracles and genealogy of Cadog, the second saint in the series, are followed by an account in a different hand of the possessions of Llancarfan and a series of its charters. The charters are on an irregular gathering[61] and have not been revised; they were most probably obtained from some outside source. The manuscript was continued in various hands, and the scribe who copied the last group of *Lives*

60 [One, presumably bearing §§ 2–3 and 5, is lost; the other, bearing §§ 18 and 32 on its recto and § 20 on its verso is now fo 32. (Wade-Evans, *Vitae Sanctorum Britanniae*, pp. 32–5, supplies §§ 2, 3, and 5 from BL MS. Cotton Titus D.XXII, fos 6or, 6ov–62r.)]
61 [Fos 38–42. (The charters start, however, at fo 37v25.)]

wrote the first two irregular gatherings, which contain the *capitula* and kalendar. After the first few *Lives* had been written, other texts came to light. Someone – call him the Master of the Scriptorium – started to go through the manuscript, making extensive additions in the margins and on odd inserted leaves, with notes at relevant points, 'Require signum scedulae', 'Require istud signum', which may have been made with an eye to retranscription. But the revision was very unevenly applied, and, for some reason to which the known evidence provides no clue, it was never completed. Only the first three *Lives* have been fully revised. The succeeding four have been partially revised, and the kalendar has likewise received a few additions, but more than three-quarters of the days in the year are still completely blank, and various saints whom one would expect to find are omitted.

The compilers of Vesp. wished to provide some record of the Celtic saints of Wales. They seem to have observed no special order in copying the *Lives*, but to have transcribed them as they came to hand. Their 'kalendar' takes a Roman framework, adds the saints of the *Lives* which they had transcribed, and uses other native sources, which almost certainly included a kalendar derived from Gloucester. In the space between kalendar and *capitula* they copied out a glossary and a Brecknock-tract for good measure. There is uneven and incomplete revision. The whole effect is extremely haphazard, as though the plan of the collection had only been worked out on the broadest lines. It contrasts sharply with the impression conveyed by the main body of the *Book of Llandaf* of a work uniformly executed and planned. Both the contents and the palaeography suggest that Vesp. may have been considered as a source-book for historical record. The interests it represents are varied and contradictory: it is in no sense a brief in support of a case, like the *Book of Llandaf*. It may not even, as we have it, be complete. It is possible that Vesp. may have been in progress for some time: the changes of hand and inks and the occasional spaces are of too common occurrence in manuscripts to act as evidence for such a suggestion, but they certainly do nothing to weaken the possibility. It looks as if the compilers must have intended to make other entries as opportunity offered. If they ever clearly formulated a detailed plan, the present manuscript can hardly be a complete expression of it; their kalendar gapes with omissions and their revision was abandoned half-way through.

The manuscript is another illustration of the interest which the Anglo-Norman settlers felt in the pseudo-historical traditions of the Celtic past. It lacks the polish of William of Malmesbury's work for Glastonbury, or the ingenuity of the *Book of Llandaf*, or the creative imagination of Geoffrey of Monmouth's *History*, but it is an industrious record of texts mainly written or rewritten in the twelfth century. It reflects the restless enterprise of this period of Norman-Welsh history – the expansion of Gloucester, the rise of Llandaf, and the preservation, though abbreviated, enfeebled and but half-understood, of the traditions of the pre-Norman Welsh Church.[62]

[62] Father Paul Grosjean, S.J., Bollandist, and Professor Francis Wormald discussed this chapter with me in a first draft. I am especially indebted to them both for help and advice.

V

The Welsh Latin chronicles:
Annales Cambriae and related texts[1]

In 1928 that great historian, John Edward Lloyd, gave the Sir John Rhŷs inaugural lecture to the British Academy on 'The Welsh Chronicles'.[2] He was mainly concerned with the Bruts, and he showed that these were translated from a Latin text which was related, in an unspecified way, to the *Annales Cambriae*. Since then, another distinguished Welsh scholar, Thomas Jones, has edited and translated the Peniarth 20 and Red Book of Hergest versions of the *Brut y Tywysogyon* and *Brenhinedd y Saesson*, and has worked out the relationship between these texts.[3] It is now clear that the Latin original of these Welsh chronicles was compiled towards the end of the thirteenth century, most probably at Strata Florida. The Peniarth 20 version and the Red Book of Hergest version are independent Welsh translations of that original. *Brenhinedd y Saesson* is a third independent Welsh version of the same text down to 1197, but after this is dependent on the other Welsh translations. The brief continuation of Peniarth 20 from 1282 to 1332 was written at Valle Crucis, as Goronwy Edwards has demonstrated.[4] So the student of the Welsh texts, largely owing to the devoted work of Thomas Jones, is now on firm ground.

But when he turns to the Latin annals all around him is still a quagmire. There are four versions of the text known as *Annales Cambriae*. The earliest, BL MS. Harley 3859, written *ca* 1100, has been well edited by Egerton Phillimore.[5] BL MS. Cotton Domitian A.1[6] and the annals on the flyleaves of the Breviate Domesday in London, Public Record Office, MS. E. 164/1 both date from the end of the thirteenth century. With the exception of fifty-five years transcribed in parallel columns by Lloyd[7] they have still to be consulted in the

---

[1] The Sir John Rhŷs Memorial Lecture to the British Academy, read on 17 October, 1973; first published in *Proceedings of the British Academy* 59 (1973) 233–58. There is a review by D. Dumville, *Studia Celtica* 12/13 (1977/8) 461–7.

[2] Lloyd, 'Welsh chronicles'.

[3] Jones, *Brut y Tywysogyon* (3 vols), and *Brenhinedd y Saesson*.

[4] In a review of Jones, *Brut y Tywysogyon: Peniarth MS. 20* in *English Historical Review* 57 (1942) 370–5.

[5] 'The *Annales Cambriæ*'; there is also a text in Faral, *Légende*, III.44–50.

[6] BL Cotton Domitian A.i is made up of two manuscripts. The section we are concerned with is fos 56–160.

[7] Lloyd, 'Wales and the coming', pp. 165–79.

edition of John Williams, Ab Ithel.[8] This is not even an accurate copy of the PRO manuscript, which Ab Ithel uses as the basis of his text after 954, and at least the Cottonian manuscript has to be completely transcribed before any comparison of the Cottonian and PRO versions can be made.[9] The annals in the fourth manuscript, the thirteenth-century Exeter Cathedral Library MS. 3514, have been well edited by Thomas Jones under the title *Cronica de Wallia*.[10] A critical edition of the *Annales Cambriae* is much needed but, meanwhile, historians need to know how the texts were put together, what sources were used, when and where the annals were compiled, and how the different texts relate to each other. This lecture is an attempt to answer some of these questions.

The starting-point of any inquiry into the Latin annals must be Harley 3859 (Ab Ithel's A). The annals here are written in an Anglo-Norman hand of *ca* 1100.[11] The last entry refers to the death of Rhodri son of Hywel (in 954) and the annals are immediately followed by genealogies which start with Owain son of Hywel. Both annals and genealogies are incorporated into a text of the *Historia Brittonum*. The Harleian annals were almost certainly completed in their present form before the death of Owain in 988 and probably in, or soon after, 954.[12]

As Lloyd pointed out, from 796 until 954 the annals must have been kept at St David's. Maredudd of Dyfed with his sons and grandsons dominates the beginning of the period, Hyfaidd of Dyfed and his son Llywarch are important towards its close, though here attention is concentrated on the great kings of Seisyllwg, Cadell, Clydog, and Hywel. Llywarch's daughter Elen married Hywel Dda, who secured Dyfed, and Hywel's son Owain was thus descended on his mother's side from kings of Dyfed. Five bishops of St David's are mentioned, as well as a burning and an attack on the city. St David's thus provides the controlling interest. But the annals were kept in a haphazard way, with spurts of activity and periods of inertia.[13]

There are strong reasons for thinking that the chronicle was started at St David's in the late eighth century, for a year-by-year chronicle nearly always

[8] *Annales Cambriæ*; or, for the period 445–1066, see Petrie & Sharpe, *Monumenta*, pp. 830–40.

[9] For comments on the edition, see Phillimore, 'Welsh historical records', pp. 140–8.

[10] '"Cronica de Wallia" and other documents'.

[11] David Dumville has very kindly sent me the following note on this manuscript: 'It is not yet possible to assign it to any centre. The contents, in this order, are: Vegetius, Macrobius, the spurious *Inuectiua* of Cicero and Sallust, the *Historia Brittonum* interpolated by the *Annales Cambriae* and the Welsh royal genealogies, part of Augustine's *De haeresibus*, Solinus, Aethicus Ister, Vitruvius. The whole is a unity, the product of a single scriptorium.'

[12] Phillimore, 'The *Annales Cambriæ*', p. 144, argues that the annals were finished in 954 or 955 because they do not mention the battle of Llanrwst, fought in 955.

[13] Between 796 and 817 there are nineteen entries, including four kings of Dyfed and a burning of St David's. Then there is a very thin phase, with only sixteen entries in forty-four years though two of these are bishops of St David's. Between 862 and 887 there is another spurt of entries, eighteen in all. The first half of this period covers the episcopate of Nobis. Then for twelve years there are three entries, followed by nine between 900 and 909 when (according to Giraldus Cambrensis) Asser was bishop of St David's. His death brings in another lean period, with only six entries in twenty-eight years. Then between 938 and 954 there are sixteen entries; two bishops of St David's are mentioned.

shows signs of localisation, and the Harleian annals point to St David's only from the late eighth century. The earlier part was a scholar's exercise compiled well after the events. There is nothing in the form of the names which requires us to assume compilation before the late eighth century.[14] Moreover the annalist was definitely interested in the Easter controversy,[15] and the later eighth century was a period when this interest was most lively in Wales. These arguments all point to annals which begin to be kept regularly at St David's in the late eighth century.

If the Harleian annals before this date are not a year-by-year chronicle, but the compilation of some scholar, one would expect to be able to trace his sources. This is possible. Up to the battle of Chester in 613 there is a close correspondence with the Irish annals. Moreover, the Harleian annals for this period with their preponderance of ecclesiastical entries look like Irish annals, for there are twenty ecclesiastical entries and eleven secular ones; and of these eleven, seven are British entries which are not found in the Irish annals.[16] Some of the Irish entries were obviously made much later in time than the events, for the births of saints are backward-looking entries. The Irish saints chosen by our annalist are ones which a Welshman much later, picking out the salient events in the history of the Irish Church, might choose to record.[17] The

[14] Professor Kenneth Jackson has very kindly advised me about these. There are three unusual forms. In *Adomnan*, the *o* points to a source not later than the first quarter of the eighth century, but this could very well have been from the *Vita Columbae* itself. The form *Cenioyd* (776) is apparently not of Irish origin, and looks as if it might have come from a Pictish source. In the reference to Kentigern, one might expect the spellings *Cintigirni* or *Centigirni* for Kentigern, instead of the *Conthigirni* which appears: but on this see Jackson, *Language and History*, pp. 669 and 676, where it is clearly shown that there is no reason to regard the *o* as archaic or strange. The very rare use of *th* for Old Welsh *t* (= /d/) is paralleled in the Life of St Cadog and in the Book of Llandaf.

[15] He starts with a change in the date of Easter by Pope Leo I (at the Fourth General Council), he notes England's adoption of the Roman Easter (in 664), and in 768 the Britons', under the influence of Elfoddw, who died in 809. The Easter question implies an interest in chronological studies, and could have stimulated a desire for a chronological record in late eighth-century Wales.

[16] On the Irish annals see Hughes, *Early Christian Ireland*, pp. 97–160; Smyth, 'Earliest Irish annals'; Mac Niocaill, *Medieval Irish Annals*. The section of the Annals of Tigernach relating to the fifth century begins in 489, but after 489 all but three entries in the Harleian annals are in both the Annals of Ulster and the Annals of Tigernach. All except three of the entries are in the Annals of Inisfallen.

[17] Patrick and Benén, Brigit and Íbar (both Leinster saints), all belong to the first phase; Ciarán of Clonmacnoise and Columcille are great monastic founders. Brendan of Birr is more of a puzzle. Gabrán son of Domangart was founder of the Cenél nGabráin in Kintyre; his son Aedán was the famous king of Dál Riata who ruled in the time of Columcille, and he fought the battle of *Eubonia*. David, Gildas, and the battle of *Cair Legion* would obviously interest a Welshman. The Irish annals mentioned in the last note are not using dating from the Incarnation, and they obviously had difficulties with their dating in this early period, so it is not surprising to find that the Harleian annals do not agree precisely with the Irish annals in their chronology. But the only wild discrepancy is over the date of St David: I think, therefore, that this entry may not be from the Irish annals but from some Welsh source. Mrs Chadwick (*Early British Church*, p. 55) sees a significant similarity between the monasteries named among the signatories of the Synod of Birr (Meyer, *Cáin Adamnáin*, pp. 16–18) and those named in the Harleian annals. But the order is not, as she claims, the same (in the annals the death of Brigit is the fourth Irish obit, while Kildare comes tenth in the *Cáin*) and houses at the beginning of the list in the *Cáin* are omitted in the annals (the Irish Bangor, Lismore, Lorrha). It may be, however, that the Irish annals and material concerning the date of Easter came into Wales by the same channels.

section of close Irish dependence stops when Isidore's chronicle comes to an end, and we know that Irish annalists were using this text.[18]

These extracts from a set of Irish annals provide the background into which the compiler has fitted eleven British entries, the seven secular ones already mentioned and four ecclesiastical entries.[19] The main interest of the British entries is certainly in North Britain and North Wales, areas which we already know were closely connected dynastically and by literary interests. The annals name three descendants of Coel Hen, the battle of Arfderydd, the death of Kentigern, two kings of Gwynedd, and the burial of Daniel of the Bangors. Cynog of Brycheiniog, who at first looks odd, is said in *De Situ Brecheniauc* to be related, by the marriage of his sister, to the line of Coel Hen.[20] The only entry definitely out of line is Dyfrig, a saint of South-East Wales; and he might well be an addition, for the entry reads *Conthigirni obitus et Dibric episcopi*. The battles of Badon and Camlann, which have caused so much discussion, are among these eleven non-Irish entries. Camlann may well be a northern battle. Badon, for good historical reasons, would seem to have been fought in the south of England.[21] But a battle of such significance would have been entered in any British chronicle, and it does not invalidate the northern orientation of the rest of the early British entries.

When we move on to the middle section of the Harleian annals which runs from the early seventh to the late eighth century, the main source seems to be this northern chronicle.[22] There is a close parallel with the northern history section of the *Historia Brittonum*.[23] Both texts give an account of the struggle between Cadwallon, king of Gwynedd, and his successors, joined by Penda of Mercia, against the Northumbrian kings Edwin, Oswald, and Oswy. Both name the battles similarly: *Meicen*,[24] *Catscaul* or *Cantscaul*,[25] *Cocboy*,[26] and *Gai*.[27] But in spite of the close correspondence, the Harleian text could not have been

[18] The Annals of Inisfallen at 612 state: 'the fifth year of the emperor Heraclius [610–41] and the fourth year of King Sisebutus, and the end of Isidore's chronicle'. It seems likely that the Irish source determined the date at which the St David's annalist chose to begin his chronicle. He used an Easter-cycle of 532 years and put in his first entry (concerning the date of Easter) at the ninth year. The beginning of the cycle would correspond to the date at which Irish annalists calculated the founding of Armagh. I am grateful to David Dumville for clarifying my ideas on this and other points. [For 445 as the first year, and for its purely Welsh significance, see now Miller, 'Disputed historical horizon', p. 23.]

[19] The death of Gildas, a British cleric, is in the Irish annals (at 570 in the Annals of Ulster).

[20] My pupil Philip Jenkins pointed this out to me. See Bartrum, *Genealogical Tracts*, pp. 14–16.

[21] See Jackson, 'Once again' and 'Site of Mount Badon'. There is an enormous literature about the Arthurian legend. Two of the most important discussions are by Jones, 'Early evolution', and Jackson, *apud* Loomis, *Arthurian Literature*, pp. 1–19. Alcock, *Arthur's Britain*, provides a good discussion of the archaeological evidence, but is sometimes misleading on the literary sources; for example, see below, p. 73, n. 41.

[22] For this whole section, see Jackson, 'Northern British section', and Dumville, 'North British section'.

[23] On the *Historia Brittonum* see the important article by Dumville, '"Nennius"'.

[24] Hatfield Chase, where Cadwallon slew Edwin and his two sons.

[25] Denisesburna, near Hexham, where Cadwallon was killed by Oswald. See Williams, 'Bellum Cantscaul'.

[26] Maserfelth (Oswestry), where Oswald fell. See Williams, 'A reference'.

[27] Winwaed, where Oswy conquered Penda and the Britons.

derived from the *Historia Brittonum*. There are entries which the *Historia* does not have[28] and, probably even more significant, fundamentally different reportings of the same events.[29] On no less than three occasions the annals substantially diverge from the *Historia* and could not have been directly derived from the *Historia*.

Nor could the *Historia* have taken its account from the annals. The different reporting argues against it, and moreover the *Historia* provides information which is not in the Harleian annals.[30] It seems certain, therefore, that there was an account of the struggle between Britons and Northumbrians which the annals and the *Historia* used independently.[31]

The other texts with which we must compare the Harleian annals during this period are the earlier recensions of the Irish annals, for though the close correspondence of Welsh and Irish annals ceases in 613, most of the entries are present in both Welsh and Irish annals, though in different guise. But the Welsh annals could not have been copying here from the Irish. Even if we put the early Irish recensions together (and the Annals of Tigernach provide the most help) the Welsh annals have a number of details and entries which the Irish annals do not give.[32] On the other hand the Irish annals give some entries which are missing from the Welsh annals but which the scribe of the Welsh text might have been expected to copy.[33] In fact the exemplar of the Harleian annals is much closer to the exemplar of the *Historia Brittonum* than to the Irish annals. It looks as if the 'Chronicle of Ireland'[34] had access to a northern chronicle, but that this was a stage removed from the exemplar of the Harleian annals and the *Historia*.

What was their prototype like? The source of the *Historia Brittonum* and the ultimate source of the Harleian annals cannot have been in chronicle-form. If it was, why did the compiler of the *Historia* have to turn to an Anglo-Saxon king-list to provide his chronological structure? It must have been North British memoranda, mainly concerning Gwynedd, Mercia, Elmet, and the area which is now the Scottish border. The author of the northern history section of the *Historia Brittonum* used these memoranda, incorporating them into an English regnal list similar to that in the Moore manuscript of Bede. These Northumbrian kings presumably meant something to him and his readers, so he was writing in a part of Britain open to English influence. Another compiler used the same memoranda, together with the obits of Strathclyde and Pictish kings and their battles,[35] entries which give his

---

[28] See below, p. 92.
[29] See below, p. 92f.
[30] See below, p. 94.
[31] For a different view of the relationship, see D. Dumville, *Studia Celtica* 12/13 (1977/8) 466–7.
[32] See below, p. 94.
[33] See below, p. 94f.
[34] For this lost source, see Hughes, *Early Christian Ireland*, pp. 99–115.
[35] The deaths of three kings of Strathclyde are recorded: Beli, his son Tewdwr, and Tewdwr's son Dyfnwal. There are four Pictish entries: the battle of Monad Carno among the Picts, the death of *Ougen* king of the Picts, a battle between the Picts and Britons in which Talorgan died, and the death of King Cinaed.

northern chronicle a more northerly orientation than the *Historia*. The compiler of the northern chronicle may therefore have come from further north, from an area in closer contact with the Picts.[36] At some time after 777 (the last of the northern entries) the northern chronicle was used by the St David's chronicler, and his annals formed the exemplar of the Harley manuscript.[37]

The northern chronicle must have looked rather different from the Irish annals. If the Welsh annals had used Irish annals to compile this central section of the Harleian text, you would expect to find certain characteristics which are absent. You would expect more entries about Iona: at least the record of her conversion to the Roman Easter (for our scribe was interested in that) and the obit of Ecgberht, whose influence achieved it. You would expect more Irish entries, especially for Leinster and southern Ireland, whereas there are only two. You would expect more ecclesiastical entries: the only three here are the obits of Adomnán, Bede, and Cuthbert of Monkwearmouth.

We cannot be sure where the northern chronicle was drawn up.[38] The compiler, using the North British memoranda, had fairly full sources for the wars of the English and Britons during the reigns of Edwin, Oswald, and Oswy on the Northumbrian side, Cadwallon, Cadwaladr, and Penda on the other. After this his sources were not very satisfactory – a few Strathclyde and English kings, a few Pictish battles, three outstanding northern ecclesiastics. It was the best he could do with the sources at his disposal. There are a few *mirabilia*-entries in this section of the Harleian annals,[39] and a few Welsh and South British entries have been inserted.[40] These cover a wide area. There are two Gwynedd entries, which were probably in the northern chronicle. The other entries concern Dyfed, Cornwall, and Hereford. They are an attempt retrospectively to provide a set of annals, and are the work of the St David's compiler in the late eighth century, or possibly of another reviser.

We may therefore conclude that from the late eighth century a record was kept at St David's, though some periods are much thinner than others and it was not always written up regularly year by year. Welsh chroniclers appear to have been nothing like so active as Irish ones in the same period. The contemporary St David's chronicle began fairly soon after Wales accepted the Roman Easter (768): but a preliminary section had to be provided, and for this the compiler used extracts from the Irish annals down to 613, and extracts

[36] I am grateful to Donald Meek for discussing this with me.

[37] It is significant that the Strathclyde entries in the Irish annals stop in 780 for nearly a hundred years – that is, at almost the same time as they do in the Harleian annals. Since they do not cease when the Iona chronicle stops in 741, I think they were entered in Ireland and did not reach the Irish annals via the Iona chronicle. The Irish annals have Strathclyde and Pictish entries not in the Harleian annals.

[38] Glasgow would be a likely place; but, if so, I think that the North British memoranda come from farther south.

[39] Mostly paralleled in the Irish annals, so they may have been in the northern chronicle. See below, p. 99f.

[40] These are listed below on p. 100. Three entries about Offa of Mercia come between the last northern entry (Abbot Cuthbert) and the first entry of the St David's group (Maredudd of Dyfed).

from a northern chronicle, into which he inserted a few other entries. The Arthurian entries of course belong to this preliminary section, and it should now be clear that there is no ground for Leslie Alcock's assurance that they go back to a contemporary source.[41] BL MS. Harley 3859 contains this set of annals down to 954. They are one of our few sources for the early history of Wales, so that the way they have been constructed, whether or not they were contemporary, what sources the compiler used, are all questions of vital interest to the historian.[42]

Now let us turn to the annals in BL MS. Cotton Domitian A.1, fos 138r–155r (Ab Ithel's C), which were transcribed at the end of the thirteenth century.[43] These begin with an Isidoran[44] section on the six ages of the world, into which have been inserted a few entries on British history derived from Geoffrey of Monmouth.[45] The Cottonian annals continue to use Isidore as their framework right down to the reign of Heraclius (610–41), citing the reign of each emperor and giving the appropriate British references under it. After Heraclius the annals change to a year-by-year format, marking each year with *annus*. This emphasises the break at the end of Isidore's chronicle which we have already noted in the Harleian annals.

The Cottonian annalist was using a text closely akin to the Harleian annals, but down to 734 he has rewritten it according to Geoffrey of Monmouth. His account of Arthur, Cynan, Godebyr (*Vortiporius*), Maelgwn, Ceredig, Cadfan, Cadwallon, Cadwaladr, and Ifor is that of Geoffrey. Arthur is treated at some length, Cadwallon's fight with Northumbria in less detail than in the Harleian text.[46] The Cottonian annals down to 734 are valueless as history, but they show the enormous influence of Geoffrey not only on romance but on historical writing. Between 734 and the end of the Harleian annals the two recensions of annals look very similar, and both show the same St David's orientation, but

---

[41] Alcock (*Arthur's Britain*, pp. 3, 45–9) believes that the fifth- and sixth-century entries were made in contemporary Easter-tables. This is not impossible, but it is much more likely that they are based on the calculations of an eighth- (or perhaps seventh-) century scholar.

[42] The preceding account of the Harleian annals is a summary of much detailed work which is thoroughly expounded in chapter VI below. For somewhat different views on two of the issues discussed, see D. Dumville, *Studia Celtica* 12/13 (1977/8) 466–7, and Dumville, 'North British section'.

[43] I am most grateful to Professor Julian Brown for advising me about the date of this hand, and about the hands of the Welsh entries in London, PRO, MS. E.164/1.

[44] I mean that he is using some text ultimately based on Isidore of Seville's chronology (as seen, for example, in *Etymologiae*, V.39).

[45] The Isidoran section was not in the early St David's manuscript which the Harleian scribe copied. The dates in Harley are approximately as they are in the Irish annals, whereas in the Cottonian manuscript some of the dates are wildly out: for example, Pope Leo's change of Easter is placed in the reign of Valentinian II, 383–92; Patrick's floruit under Arcadius, 395–408; the Synod of Urbs Legionis under Anastasius, 491–518; the death of Gildas under Justin I, 518–27; the battle of Chester under Justin II, 565–78. The compiler of the Cottonian version had an Isidoran framework. Into this he put material from Geoffrey of Monmouth and entries from the St David's annals (from a text similar to Harley).

[46] There can be no doubt that this is derived from Geoffrey. There is nothing which cannot be found in Geoffrey except the date of the *aduentus Saxonum*, 438. The other calculation from the Incarnation, 542, the end of Arthur's reign, is in Geoffrey. The order of events is Geoffrey's order.

the Cottonian recension is not copying the Harleian annals.[47] There must have been a St David's text from which both were derived.

At this point we must turn to the text transcribed on the flyleaves of the abbreviated Domesday Book in London, PRO, MS. E. 164/1 (King's Remembrancer Misc. Books Series I), pp. 2–26 (Ab Ithel's B); for the PRO-text and the Cottonian text are closely related down to 1202. The PRO annalist also started with an Isidoran section,[48] but he saw British history as beginning with Julius Caesar,[49] and from this time on marked each year with *annus*, until *s.a.* 1097 he started to date from the Incarnation. Though he includes a few entries from Geoffrey, after Pope Leo's change of the date of Easter his text is closely similar to that of the Harleian annals. He gives a few entries not in the Harleian text which look as if they may be genuine early entries[50] and has some better readings than the Harleian manuscript,[51] so he too seems to be copying the text from which the Harleian annals are derived. He is a much more accurate, less individualist, copier than the scribe of the Cottonian annals. The Cottonian and PRO annals are, then, independent recensions of a St David's text, and continue to be so until they part company after 1202.

From the end of the Harleian annals in 954 until 1202 it is necessary to consider the Cottonian and PRO recensions together. The original of both continues to be a St David's text. From 1040 onwards we have what seems to be a continuous list of St David's bishops.[52] Between 954 and 1040 three obits are given merely with the title *episcopus*, but these are in Giraldus's list of St David's bishops.[53] Though the annals do not give a continuous list of bishops for this century they record eight attacks on St David's and there can be no doubt that we are still dealing with a St David's chronicle.

But our two manuscripts are independent derivations from a St David's original. Each records a number of events absent from the other, and, though the vocabulary is similar, the wording is not identical.[54] I give the following specimen as an example:

---

[47] Cotton has ten entries not in Harley, and Harley has thirty-three entries which Cotton does not give.

[48] Again, this is an addition to the St David's annals as they were in 954. The PRO Isidoran preface goes down to the reign of Leo I (457–73), so that the chronological join with the main text is very clumsy.

[49] So did Bede, *Historia Ecclesiastica*, V.24, whose annal for 60 B.C. begins the PRO-text.

[50] 565: 'Nauigatio Gilde in Hibernia';
    569: 'Sinodus Uictorie apud Britones congregatur';
    649: 'Guentis strages';
    880: 'Gueit Conani';
    889: 'Subni Scotorum sapientissimus obiit'.

[51] At 865 he has the correct reading and the Harleian annals a corrupt reading, for example.

[52] Erfyn, Joseph, Bleddyn, Sulien, Abraham, Wilfrid, Bernard.

[53] Giraldus Cambrensis, *Itinerarium Cambriae*, II.1, though Rhydderch seems too early there. The possibility is not to be overlooked, however, that Giraldus was himself drawing on the St David's annals.

[54] Williams Ab Ithel, *Annales Cambriæ*, pp. 34–5.

Annus MCXI. Iorwert filius Bledint de carcere rediit. Owinus et Madocus filii Ririt combusserunt Meirionnith. Owinus diuertens ad Keredigeaun irruptiones fecit in Flandrenses; pro quo Cadugaun pater eius Keredigeaun amisit, et Gilberto filio Ricardi traditur. Owinus et Madocus Hiberniam petunt. Madocus rediit, et in siluis latuit.

Annus: Iorwerth filius Bledin iussu regis de carcere in patriam suam rediit. Oweyn filius Cadugaun et Maredut filius Ririd combusserunt Meyronnith, hominesque ibi et armenta occiderunt. Postea Owein uenit de Keredigaun et irruptiones fecit in Flandrenses, quapropter Cadugaun eius pater Kereticam terram amisit et Gilberto filio Ricardi traditur. Ipse uero Owein et Madauc expulsi Yberniam petunt. Sed Madauc iterum de Ybernia rediit et latuit in siluis.

Annus MCXII. Iorwarth a Madoco nepote suo occisus est. Owinus de Hibernia rediens terram suam a rege accepit. Mortalitas hominum maxima.

Annus: Jorwerth a Madauc nepote suo occiditur, et ab eodem Madauc Cadugaun suus auunculus occiditur. Interea Owein de Ybernia rediit et terram suam a rege accepit.

From 1136 to 1167 the differences of wording are much more marked, but many of the same incidents are recorded in both Latin recensions and in the vernacular recensions, the Bruts, so that the same text seems to lie behind all the manuscripts. At 1168 the two Latin recensions again become very similar. This continues until 1188. At 1189 the PRO-text begins to take on independent features, though the St David's original remains in the background until 1202. After this the texts diverge.[55]

The Anglo-Normans moved into South-West Wales in the 1090s, and after this English entries in the Cottonian annals become more frequent. They are about the crusades, royal visits to Normandy and Gascony, the struggles between kings and their sons and barons, John's contest with the Church (he is *maliciosus opressor ecclesiarum et optimatum . . . odiosus Domino et hominibus*), notices of royal births and deaths, papal councils and succession and the visits of papal legates, and a few ecclesiastical obits. These are not tacked on to the end of Welsh entries, but often take a central place. The material is commonplace, but though I have compared it with twenty-five sets of English

---

[55] In the late eleventh and early twelfth centuries the interest of the annals is quite widespread, concentrating especially in Dyfed, Ceredigion, and Powys. The annals are also concerned with the family of Sulien, but other than this they show no special intimacy with Llanbadarn, whereas there are fairly frequent entries about the city of St David's (between 1073, when Sulien was appointed, and 1099, when Rhigyfarch died, there are six references to St David's, other than to its clerics). It should be remembered that the *paruchia* of St David spread over Dyfed, Ceredigion, and Southern Powys. There must have been a close connexion between Llanbadarn and St David's in this period, which no doubt facilitated the transmission of news.

annals,[56] I cannot find that it is directly borrowed. The English element becomes marked from the 1160s, was present before the texts diverged after 1202, and continued sporadically throughout the St David's chronicle. I think therefore that it probably originates at St David's; but it must first have been entered as rather jumbled memoranda, perhaps from memory and not immediately, because the sequence is in some cases confused. It shows that the St David's scribes were at work in an anglicised society.

The St David's annals are really Anglo-Welsh from the 1160s onwards. In the thirteenth century they sometimes give the deaths of English lords in battle without even naming the independent Welsh ruler on the opposing side. The amount of detail about St David's grows. For example, when the annalist records a St David's appointment in the later period he sometimes supplies the string of changes which it brings about, together with precise information about the date of a man's death, the exact place of the tomb within the church, and so on. There is no doubt that the Cottonian annals remain throughout a St David's chronicle, though there are lean years when little or nothing was recorded. They are especially valuable as a source for the Anglo-Norman south-west, interested in Pembroke, the Marshall family and other Anglo-Norman lords, Carmarthen, and the St David's area.

For the period between the death of Æthelred and the coronation of King John two bifolia and one single leaf have been inserted into the Cottonian annals.[57] They are in the same hand as the main text, but were put in as an afterthought. The leaves bear rather scrappy and laconic English entries with marks to show where they were to be fitted into the main text. They are derived from John of Worcester up to 1138.[58] After this they are still derived from a Worcester text. This shows that a Worcester chronicle (or extracts from it) was available at St David's, and that the idea of combining Welsh and English entries, later to be adopted in *Brenhinedd y Saesson*, had already been conceived at St David's by the late thirteenth century, probably under the influence of Geoffrey of Monmouth.

Now let us turn to Exeter Cathedral MS. 3514, and to the second of the two chronicles transcribed there.[59] This has no independent historical value, but it shows us how one Welsh annalist worked, and what sources he had at his disposal. Up to 1172 the entries are very short and scattered. From 1172 to 1265

---

[56] BL MS. Cotton Vespasian E.IV; the annals of Worcester, Winchester, Waverley, Tewkesbury; the *Flores Historiarum*, Roger of Wendover, the Major and Minor Chronicles of Matthew Paris, the Bury chronicle, the Peterborough chronicle, Roger of Hoveden, William of Newburgh, Ralph de Diceto, Gervase of Canterbury, Bartholomew de Cotton, Ralph of Coggeshall, Walter of Coventry, Thomas Wykes; the annals of Osney, Dunstable, Bermondsey, Burton, Southwark, and Winchcombe. Professor Christopher Cheney very kindly lent me his transcript of BL MS. Cotton Faustina B.I (Winchcombe) and discussed the English annals with me. There are some verbal similarities between the St David's annals and the Battle annals edited by Liebermann (*Anglo-normannische Geschichtsquellen*, pp. 50–5), but these stop in 1206; Brecon was a cell of Battle.

[57] Fos 142, 144, 146, 148, 150.

[58] On John of Worcester see Darlington, *Anglo-Norman Historians*. Between 1104 and 1121 there is a close association between the Cottonian Annals of St David's and the extracts from John in the Annals of Worcester (ed. Luard, *Annales Monastici*, IV.355–564, esp. 374–7).

[59] MS., pp. 523–8: edited for 1254–85 by Jones, '"Cronica de Wallia" and other documents', pp. 42–4.

they are abstracted from the Bury chronicle.[60] 1265 is where the original Bury chronicle by John of Tayster ended. From 1274[61] until the annals end in 1285 they are abstracted from the St David's text. But since they leave out much of the detail about St David's this does not look like a chronicle compiled there, although the St David's annals were accessible to the scribe. We shall return to this question later.

The other chronicle in the Exeter manuscript, known as the *Cronica de Wallia*,[62] is a much more important and interesting one. Unfortunately it does not begin until 1190. It is about Welsh Wales, especially the areas ruled by Rhys and his descendants, and it is a Cistercian document.[63] Up to 1216 it is closely paralleled by *Brut y Tywysogyon*. The next ten years are missing, but the entries for 1228 and 1230 have correspondences with the *Brut*. From 1231 to 1246 it is almost identical with the PRO annals, and 1248 is similar. The years 1249–53 are missing. Then from 1254 onwards the character of the entries changes, and with the exception of one entry in 1255 they are a conflation of extracts from the St David's and the Bury annals.[64] The scribe therefore seems to have used a defective manuscript, and his independent Welsh source came to an end in 1255.

There are indications that the section from 1231 to 1255 had a Strata Florida origin, though all the Strata Florida entries which we find in the PRO annals are not present. But the death of Owain son of Gruffydd is recorded in 1235, with the exact date and the information that he was buried next to his brother Rhys in the monks' chapter at Strata Florida.[65] 1236 reports, with the date (*circa festum Sancti Michelis*), a transaction of Maelgwn son of Maelgwn by which he made ready to despoil the monks of Strata Florida of Ystrad Meurig, which his ancestors had given them. This reference to monastic property in the vicinity of the monastery points clearly to Strata Florida. The annalist also mentions that the princes of Wales swore fealty to David in 1238 at Strata Florida. Mr Beverley Smith has considered and rejected the possibility that these Exeter annals were put together at Talley in Ystrad Tywi.[66] Talley

---

[60] Printed by Thorpe, *Chronicon ex Chronicis*, II. 151–96, as the continuation of 'Florence' of Worcester or, for the period after 1212, by Gransden (ed. & tr.), *Chronicle*. See Galbraith, 'St Edmundsbury'.

[61] There are entries at 1266 and 1273, but they are not from the St David's annals as we now have them.

[62] Exeter, Cathedral Library, MS. 3514, pp. 507–19. Edited by Jones, '"Cronica de Wallia" and other documents', pp. 29–41.

[63] Apart from the references to Strata Florida, it is concerned with King John's exactions as they affect the Cistercian order (see 1209).

[64] 1254 and 1255 are overlap-years. 1255 has some correspondences with PRO and the *Brut*, some extracts from the Bury annals.

[65] Rhys died in 1220, but this section is missing from *Cronica de Wallia*.

[66] Smith, 'Dynasty', p. 277, states: 'There does not appear to be any good reason to associate the *Cronica de Wallia* with Strata Florida'. But the evidence I am citing seems to me very good evidence. The only reference to Talley in the *Cronica* (and comparably in the *Brut*) is at 1214: 'Hoc anno duo Walenses episcopi Deo donante preficiuntur Meneuensi et Bangorensi ecclesiis. Geruasius uero abbas de Tallelecheu Premonstracensis ordinis sedis Meneuie, Caduganus uero abbas de Alba Domo Bangorum preficitur, uir mire facundie et sapientie.' This seems to me to show much greater intimacy with and enthusiasm for Whitland than Talley. Smith also recognises Whitland as the possible home of the *Cronica*, and prefers it.

seems impossible, for although there are several eulogies accompanying obituary notices in this part of the annals, Rhys Gryg, lord of Ystrad Tywi, does not get one (1234),[67] nor does his son Rhys Mechyll (1244). On the other hand Owain son of Gruffydd, lord of South Cardigan, who was buried at Strata Florida, does. So, more surprisingly, does Richard Marshall, earl of Pembroke.[68] In the section from 1190 to 1216 eulogies go to the Lord Rhys, sufficiently outstanding to deserve a special mention in any South-West Welsh annals, and to his sons Gruffydd and Hywel, both of whom were buried at Strata Florida.[69]

There is a significant detail in the entry for 1207 which also points to Strata Florida. The earl of Gloucester then came from Buellt to devastate the land of the sons of Gruffydd. *He stayed the first night at the grange of Aberdehoneu*. Aberdehoneu was a Cistercian grange near Builth and part of the possessions of Strata Florida. This is probably why it receives mention.

I think therefore that from 1190 to 1255 these annals are from a Strata Florida source.[70] They are the nearest we can come to the Latin original of *Brut y Tywysogyon* in its earliest known version, before it became conflated with supplementary material. They are in a rhetorical style similar to that of the *Brut*. Here is a passage describing how, after Rhys had burned Radnor, Roger de Mortimer and Hugh de Sai set out their hosts against him, and how Rhys, like a lion, defeated them (A.D. 1196):

> Qua combusta eadem die Rogerus de Mortuo Mari et Hugo de Sai cum maximo apparatu in ualle eiusdem uille turmas magnas bellicis armis munitissimas, acies instauratas loric<at>as, clipeatas, galeatas, contra Resum principem exposuerunt. Quos ut Resus uir magnanimus asspiciens manu ualida, corde audaci leonem induens, in hostes irrumpens eosdemque actutum in fugam conuertens, fugatos instanter persequens uiliter, sed uiriliter tractauit. Omnesque Marchenses tremore affecti non modico stragem ibidem factam complanxerunt.

---

[67] Smith (*ibid.*, pp. 262–6) argues that the *Cronica* shows a partiality for Rhys Gryg, but I do not find his arguments convincing. In 1213 *Cronica de Wallia* gives a short statement which has been very much amplified in the Peniarth 20 version of the *Brut*: it is dangerous to argue from the omissions. In 1215 the annalist says the territory was divided 'in tribus partibus licet inequalibus': he seems to think that Maelgwn gets the biggest, and cites Rhys Gryg third. Smith suggests that the *Cronica* was compiled, perhaps in Ystrad Tywi, between 1277 and 1283, when there seemed good hope that Rhys ap Maredudd might reestablish control over all Ystrad Tywi. But the derived entries for the years 1254–66 in *Cronica de Wallia* (see below, pp. 79, 85) are quite inconsistent with this kind of political motivation. Here the St David's text is fuller. *Cronica de Wallia* is giving brief extracts, and the omission of much of the detail of the St David's annals does not strike me as significant in the same way as it does Mr Smith.

[68] And, very briefly, David of Gwynedd (1246), buried at Aberconway, daughter-house of Strata Florida.

[69] And briefly to Cedifor ap Gruffydd (1206).

[70] Jones points out (*Brut y Tywysogyon . . . Peniarth MS. 20 Version*, p. xli) that the Exeter and PRO texts both omit a reference in 1248 to the settlement of a debt owed by Strata Florida to King Henry III, which the *Brutiau* say was recorded in the monastic annals. PRO seems to have a lacuna here, with no Welsh entries for 1247–50, and a very brief foreign entry for 1249. The Strata Florida part of *Cronica de Wallia* is also lacunose at this point. So I do not think that the absence of this entry argues against Strata Florida origin. The entry about the Strata Florida grange of Aberdehoneu is not in the Peniarth 20 *Brut*, which on other grounds must be a Strata Florida document.

The late thirteenth-century scribe had, then, a Strata Florida document which took him down to 1255. But he seems not to have compiled his annals at Strata Florida, because he used no Strata Florida material later than this. He had to make up with a conflation of extracts from the Bury chronicle and the St David's annals. They are the same extracts as those which appear in the second set of annals in the Exeter manuscript which I have already mentioned, and the two sets must have come from the same house. There is nothing in them to indicate which house. But the third text printed from this manuscript by Thomas Jones concerns the lords of Carew, just to the south-west of the Cistercian house of Whitland. The land for Whitland was granted by Bishop Bernard of St David's, and Strata Florida was Whitland's daughter-house. Whitland was therefore in a good position to obtain material from Strata Florida and from St David's and to show a keen interest in Welsh Wales, in the descendants of Lord Rhys and in the lords of Carew. It is impossible to prove definitely that the Exeter annals came from Whitland, but Whitland is by far the most likely place for their compilation.[71]

Now we turn to the most complicated of all the texts, the PRO annals. Up to 1202 they were using the St David's chronicle, but their character changes in 1189. From this time on, until 1263, they speak with the voice of independent Wales. The English are *dolosi et in omnibus fere odiosi* (1216); after a Welsh victory (1214) the Welsh returned joyful to their homes and the doleful Franks were everywhere ejected and dispersed hither and thither like birds. When Rhys son of Maelgwn died untimely in 1255, his panegyric says that people hoped he would have freed Wales from the yoke of the English. There is no doubt where the sympathies of the annalist lie.

We can best discuss the PRO annals after 1189 in four sections. In the second of these, between 1231 and 1255, four deaths or burials at Strata Florida are noted, three with dates. Maelgwn's attempt to despoil the Strata Florida monks of their property in 1236 is also recorded. This section is very similar to the *Cronica de Wallia*, which we saw had a Strata Florida source. But the first section, before 1231, is different from the *Cronica* and the *Brut*. We know from the *Brut* that two people whose obits are mentioned during this period were buried at Strata Florida, but the PRO annals do not mention the place of burial.[72] The absence of one of these is especially notable, since later, in 1235 (in the second section), the annals say that Owain was buried in the chapter there next to his brother: but the first section had not noted the brother's burial. Nor does the first section of the PRO annals mention the incident involving the Strata Florida grange at Aberdehoneu. So the section before 1231 does not show special intimacy with Strata Florida. The PRO annals report many of the same incidents as the *Cronica de Wallia* and the *Brut*, but they seem to be using a different text, and there is a substantial amount for which there is no parallel in the *Cronica* or the *Brut*. There is,

[71] This is the conclusion which Beverley Smith finally reaches. Thomas Jones stressed the Strata Florida *origin* of the text.
[72] 1201, 1220.

however, quite a lot of detail about campaigns in the south-west, areas within easy reach of Whitland. The milieu of the first section is definitely Cistercian.[73]

After the second – Strata Florida – section (1231–55) we come to the fullest and most interesting part of the PRO annals. This certainly gives the impression of contemporary reporting. The annalist writes with enthusiasm: his rhetoric is that of the Welsh nationalist. His vivid narrative moves forward purposefully, supported with convincing dates and details. Under the leadership of Llywelyn the Welsh surge on in a series of victories. Much of this section concerns events in Central Wales: Maelienydd, Arwystli, Ceri, Radnor, Elfael, Buellt. These areas are all in the neighbourhood of the Cistercian house of Cwm Hir, a daughter of Whitland. The death of Abbot Gruffydd of Cwm Hir is given, with a date, at 1261, a very unusual type of entry in the PRO annals. The events of these years are either not in the *Brut* at all, or are very differently reported there, so that the Welsh translators seem to have had quite a different text. The only mention of Strata Florida in the PRO annals during these years is the burial of David ap Hywel there in 1258, and he was a noble of Arwystli.[74]

All these three sections of the PRO annals after 1189 – the first which has a good deal of material from the neighbourhood of Whitland, the second from Strata Florida, and the third which seems to be interested in Central Wales round Cwm Hir – have brief additions from English annals.[75] These are in a markedly different style from some of the Welsh entries. Look at the year 1231. There is a longish narrative account of how Llywelyn attacked Montgomery, Brecon, Hay, and Radnor, then Caerleon, Neath, Kidwelly, and Cardigan. Meanwhile the English king had taken an army to the Marches and built Painscastle. Then we have appended three brief sentences: 'Obiit Willelmus Marescallus vii Iduum Aprilis et Ricardus frater eius factus est comes Penbrochiae. Ricardus comes Cornubiae desponsauit Isabellam comitissam Gloucestriae. Henricus rex firmauit castrum Matildis.' Here the compiler does not seem to have realised that Painscastle and *castrum Matildis* are one and the same place, so he has repeated his information. In the PRO annals we are in fact dealing with a composite text, made up of material of various origins, a text at a later stage of evolution than the Strata Florida part of *Cronica de Wallia*.

The PRO compiler, for the period before 1203, took over a St David's text which already had an English element, but he proceeded to append brief entries from an English chronicle which he had beside him. Some of these are

[73] See 1201, 1207.

[74] There is an interesting reference to Whitland, with the date, in 1257. This describes how four Anglo-Welsh lords and their knights broke into the abbey, beat up the monks, despoiled the *conuersi*, killed the servants, and made off with some of the monastic property. But I think this could have entered the annals of a daughter-house.

[75] See, for example, PRO 1229 (cf. Vesp. E.IV and Wint.); end of PRO 1231 (cf. Vesp. E.IV, Wint.); end of PRO 1235 (cf. Vesp. E.IV); etc.

verbally identical with those in BL Cotton Vespasian E.IV,[76] a set of Winchester annals augmented at Waverley. As Liebermann has shown,[77] Vesp. E.IV was used by the Worcester annals, was descended from a lost Winchester manuscript, and is related to the extant annals of Winchester, Waverley, and Tewkesbury. The text our scribe used was not Vesp. E.IV, because he has entries which are not in Vesp. but are in the related annals, often those of Waverley.[78] There can be no doubt that the Welsh compiler had an English set of annals which probably reached him through the Cistercian house of Waverley, and which lies behind his English additions.

The contemporary narrative breaks off in 1263, right in the middle of the triumphant career of Llywelyn. The point of view completely changes. In the fourth and final section Edward is *rex illustris*. Llywelyn, the hero of the immediately preceding part, gets a very brief obituary notice in the wrong year (killed by the English, but *fraude suorum*) without a word of panegyric. There is similarly no praise for David. Llywelyn was in fact buried at Cwm Hir, so the annals can hardly have any connexion now with that house. The Waverley chronicle which had provided the additions in the earlier sections now gives the main structure of the annals. The annalist now is simply not interested in Welsh Wales, unless it is to record English victories or the submission of Welsh princes to the king.[79] He misdates the death of the great Llywelyn. Apart from Llywelyn and David, he mentions the obits of only two Welsh princes, both lords of Ystrad Tywi. Both these are wrongly dated. Maredudd son of Rhys died in 1271, not 1273, and Rhys son of Maredudd, whose obit our compiler gives in 1270, was attacking Gower as late as 1287. He must be confusing him with Rhys Fychan (son of Rhys Mechyll) who died in 1271. This section does not look as if it was written by a Welshman at all.

To interpret this evidence we have to turn to the rest of the material on the flyleaves of the Breviate Domesday. It is almost all of South Welsh interest, written in various hands, one recurring, all of the same date. They can be dated precisely by the contents to the time between 1300 and 1304. On the flyleaves following *Annales Cambriae* there is a second chronicle[80] interested

---

[76] PRO 1168: 'Episcopi et fere omnes magnates Angliae scripserunt domino papae contra Thomam archiepiscopum. Galfridus Foliot archiepiscopus Eboracensis ab archiepiscopo Thoma excommunicatus est.'

PRO 1173: 'Rex pater et rex filius discordes facti sunt. Comes Leicestriae captus est.'

PRO 1181: 'Philippus rex Francorum a Francia Iudeos expulit'.

PRO 1182: 'Henricus rex .xlii. millia marcarum misit Hierosolimis'.

All these are identical with Vesp. E.IV. I am most grateful to Professor Cheney for drawing my attention to this group of annals; he had already noted similarities.

[77] *Anglo-normannische Geschichtsquellen*, pp. 173–202.

[78] For example, PRO 1176: 'Pons lapideus Londoniae inceptus est'.

[79] At 1276, 1277, and 1280. Williams Ab Ithel, *Annales Cambriæ*, p. 105, omits the entry for 1276 and misdates 1277. 1276 reads: 'Hoc anno uenit Paganus filius Patricii de Chauard cum magno exercitu ad uillam de Kermerdin et subiugauit domino regi Anglie totam terram de Stratewi et de Kardigan et uastauit omnia castella eiusdem patrie. Omnes barones Sudwallie Angliam intrauerunt et omagium domino regi Anglie fecerunt.'

[80] London, PRO, MS. E.164/1, pp. 29–35: edited Anon., 'Chronicle of the thirteenth century'.

mainly in Glamorgan.[81] After a few introductory sentences it starts in 1081 with extracts from the Annals of Margam; then in 1142 it transfers to a text similar to the Annals of Tewkesbury, but leaves them in the 1240s. After 1256 the material of Welsh interest increases in quantity. From the death of Herewald in 1104 until 1266 there is an almost complete list of the bishops of Llandaf,[82] but these cease quite abruptly. Cistercian interests are present throughout, but after 1250 there is only one Margam entry. Neath is mentioned twice towards the end of the chronicle, in 1283 and 1289, each time with an entry referring to property. The chronicle terminates in 1298 with an entry about the betrothal of Lady Anna, daughter of William de Breose. The Cistercian abbey of Neath would be a suitable place for its compilation.[83]

Much of the material on the rear flyleaves is a collection of evidence relating to the dispute, about the marcher-rights of the De Breose lords of Gower, which came to a head in 1299 and was not terminated until 1306.[84] The latest of the documents copied there is an *inspeximus* by William de Breose dated 6 May, 1300. But the collection does not contain the confirmation of John's charter to William de Breose by Edward on 16 October, 1304, which would almost certainly have been included, had it then been issued. Whoever ordered the compilation of this section was interested in the history of the English conquest, in Carmarthen and Gower, and especially in the De Breose family, for on pp. 481–2 there is yet another short set of annals relating directly to these subjects. Most of the material in them comes from the West Welsh annals we have been discussing, but here the entries end with Maredudd's revolt in 1287.

The hands in which these documents are copied are not practised chancery hands, but rather the kind of hands you would expect in a monastic cartulary.[85] The flyleaves also include a grant to Neath abbey by Henry II, a confirmation by Peter de Leia of St David's of grants to Neath, a grant by John de Breose to Neath, and an *inspeximus* by William de Breose of a grant to Neath. Neath was on the edge of Gower and had lands in Gower. Neath is almost certainly the place where the following texts on the flyleaves of the Breviate Domesday were transcribed: the Glamorgan chronicle compiled at Neath, the

[81] Other annals relating to South-East Wales are the Annals of Margam, 1066–1232 (ed. Luard, *Annales Monastici*, I.1–40), and the annals in London, BL MS. Royal 6.B.XI, fos 105r–108r, 112r. These latter extract their entries from the Annals of Tewkesbury (more precisely than do the PRO annals) down to 1248. After this they are independent, with much detail about appointments at Llandaf. Some years are given very fully (e.g., 1256), others very meagrely. They stop in 1268. Ker, *Medieval Libraries*, p. 48, lists this manuscript as part of the library of Cardiff, a Benedictine priory and cell of Tewkesbury, three or four miles from Llandaf. A copy of the Tewkesbury annals up to 1248 may well have reached Glamorgan through Cardiff. Both Royal 6.B.XI and the PRO annals copied them only up to the 1240s.

[82] Of the twelve bishops between these dates only William of Saltmarsh is missing.

[83] J. B. Smith & T. B. Pugh, *apud* Pugh, *Glamorgan County History*, III.241, say 'almost certainly compiled at Neath or Margam'. But were it Margam, you would expect the Margam entries to increase in the later stages, not to fade out.

[84] It is discussed by Seyler, 'Early charters', and by Smith & Pugh, *apud* Pugh, *Glamorgan County History*, III.231–40.

[85] Here I am glad to quote Professor Brown's opinion.

Neath grants, the short annals concerning the English conquest and De Breose activities, the evidence about De Breose rights in Gower and the related documents.

There is a strong presumption that our West Welsh annals were also copied into the Breviate Domesday at Neath or for Neath. The scribes who put together the evidence on jurisdiction in Gower were interested in them and, largely from them, made the extracts giving the history of Carmarthen, Gower, and the De Breose family. They must have been familiar with such a technique. Rishanger says that in 1291 King Edward, trying to assert his right as superior lord, had the monastic chronicles of England, Scotland, and Wales scrutinised,[86] and the Great Roll for 1292 contains a list of relevant extracts.[87] Our manuscript is interested mainly in De Breose claims, but so it would be if the material was compiled by Neath monks rather than by the king's clerks. After 1291, annals must have been clearly recognised as not only interesting but potentially useful, and Neath could have sent to Strata Florida to borrow its annals. Or the annals could have been copied at Strata Florida for Neath and bound into the Breviate at Neath, for the vellum of the flyleaves is not nearly so well prepared as that of the main manuscript, being browner, stiffer, less carefully cut, and containing holes.[88]

One entry in the annals suggests transcription either at Neath or under the auspices of Neath. Although there is no record in the annals of the foundation of Strata Florida, Whitland, or Cwm Hir, the western Cistercian houses,[89] the foundation of Neath and Tintern has been put in.[90] These entries look very odd in so predominantly West Welsh a context: but if the annals were copied at Neath their presence is explained.

The independent Welsh annals probably obtained from Strata Florida broke off at 1263. I think they may have been continued at Neath, possibly by an English scribe. This would explain the ignorance of independent Welsh affairs. Ystrad Tywi, the neighbouring Welsh kingdom, meant something to the compiler, but even here he got his facts wrong. It was this man who added the material from the Waverley chronicle, for it does not appear in the *Brut*.[91]

---

[86] Riley, *Chronica Monasterii S. Albani*, pp. 123–4.

[87] Rymer, *Foedera*, I/3.99–102. Cf. Stones, *Anglo-Scottish Relations*, pp. xxvi–xxvii: 'Closer study of the text shows that Edward's clerks almost certainly possessed texts of some complete chronicles'. I owe these references to Professor Cheney.

[88] The De Breose documents start on the last leaf of the Breviate and continue on pp. 474–87 on a separate gathering. The two long sets of annals are on the fore flyleaves, on gatherings separate from the Breviate, but the hand of the Glamorgan chronicle recurs in the De Breose documents at the end. When the name De Breose occurs in the text of the Breviate it has sometimes been noted in the margin. At first this is very frequent; it becomes less so and then stops altogether. According to Galbraith (*Herefordshire Domesday*, p. xxviii) the thirteenth-century PRO Breviate 'appears to be a line for line copy' of the one kept at Margam. Smith (*apud* Pugh, *Glamorgan County History*, III.620, n. 197) notes: 'The possibility must be admitted that the text itself was executed on behalf of the De Breoses'.

[89] Nor of Llantarnan, Strata Florida's daughter in Glamorgan.

[90] 1130: 'Fundata est abbatia de Neth; eodem anno fundata est abbatia de Furneis' (Furness was founded in 1127). 1131: 'Fundata est Tinterna'.

[91] The burning of Strata Florida in 1286 would be of sufficient interest for a Cistercian scribe from Neath to enter. It is not in *Brut y Tywysogyon*.

We can now see how our texts evolved and what historical influences governed their development. St David's was the early centre of annalistic writing. Contemporary annals were kept here from the late eighth century on, and soon after they were started earlier sections were compiled, based on Irish annals and a northern chronicle. The Harleian annals are copied from this St David's text. Cotton Domitian A.i, itself a St David's manuscript,[92] is based on the same St David's annals, and so are the PRO annals up to 1202.[93] Up to the twelfth century St David's had a wide range of interests over much of Wales: after the English conquest the annals gradually adopt an anglicised orientation and their interest in Welsh affairs is narrowed. Strata Florida started to keep annals soon after its foundation in 1164: so *Brut y Tywysogyon* indicates. The *Cronica de Wallia* in the Exeter manuscript is the earliest version now known of a Strata Florida text. It stopped in 1248, or perhaps 1255.[94] The PRO manuscript after 1189 is much the most complicated. The section from 1231 to 1255 was definitely a Strata Florida text; the parts preceding and following it, with material from Whitland and Cwm Hir, were possibly compiled there.[95] But I believe the PRO annals were transcribed at or for Neath, together with the other chronicle and the material relating to the dispute over jurisdiction in Gower. They were conflated with a Waverley chronicle and the last section may have been added by an Englishman at Neath. The Latin texts therefore show us Welsh annals at various stages of composition, in several houses, under different political influences, all earlier than the Welsh Bruts.

In this lecture I have tried very briefly to indicate how the Welsh annals were put together. Some of the problems I have not had time to deal with and some I cannot answer. I am sure, however, that if we are to reach sound conclusions we must look at all the evidence together, see the annals in their relation to each other, to other relevant material, and to English annalistic writing of the twelfth and thirteenth centuries. Tracking down the sources of our Welsh Latin annals is an exacting task, but if it is not done significant details and omissions will be imagined in what was just slavish copying, or a source compiled before the end of the eighth century will be seen as a contemporary fifth-century record. Parts of the Welsh Latin annals are original and contemporary, parts are rather sluggishly kept, parts are compiled long after the events from material the annalist happened to have to hand. What I have said today is the dry bones of history. But before dry bones can live, someone must collect the pieces and put together the skeleton. This is what I have tried to do.

[92] Ker, 'Sir John Prise', pp. 21–2.

[93] Both these sets of annals, and especially those in the Cotton manuscript, show that Geoffrey of Monmouth was taken seriously as an historian of early Britain. See Keeler, 'Four mediaeval chroniclers'.

[94] See above, p. 77. In *Cronica de Wallia*, 1254–5 are overlap years, with one passage like the Strata Florida annals, others from St David's and the Bury chronicle.

[95] For a different view, see D. Dumville, *Studia Celtica* 12/13 (1977/8) 464.

APPENDIX

A synopsis of proposed stages in the development of the Annales Cambriae

1. Annals began to be kept at St David's in the late eighth century.

2. Soon after this the annals were extended backwards by drawing on the following sources: (*a*) Irish entries up to the end of Isidore's chronicle, (*b*) a northern chronicle with North Welsh entries. A few other scattered British references were added, and the annals were arranged probably now, if not in 954, in the form of a 532-year cycle.

3. It was copied out in 954 and genealogies were attached to the annals.

4. After 954 the annals were continued at St David's.

5. *Circa* 1100 the Anglo-Norman scribe of BL MS. Harley 3859 (origin and mediaeval provenance unknown) transcribed the text described in §3 (Ab Ithel's A).

6. Some time between 954 and 1202 someone at St David's added a preliminary Isidoran section starting at the creation of the world.

7. Annals began to be kept at Strata Florida soon after its foundation in 1164.

8. Material from Whitland, Strata Florida, and Cwm Hir was added to a version of the St David's annals which went down to 1202 (see §§ 1, 2, 4, 6). The independent material began in 1189 and ended in 1263.

9. After 1266 someone, most probably at Whitland, compiled a set of annals, using a Strata Florida text from 1190 to 1255, and conflating an abstract of the St David's annals with the Bury chronicle for the years 1254–66. This is the *Cronica de Wallia*. In the same house another set of annals was drawn up, based on extracts from the Bury chronicle down to 1265 and an abstract from the St David's annals from 1274 to 1285 (the same abstract as in the annals just mentioned). Notes were added about the sons of Rhys and the sons of William Fitzwilliam of Carew. This is all in Exeter MS. 3514.

10. A Breviate Domesday Book was copied for Neath in the second half of the thirteenth century. Some time after 1286, probably after 1291 and possibly not until 1299, the Neath monks secured the material listed in §8. One of them copied it on to what are now the flyleaves of the Breviate Domesday, conflating it with a set of annals from Waverley. He used the Waverley annals to bring his chronicle up to 1286. This is the text of the *Annales Cambriae* in PRO E.164/1, pp. 2–26 (Ab Ithel's B).

11. Between 1300 and 1304 a Glamorgan chronicle compiled at Neath and documents of De Breose interest relating to a dispute concerning the marcher-rights of the De Breose lords in Gower were copied on to the flyleaves of the Breviate Domesday at Neath.

12. In 1288 a St David's scribe made a copy of the St David's annals. He intended to continue (the *annus* for the year 1289 is entered), but never did. When he had copied the annals he inserted two bifolia and a single leaf to take extracts from a Worcester chronicle. This is the text of the *Annales Cambriae* in BL Cotton Domitian A. 1 (Ab Ithel's C).

VI

The A-text of *Annales Cambriae*

The man who put together the version of *Annales Cambriae* which now survives in London, British Library, MS. Harley 3859, fos 190r–193r,[1] was not using a system of dating from the Incarnation. He began in the year 445 of our era, marked each year *an'* and recorded the tenth, twentieth, thirtieth year, and so on up to 530 of his reckoning. Then there are three more *an'* markings. His first entry was at his year 9, 453 of our era, and his last at his 510th year or our 954. I shall refer to our dating.[2]

Between 445 and 500 there are only four entries. The first of these reads: 'Easter is changed on the Lord's Day by Pope Leo, bishop of Rome'. It looks as if the man who put the annals into their present form was interested in the date of Easter.[3] There is another paschal entry at 768: 'Easter is changed among the Britons, Elbodugus a man of God emending it', and the death of this Elfoddw is noted at 809, where he is called *archiepiscopus* in the region of Gwynedd (*Guenedote regione*). The last entry, in 954, is of the death of Rhodri son of Hywel, and the Welsh royal genealogies which follow the annals in BL Harley 3859 (fos 193r–195r)[4] start with Owain son of Hywel. The genealogies refer to no one later than Owain, and those of Rhos (§ 3), Strathclyde (§ 5), Dyfed (§ 13), Ceredigion (§ 26), Powys (§ 27) and Gwent (§ 29) are all traced back from ninth-century kings. So the assumption is that the compiler was working soon after 954, the date of his last entry.

When do the *Annales Cambriae* become contemporary and where were they drawn up? A contemporary chronicle nearly always shows traces of its origin. Round about 790 the Irish annals become fuller and provide detailed entries about Armagh. It is almost certain that, at that time, a year-by-year record was being kept at Armagh.[5] The *Annales Cambriae* are much thinner, but there is quite a spate of entries after 795, and for the first time the monastery of St David's and the kingdom of Dyfed come consistently into the news. From 796

---

[1] Ed. Phillimore, 'The *Annales Cambriæ*', pp. 152–69.

[2] The dates are purely conventional. Greater accuracy must await a full study of the chronology of these annals.

[3] One may add to the points made here (i) the 532-year 'Great Cycle' form of this chronicle, and (ii) the entry at 665 on the first official Roman Easter in Northumbria – 'Primum pasca apud Saxones celebratur'.

[4] Ed. Phillimore, 'The *Annales Cambriæ*', pp. 169–83, and by Bartrum, *Genealogical Tracts*, pp. 9–13 (with notes on pp. 125–9).

[5] On the Irish annals see Hughes, *Early Christian Ireland*, pp. 97–159, esp. 129–35.

to 954 interest is not constant. In the first twenty-two years (up to 817) there are nineteen entries, spread over twelve of those years, including four kings of Dyfed (Maredudd, Rhain, Owain ap Maredudd, Tryffin ap Rhain) and the burning of St David's. Then there is another very thin phase, with only sixteen entries spread over twelve of the next forty-four years (818–61), though two of these are about bishops of St David's (Sadwrnfyw Hael, Nobis). From 862 to 887 there is another spurt of entries, eighteen in all, spread over sixteen of these twenty-six years. Then for twelve years (888–99) there are three entries, followed by nine entries covering eight of the ten years from 900 to 909, when (according to Giraldus Cambrensis) Asser was bishop of St David's.[6] His death is followed by another lean period, with only six single annals in twenty-eight years (910–37); then, from 938 to 954 there are sixteen entries spread over eleven of these seventeen years, in which two bishops of St David's (Lunberth and Eneuris) are mentioned. Maredudd of Dyfed, his sons and grandson dominate the beginning of the period, Hyfaidd and his son Llywarch are important towards its close, though here attention is concentrated on the great kings of Seisyllwg, Cadell and his sons Clydog and Hywel. According to the genealogies Llywarch's daughter Elen married Hywel, and their son Owain was thus descended on his mother's side from the native kings of Dyfed. We know of no kings of the native line after Llywarch (*ob.* 903). So a St David's annalist *ca* 950 (or at any time from the beginning of the tenth century) would inevitably be concerned with Hywel. It looks as if the controlling interest between 796 and 954 was St David's, though the annals were kept in a very haphazard way with spurts of interest and periods of inertia. It does, however, seem likely that from about 796 contemporary entries were made at St David's. This has been said before on various occasions.[7]

The subject-matter of these last 160 years of the A-text is mainly Welsh, and it is almost entirely secular in character. This differentiates it sharply from the Irish annals. Apart from the bishops of St David's[8] the only other men specifically mentioned as ecclesiastics are Jonathan, abbot (*princeps*) of Abergele (*ob.* 856), and the Elfoddw, *archiepiscopus* in Gwynedd (*ob.* 809), who in 768 corrected the date of celebration of Easter.[9] Apart from the kings of Dyfed,[10] the annalist mentions kings of Gwynedd,[11] Ceredigion,[12] Powys[13] and

---

[6] During the episcopacy of Nobis (840–73) there are twenty-two entries spread over seventeen of these thirty-four years. For Giraldus on Asser, see *Itinerarium Cambriae*, II.1 (edd. Brewer *et al.*, *Giraldi Cambrensis Opera*, VI.102–3).

[7] For example, by Phillimore,'The *Annales Cambriæ*', p. 145; Stevenson, *Asser*, p. 316; Lloyd, *History of Wales*, I.263–4.

[8] At 831, 840, 873, (908), 944, 946. St David's is also mentioned at 810 (*Combustio Miniu*) and 906 (*Miniu fracta est*).

[9] Guorchiguil (*ob.* 907 A) is called *episcopus* in B. Laudent (*ob.* 831 A) looks like a cleric, too.

[10] At 796, 808, 811, 814, 892, 903.

[11] Of the first dynasty at 798, 813, 814, 816, 825. Of the second dynasty (and therefore not necessarily holding kingship in Gwynedd itself) at 844, 877, 880, 894, (904?), 909, 915, 919, 928, 939, 943, 950, 951, 954.

[12] 807, (?849?), 871.

[13] 808, 814, 854.

Gwent.[14] There are records of the devastation of areas by English[15] and by Norse,[16] of conquests[17] and expulsions,[18] of the destruction of fortresses,[19] of various battles (often introduced by the Old Welsh word *gueith*),[20] and of the drownings[21] and poisonings[22] of kings. In addition, there are obits of two Irish kings, Aed mac Néill (this is Aed Findliath) in 878 and Cerball of Osraige in 887,[23] of five English rulers, Offa (796), Alfred of Wessex (900), Æthelflæd of Mercia (917), Æthelstan (940) and Edmund (947), and of Cinaed mac Alpin (856), *rex Pictorum*. In character it is not unlike the Iona chronicle, though it has not the same detail. It looks quite unlike the annals kept at Armagh, with their concentration on ecclesiastical affairs.

The construction of the annals before about 796 was artificial. These annals were put together from written sources to provide a history of the period before the date when the contemporary year-by-year chornicle began. We need therefore to see what were the written sources used. If anyone will copy out the annals of the A-text, with the entries from the Irish annals alongside,[24] he will immediately see that there is a close correspondence with the Irish annals up to 613, but after this much greater independence. Moreover the *Annales Cambriae* for this first section look like Irish annals. Of the thirty-three entries spread over twenty-four different years there are twenty which may be described as ecclesiastical and ten secular ones.[25] Of these ten, seven are British entries which are not found in the Irish annals at all.[26]

[14] 848, (?873? – thus Bartrum, *Genealogical Tracts*, p. 204), 943.

[15] 798, 822, 849, 864, 877, 880, 894, 943, 946, 951.

[16] (844?), 850, 853, 866, 870, 876, 895, 902, 913.

[17] At 822.

[18] 814, 816, 862.

[19] 822, 871.

[20] *gueith*: 817, 844, 848, 873, 876, 880, 906, 921. *cat*: 866, 869. Latin *bellum* is also used: 796, 813, 938, 951. The battle-entry at 814 fits into none of these categories.

[21] At 871, 875.

[22] At 943, 946.

[23] Perhaps also one Hiberno-Norse king (Abloyc, 942), but only – since Afloeg is known elsewhere as a Welsh name – if a number of conjectures be allowed. [First, we must suppose that *Abloyc* (Afloeg) was written by error for **Abloyt* (Afloedd). But all versions of *Brut y Tywysogyon* (*s. a.* 940) offer *Abloyc brenhin* (*Iwerdon* is added by the Peniarth version and *Brenhinedd y Saesson*), thus confirming, it would seem, the accuracy of Harley 3859 and requiring the supposed error of -*c* for -*t* to be very early. Secondly, on the evidence of *Hanes Gruffud vab Kenan* (§ § 3, 4) and *Achau Brenhinoedd a Thywysogion Cymru* (§ 6 a, c, e), we must suppose that a Welsh Afloedd was created to represent Irish *Amlaib*, itself the Irish representation of Norse Óláfr; unfortunately, neither of these texts is earlier than the late thirteenth century in its present form, and we cannot tell whether such an equation represents tenth-century usage also.]

[24] The principal texts are the Annals of Ulster, the Annals of Inisfallen, the Annals of Roscrea, and the three constituents of the Clonmacnoise group of annals (*Chronicum Scotorum*, the Annals of Clonmacnoise, and the Annals of Tigernach). Details of the editions are given by Hughes, *Early Christian Ireland*, pp. 306–7.

[25] The plague recorded for 537 is not here assigned to either class. The notice under 613, 'Et Iacob filii Beli dormitatio' is conjecturally ecclesiastical, on the grounds that *dormitatio* in the Irish annals usually refers to a death in religion.

[26] The entry for 547, not counted as one of the seven, is very likely modelled on the entry represented by that *s. a.* 549 in the Annals of Ulster. See below, pp. 89, 91.

The Irish annals in question go back to a common text which we may call the 'Chronicle of Ireland'.[27] A chronicle of Dalriadic and Pictish events, kept at Iona, forms the core of the early entries until 741, when it comes to an abrupt halt. Chronicles and entries from different areas and monasteries in Ireland were added to this, and from the 790s a major chronicle was kept at Armagh. Not earlier than the early tenth century a copy of this went to Clonmacnoise, where it became the ancestor of the Annals of Tigernach and related texts. Another stayed at Armagh, and from it are descended the Annals of Ulster. Both these texts are necessary to reconstruct the lost 'Chronicle of Ireland'. Another manuscript travelled south to Munster, where it was amalgamated with a southern chronicle to form a history for the period before 972, when the Dál Cais rulers Mathgamain and Brian rose to power. It was later savagely abbreviated and became the Annals of Inisfallen.

The first section of the A-text of *Annales Cambriae*, for the years 453 to 613, receives its structure from the Irish annals. There are thirty-three entries, of which twenty are in the Irish annals.[28] The Annals of Tigernach are fragmentary, and start only in 489, but, after 489, all but three of the seventeen entries derived from the Irish annals are in both the Annals of Ulster and the Annals of Tigernach.[29] All except three of these seventeen entries are in the Annals of

---

[27] On this, see Hughes, *Early Christian Ireland*, pp. 99–115, which is summarised in this paragraph.

[28] The twenty are as follows:

454 Brigida sancta nascitur.
457 Sanctus Patricius ad Dominum migratur.
468 Quies Benigni episcopi.
500/1 Episcopus Ebur pausat in Christo, anno .cccl. etatis suæ.
521 Sanctus Columcille nascitur.
521 Quies sanctæ Brigidæ.
544 Dormitatio Ciarani.
547 Mortalitas magna in qua pausat [Mailcun rex Genedotæ].
558 Gabran filius Dungart moritur.
562 Columcillæ in Brittannia exiit.
570 Gildas obiit.
574 Brendan Byror dormitatio.
584 Bellum contra Euboniam. . . .
589 Conuersio Constantini ad Dominum.
595 Columcille moritur. . . .
595 . . . Agustinus Mellitus Anglos ad Christum conuertit.
601 . . . Gregorius obiit in Christo.
601 Dauid episcopus Moni iudeorum.
607 Aidan map Gabran moritur.
613 Gueith Cair Legion et ibi cecidit Selim fili<us> Cinan.

The entry for 453 requires a brief comment. It refers to an event of 455 ('Pasca commutatur super diem dominicum cum papa Leone episcopo Rome') which is also reported in the Annals of Ulster (451: Pasca Domini .uiii. Kl. Maii celebratum est) and the Annals of Inisfallen, but the wording of these Irish annals (very close to that of Prosper's chronicle) is so different from that of *Annales Cambriae* that we can hardly suppose a direct relationship.

[29] The following three entries cannot be found in the Annals of Ulster in the primary hand:

562 Columcillæ in Brittannia exiit.
595 Agustinus Mellitus Anglos ad Christum conuertit.
601 Dauid episcopus Moni iudeorum.

Inisfallen.[30] So we may safely conclude that all the twenty entries were in the 'Chronicle of Ireland'.[31] What made the annalist choose these entries? Some are entries obviously made much later in time than the events, for the births of saints are backward-looking entries, made when the reputation of that saint had become well established. These Irish saints are the ones whom a Welshman, wishing, much later, to pick out the salient events in the history of the Irish Church, might choose to record: Patrick and Benén (Armagh), Brigit and Bishop Íbar (both Leinster saints) all belong to the first phase of Irish christianity; Ciarán of Clonmacnoise and Columcille of Iona are two of the great monastic founders. Brendan of Birr is more of a puzzle. He is known as 'the eldest of the saints of Ireland',[32] but Brendan of Clonfert, the Navigator, is far better known, and would have been a more obvious choice. Gabrán son of Domangart was the founder of Cenél nGabráin in Kintyre; Aedán, his son, was the famous Dalriadic king who ruled in the time of Columcille, and the battle of *Eubonia* (the Isle of Man) was fought by him. David, Gildas, and the battle of *Cair Legion* where Selyf died would obviously interest a Welshman. With the possible exception of Brendan of Birr, I think these are all entries which a Welshman in the ninth or tenth century, wishing to provide a preliminary section for his chronicle, would pick out as salient events to provide the chronological structure into which he might fit his Welsh entries. Consequently, I think that the A-text entry at 457, 'Sanctus Patricius ad Dominum migrauit', has as much or as little authority as that in the Annals of Ulster, 'Quies senis Patricii ut alii libri dicunt'.

As I have said elsewhere,[33] the dating of the Irish annals in the period before 585 is by no means consistent. The order of events in the Annals of Ulster is not always the same as the order in the Annals of Tigernach. Both of these texts sometimes enter the same event at different dates, with the additional clause *ut alii (libri) dicunt*. Irish scholars were aware of discrepant dates. They use no *anno Domini* dating. The Annals of Tigernach, from their beginning in 489 until 710, record Continental events such as the reigns of Roman emperors and popes, and it was probably these which gave chronological structure to the Irish annals. Our manuscripts of both the Annals of Tigernach and the Annals of Ulster are late. Since their order of events is not identical and since they obviously had difficulties with dating in this early period, it is not surprising to find that the *Annales Cambriae*, using a manuscript of the 'Chronicle of Ireland', do not agree precisely in their chronology with the extant Irish annals. The Welsh annals are mostly one, two, even three years later than the Annals of Ulster in dating events, but sometimes they are a year or more earlier. But the only wild discrepancy is over the date of St David which the *Annales Cambriae*

[30] 547 Mortalitas magna in qua pausat. . . .
589 Conuersio Constantini ad Dominum.
595 Agustinus Mellitus Anglos ad Christum conuertit.
[31] Of the three entries before 489, all are in the Annals of Ulster and *Chronicum Scotorum*, but one (457: Sanctus Patricius ad Dominum migratur) is not in the Annals of Inisfallen.
[32] Plummer, *Bethada Náem nÉrenn*, I.96 and II.93.
[33] Hughes, *Early Christian Ireland*, pp. 142–4.

(A) give at 601, the Annals of Tigernach and the Annals of Inisfallen at 589.[34] (It is not in the Annals of Ulster.) I think therefore that this entry may not be drawn from the Irish annals, but from some other source.[35] Otherwise, the discrepancies are what anyone who is familiar with the problems of the early Irish annals might expect.[36]

These extracts from a set of Irish annals provided the background into which are fitted eleven British entries, as follows:

516 Bellum Badonis in quo Arthur portauit crucem Domini Nostri Iesu Christi tribus diebus et tribus noctibus in humeros suos et Brittones uictores fuerunt.

537 Gueith Cam lann in qua Arthur et Medraut corruerunt. Et mortalitas in Brittannia et in Hibernia fuit.

547 [*After the* mortalitas magna *entry, which is shared with the Irish annals, our text continues*] in qua pausat Mailcun rex Genedotæ.

573 Bellum Armterid.

580 Guurci et Peretur moritur.

584 . . . Et dispositio Danielis Bancorum.

595 . . . Dunaut rex moritur.

601 Sinodus Urbis Legion. . . .

606 Dispositio Cinauc episcopi.

612 Conthigirni obitus et Dibric episcopi.

613 . . . Et Iacob filii Beli dormitatio.

The main interest of these entries seems to be in north Britain and north Wales, with three descendants of Coel Hen, the battles of Arfderydd and Camlann (*if* this latter is to be identified with Camboglanna, the fort north of Hadrian's Wall), St Kentigern of Glasgow and Llanelwy, two kings of Gwynedd (Maelgwn, Iago) and the burial of Daniel of the Bangors from north Wales.[37] Cynog, saint of Brycheiniog, and Dyfrig, of the south-east, do not fit into this picture.[38] The whereabouts of the battle of Badon has been a subject

---

[34] It is at the same date in the Annals of Roscrea, and under 588 in *Chronicum Scotorum*.

[35] [See now the discussion by Miller, 'Date-guessing and Dyfed', pp. 41–50.]

[36] [Three more complex chronological problems should be mentioned, however. (1) 454 as the date of the birth of Brigit agrees well enough with the Annals of Ulster's 452 and 456, and with the computed 455 of the Annals of Inisfallen: all these Irish entries are qualified by the *alii dicunt* formula, however. On the other hand, the Annals of Clonmacnoise, the Annals of Roscrea, and *Chronicum Scotorum* all attest to a date 439. (2) The date 544 for the death of Ciarán is paralleled in *Chronicum Scotorum* and the Annals of Tigernach. The Annals of Ulster give 549, on the other hand (and the editorial date of the Annals of Inisfallen is 548). This position is complicated by the closer agreement of *Annales Cambriae* with the two latter in wording. (3) The obit of Brendan of Birr at 574 presents a situation comparable to that of the Brigit-date, albeit with a further complexity. The Annals of Inisfallen, the Annals of Roscrea, the Annals of Tigernach, and *Chronicum Scotorum* all seem to agree on a date of 573. This has no counterpart in the Annals of Ulster which give instead, at 565, an *alii dicunt* entry found also at that point in the Annals of Roscrea and the Annals of Tigernach. The complexities in these three cases should serve to underline the caution which is needed in studying the text-history of these annal-collections.]

[37] Possibly also *Sinodus Urbis Legionis* (612) if this is Chester, not Caerleon-on-Usk.

[38] [On these entries relating to Welsh saints, see now Miller, 'Date-guessing and Dyfed', pp. 41–50.]

of immense speculation.[39] As Thomas Jones pointed out,[40] the entry *Bellum Badonis* would be completely in keeping with the laconic brevity of the Welsh annals, but the remainder of the sentence reads like a gloss: 'in which Arthur carried the cross of Our Lord Jesus Christ for three days and three nights on his shoulders and the Britons were victors'. The style is quite out of keeping with the annal-entries. All we can say is that a story something like this (though not identical with it) was known to the author of the *Historia Brittonum* in the early ninth century, to be repeated in a different form in the twelfth century by Geoffrey of Monmouth.

We *may* have here some entries from a north British source which had an interest in north Wales. They are, however, too few to be regarded as a set of annals. They are not in the Irish annals.

The close correspondence between the *Annales Cambriae* and the Irish annals stops at 613. After this, until the year 777, the *Annales Cambriae* take their backbone from a north British chronicle. Between 617 and 682 there is a close parallel in the *Historia Brittonum*[41] to this series of entries. This section of the *Historia Brittonum*, and the corresponding entries in the *Annales*, are an account of the struggle between Cadwallon, king of Gwynedd, and his successors, joined by Penda of Mercia, against the Northumbrian kings Edwin, Oswald, and Oswy. The *Annales Cambriae* (A) and the *Historia Brittonum* have close correspondences. They name the battles similarly. Hatfield Chase, where Cadwallon slew Edwin, is the battle of *Meicen*. *Denisesburna* near Hexham (also called Heavenfield), where Cadwallon was killed by Oswald, is the battle of *Cantscaul* (or *Catscaul*). Oswald's death in the battle of *Maserfelth* (Oswestry) is in the battle of *Cocboy*. Oswy's conquest of Penda and the Britons at *Winwaed* is 'the slaughter of the field of *Gai*'. Both texts record that Rhun son of Urien baptised Edwin.

Nevertheless, the *Annales Cambriae* could not have been taken from the *Historia Brittonum*. There are entries which the *Historia Brittonum* does not have: the death of Belin in 627,[42] the siege of Cadwallon in the island of *Glannauc* in 629, the 'slaughter of the Severn' and the slaying of Idris in 632. What is more conclusive is the different reporting of the same events. The *Historia Brittonum* says, 'Edwin son of Ælle reigned seventeen years, and he took Elmet and drove out Ceredig the king of that region'. The inescapable inference is that this happened during Edwin's reign, but the *Annales Cambriae* report the death of Ceredig in 616 and the beginning of the reign of Edwin in 617. This could hardly have come direct from the *Historia Brittonum*.[43] There is a confusing passage in the *Historia Brittonum* recounting the final defeat of Penda by Oswy

[39] See Jackson, 'The site of Mount Badon'.
[40] 'Early evolution', p. 5. See, further, Bromwich, 'Concepts', pp. 172–3.
[41] The two texts may be studied together in Faral, *Légende arthurienne*, III.3–63.
[42] Who may perhaps have been King Beli of Strathclyde, great-grandfather of the Beli who died in 722.
[43] Bede, *Historia Ecclesiastica*, IV.23 (21), shows King Ceredig ruling after (though not necessarily long after) 614. We have no information, independent of our Welsh sources, about his expulsion or death.

and the escape of *Catgabail* (Cadafael) and looking back in the middle of the account to an event known in Old Welsh as *Atbret Iudeu*,[44] where Oswy, who had made a sack, had to restore the booty to Penda, who distributed it to the kings of the Britons. The passage in the *Historia Brittonum* runs:

> Osguid [Oswy] son of Eadlfrid [Æthilfrith] reigned twenty-eight years and six months. . . . And he killed Pantha [Penda] in the field of Gai and the kings of the Britons were slain

—and now the sequence is interrupted by a backward look—

> who had gone out with King Pantha on an expedition as far as the city which is called Iudeu. Then Osguid restored all the riches which were with him in the city even into the hand of Penda, and Penda distributed them among the kings of the Britons, that is *Atbret Iudeu* ['the restoration of *Iudeu*'].

At this point the account of the battle of *Gai* (in which Penda was killed) is resumed:

> Catgabail alone, king of Gwynedd, escaped with his army, rising up in the night, for which reason he was called *Catgabail Catguommed*.

If a scribe had been drawing up annals from this he would have put the sack by Oswy and the restoration first, the slaughter of the field of Gai and the killing of Penda together. The *Annales Cambriae* give:

656 Strages Gaii campi
657 Pantha occisio
658 Osguid uenit et predam duxit.

Both the *Historia Brittonum* and the *Annales Cambriae* record the sack by Oswy *after* the battle, though the sense of the *Historia Brittonum* makes it necessary to assume that it happened before it, during Penda's lifetime. It looks as if both were copying a text where the order of events was not absolutely clear. There is one other difference between the *Annales Cambriae* and the *Historia Brittonum*. The latter puts the pestilence, in which Cadwaladr died, during Oswy's reign. But the *Annales Cambriae* read:

669 Osguid rex Saxonum moritur
682 Mortalitas magna fuit in Brittannia <i>n qua Catgualart filius Catguo-lau<ni> obiit.

Since, then, on three occasions the *Annales Cambriae* substantially diverge from

---

[44] Discussion of the location of this event may be found in Graham, 'Giudi', and Rutherford, '*Giudi* revisited'. Bede, *Historia Ecclesiastica*, III.24, is probably making reference to this episode, though his account is quite different. He says that Oswy promised Penda a great store 'of royal treasures and gifts' on condition that Penda would return home and cease to devastate. Penda refused, and they fought at *Winwaed*, near Leeds, where Oswy was the victor.

the account in the *Historia Brittonum*, I think they could not have been taken from it.

Nor would the author of the *Historia Brittonum* have taken his account directly from the *Annales Cambriae*. The different reporting argues against it. Moreover the *Historia Brittonum* provides information which is not in the *Annales Cambriae*: the names of the two sons of Edwin slain by Cadwallon in the battle of Meicen, *Osfird* (Osfrith) and *Eadfird* (Eadfrith);[45] the British nickname of Oswald, *lamnguin* ('white blade'); the fact that *Eoba* (Eowa) who fell at Cocboy (Cogfwy) was son of *Pippa* (Pybba) and brother of Penda;[46] Penda's killing 'by craft' of Anna, king of the East Angles; the flight of *Catgabail* (Cadafael) and his nickname *catguommed* ('battle-shirker');[47] events at the end of the series which the *Annales Cambriae* omit altogether. It seems certain, therefore, that there was an account of the struggle which the *Historia Brittonum* and the *Annales Cambriae* used independently. Kenneth Jackson notes that the peculiar spelling (*Catgualart*) of the name Cadwaladr in both the *Annales Cambriae* and the *Historia Brittonum* suggests that the scribes are copying the same text or that one is derived from the other.[48] I think, as he does, that each is copying independently from the same text.

The other source with which we must compare the *Annales Cambriae* during this period is the Irish annals, for, though the close correspondence of the *Annales Cambriae* with the Irish annals ceases in 613, most of these entries are present in both sets of annals, though in a different guise. The *Annales Cambriae* could not have derived these from the Irish annals. Even if we put all the early recensions together (and the Annals of Tigernach provide the most help), the *Annales Cambriae* have details and entries which the Irish annals do not give. Where the *Annales Cambriae* give the name of the battle, the Irish annals say 'the battle of Edwin', or 'the battle of Cadwallon', or 'the battle of Oswald', or 'the battle of Penda', usually meaning that the man named was killed in the battle.[49] The Irish annals do not record the death (616) of Ceredig (of Elmet), the beginning of Edwin's reign (617), the name of the man who baptised Edwin (626), the death of Belin (627), the siege of Cadwallon in *Glannauc* (629), the cryptic entry 'Guidgar uenit et non redit' (630), the first (Roman) Easter among the English (665), the second battle of Badon (665) and the death of Morgan (665). On the other hand they do give some entries in this period which the scribe of the *Annales Cambriae*, with his northern interests,

[45] Bede, *Historia Ecclesiastica*, II.20, says that Osfrith was killed in the battle, but that Eadfrith was compelled to desert to King Penda who afterwards murdered him.

[46] Bede, *Historia Ecclesiastica*, III.9, does not mention him in connexion with this battle. Lot (*Nennius*, I.71–80) argues that some of this part of the *Historia Brittonum* comes from Bede. But there are such discrepancies that it seems an unlikely theory.

[47] On which see Jackson, 'Brittonica', p. 69.

[48] 'Northern British section', p. 35. [But this overlooks the fact that both texts occur together in BL MS. Harley 3859, sharing a common immediate Welsh exemplar, probably of the mid-tenth century. The shared orthographical peculiarity could as well be ascribed to that stage of the texts' history. This is made more likely by the different spelling in the other manuscripts of these texts.]

[49] An exception may be found in the Annals of Ulster, *s. a.* 649 (= 650), which reads 'Bellum Ossu fri Pante'. The Annals of Tigernach understood this as the battle of *Winwaed*, where Penda was killed.

might have been expected to copy: 'Congregacio Saxonum contra Osualt' (AT 635); the slaying of Oswine (son of Osric), king of Deira (AU/AT 651); the battle of Anna (AU 656); the death of King *Guret* (Gwriad) of Strathclyde (AU 658);[50] the death of the son of Penda (AU 675); a battle of the English in which *Ailmine* (Ælfwine) son of Oswy was slain (AU/AT 680). This brings us down to 681. Had the compiler of the *Annales Cambriae* been copying Irish annals, one would expect some of these entries to have been included. In fact his exemplar must have been more like that of the account in the *Historia Brittonum*.

We may therefore conclude again that the prototype of the Irish annals and the compiler of the *Annales Cambriae* had an account of the struggle of British and English in the seventh century on which they drew independently. The dating of the Irish annals is within a year or two years of the *Annales Cambriae* until Cocboy which the Annals of Ulster put five years earlier (at 638=639, as against 644); the Annals of Inisfallen give 645. There seem to be two dates in the Irish annals for Winwaed: the entry *s. a.* 655 (=656) in the Annals of Ulster corresponds with the date (656) in the *Annales Cambriae*, while that *s. a.* 649 (=650) may be a duplicate.

What was this common prototype like? The dating was not clear. The author of the *Historia Brittonum* (or his source) decided to clarify things by fitting the British events into the regnal years of English kings. (This was a well recognised annalistic custom, applied to imperial reigns.) He seems to have added, independently of the chronology followed by the *Annales Cambriae*,[51] his dating by English reigns. We have to imagine these entries made originally in the margins of a manuscript, with only vague indications of the precise year to which they should be assigned. A scribe trying to draw up annals, putting *annus* or *kl.* at the beginning of each year, must have entered them as he thought best. '*Annus*' was little use to someone drawing up a coherent narrative, so the author of the *Historia Brittonum* turned to English king-lists.

This part of the *Historia Brittonum* has been called the 'northern British section', and though its account stops with the reign of Ecgfrith who died in the battle of Nechtanesmere in 685, the *Annales Cambriae* continue to show a definite interest in north British affairs until 777. They record the deaths of three kings of Strathclyde – Beli son of Elffin (722), Beli's son Tewdwr (750) and Tewdwr's son Dyfnwal (760). There are four Pictish entries – the battle of *Mons Carno* (among the Picts) in 728; the death of *Ougen*, king of the Picts, in 736;[52] a battle between Picts and Britons in 750 in which Talorgan king of the Picts died; and the death of King *Cenioyd* in 776. The obit of Adomnán (of

[50] He is not in the Harleian genealogies.

[51] For example, the *Annales Cambriae* say that Edwin began to reign in 617. The *Historia Brittonum* says he reigned for seventeen years. If this figure had been available to the chronicler he would not have put Edwin's death at 630, as he does (assuming that there has not been a major chronological dislocation at this point in the extant text). There are other, smaller discrepancies of this sort.

[52] This *Ougen* is not in either the Irish annals or the Pictish king-lists. Thomas Jones, in his notes to his translation of *Brut y Tywysogyon* (Peniarth MS. 20 version), p. 132, offers two hypotheses, neither of which seems to me very credible. For Oengus son of Fergus see below, pp. 97–8.

95

Iona) is entered at 704, and we have four Anglo-Saxon entries: the deaths of Aldfrith (704) and Osred (717), both kings of Northumbria, the death of King Æthelbald of Mercia (757), and the death of Abbot Cuthbert in 777. This Cuthbert provides one of the few ecclesiastical entries of the northern chronicle. He must be the abbot of Wearmouth, who wrote a letter to Lul about 764.[53] He says he was a disciple of Bede, had been 'reared at his feet', and had lived in the monastery for forty-six years. If he came to the monastery at the age of seven, this means that in 764 when he wrote to Lul he was fifty-three, and in 777 (where the *Annales Cambriae* record his death) he was sixty-six. He seems to be the disciple of Bede who wrote an account of his death.[54] If he was sixty-six in 777 when he died, he was twenty-four at Bede's death in 735.

Most of these north British entries are also in the Irish annals. Only one of the three kings of Strathclyde is there,[55] but three of the four Pictish entries,[56] the obits of Adomnán, of the two kings of Northumbria,[57] and of the king of Mercia, though not Abbot Cuthbert's. However, the Irish annals give not only a mass of Dalriadic and Pictish entries, but a number of north British and English entries not mentioned by the *Annales Cambriae* – for instance, in 694 the death of Domnall mac Auin (Dyfnwal son of Owain), king of Strathclyde; a battle between the English and Picts in 698 where 'Brectrid son of Bernith' fell; the death of the daughter of Oswy in Hild's monastery (713); the entry into religion and imprisonment of Echaid *filius Cuidini* (Cuthwine), 'king of the English' (731);[58] the burning of Dumbarton on 1 January (780). This is in fact the last of the independent Strathclyde entries[59] in the Irish annals (up to 910), and it seems significant that the north British entries in both the *Annales Cambriae* and the Irish annals stop at almost the same time.

Moreover this middle section of the *Annales Cambriae* looks quite different from the Irish annals. If the Welsh annals had used the Irish annals here you would expect certain characteristics which are in fact absent. You would expect more entries about Iona, at least the record of her conversion to the Roman Easter in 716 (for our annalist was interested in that issue), and the death in 729 of Ecgberht, whose influence achieved it. In fact the only Iona entry here is the death of Adomnán. You would expect more Irish entries, especially for Leinster and southern Ireland. Only two entries relate to

---

[53] Edited by Tangl, *Briefe*, no. 116; translated by Whitelock, *English Historical Documents*, no. 185.

[54] Edited and translated by Colgrave and Mynors, *Bede's Ecclesiastical History*, pp. 579–87.

[55] Beli son of Elffin is in the Annals of Ulster (722), but not Tewdwr son of Beli (750) or Dyfnwal son of Tewdwr (760).

[56] Not the obit of *Ougen* (736), but the three other entries listed above (p. 95) are found in the Annals of Ulster at 729, 750, and 775.

[57] Osred is at 716 in the Annals of Ulster, as against 717 in *Annales Cambriae*.

[58] This is presumably King Ceolwulf of Northumbria: cf. Plummer, *Venerabilis Baedae Opera Historica*, II.340.

[59] The Annals of Ulster note that Dumbarton was besieged for three months and sacked by the Norse in 870, and (supported by *Chronicum Scotorum*) that King Arthgal of Strathclyde was killed in 872 by the advice of Constantine, king of Scots; but both these entries probably came into the Irish annals via another route.

Ireland.[60] You would certainly expect more ecclesiastical entries. The only three here are the deaths of Adomnán, Bede and Cuthbert. Whereas the first section of the *Annales Cambriae* shows its Irish origin clearly, this middle section with its northern backbone looks quite different, even though several of the entries are in the Irish annals.

It seems as if the Irish annals were themselves using a north British chronicle. But John Bannerman, in arguing very effectively for the existence of an Iona chronicle, has shown that, while it was mainly interested in Dalriadic and Pictish affairs, it nonetheless entered some of the contemporary happenings of Northumbria and north Britain.[61]

If one abstracts all the Dalriadic, Pictish, English and north British events in the 'Chronicle of Ireland' some interesting conclusions emerge. Between 616 and 724 there are fifty-seven entries about Scottish Dál Riata, twenty-three about Pictland, eighteen about the English and seven about the Britons.[62]

In the short period between 724 and 741, when the Iona chronicle ceases, the Dalriadic entries continue, but there is now a thicker spate of Pictish entries. We here have a chronicle of the reign of the Pictish king Oengus son of Fergus and its immediate antecedents,[63] which is incorporated into the Scottish annals.[64] Let me give a resumé of these eighteen years, in order to show how much detail is provided.

In 724 Nechton king of the Picts entered religion and Drust succeeded him on the throne. The following year Simul son of Drust was fettered. We do not know who was responsible for this. Drust was still in power in 726, when he fettered Nechton the former king. But after that Drust was turned off the throne, which was taken by Alpin.

Now comes the rise to power of Oengus son of Fergus. He and Alpin fought at Monid Croib in 728 and Oengus was victor. The Annals of Tigernach say that Oengus now assumed royal power. But his position was not yet established. There was another battle at *Castellum Credi* between Oengus and Alpin, when Alpin fled. Now Nechton (whom we last heard of as fettered by Drust in 726) took the kingship. Nechton and Oengus fought it out in 729 at Monith Carno, where Oengus was victorious. It was a crucial battle, and the *Annales Cambriae* were right to record it. Oengus followed this up by slaying Drust at

[60] 661 Commene fota.   683 Mortalitas in Hibernia.

[61] Bannerman, *Studies*, pp. 9–26.

[62] This is a minimum number. There are a few people and places whom I have not been able to identify. And I have not counted entries about Skye, etc., because I do not know whether to count them as Dalriadic or Pictish. Some of the British entries may have been made because the Britons were fighting the Scots of Dál Riata or the Picts or the Irish.

[63] Cf. Henderson, *The Picts*, p. 168, and 'North Pictland', pp. 44–5.

[64] [Dr Hughes's manuscript leaves unclear the precise process which she envisaged here. It is at least a curious coincidence that the reconstructed Iona chronicle and the Pictish annals which Dr Hughes here hypothesises stop at much the same point. On the other hand, it seems unlikely that the Pictish annals would have been incorporated into the Iona chronicle *at Iona* if both sets of annals were still productive in 740–1. We might, as a somewhat desperate compromise, choose to suppose that an Irish chronicler was at this date requesting *and receiving* copies of annals from centres known to be keeping them.]

the battle of Druim Derg Blathuug on 12 August, 729. He had thus defeated three rivals, Alpin, Nechton and Drust. Nechton was possibly allowed to return to religion, for he died in 732.

The son of Oengus and the son of Congus fought in 731. The son of Congus is named in 734, Talorg. He was then manacled by his brother, delivered to the Picts, and drowned. Oengus was making inroads on Scottish Dál Riata, for Dúngal 'fled to Ireland from the power of Oengus' in 734. Oengus devastated Dál Riata in 736, seized the fort of Dunadd, burned Creich and bound the two sons of Selbach, Dúngal and Feradach. In the same year, at Cnoc Coirpri, there was a battle between Dál Riata and the Picts of Fortriu, when Talorgan son of Fergus (and brother of Oengus) put to flight the king of Dál Riata. A Pictish sub-king, Talorgan son of Drostan, king of Atholl, was drowned by Oengus in 739. In 741 the last entry reads, 'The smiting of Dál Riata by Oengus son of Fergus'. Here the detailed account breaks off, though Oengus reigned for another twenty years.

This degree of detail must imply a separate Pictish chronicle. So I do not think that the Iona chronicle merely changed its place of composition. I think the Iona chronicle went on during this period: there are four Iona entries in these seventeen years, as well as entries about Kingarth (in Bute), Applecross and Islay and a number of entries about Dál Riata. As a location for a separate Pictish chronicle we need somewhere in the heart of southern Pictland, near the royal court and the scene of the action. St Andrews (*Cenrigmonaid*) is mentioned for the first time with the death of its abbot in 747, and this would be in the right geographical position.[65]

So an examination of the *Annales Cambriae*, and a reexamination of the Dalriadic, Pictish, English and British entries in the Annals of Ulster and the Annals of Tigernach, makes us realise that the composition of the early Irish annals is even more complicated than had been thought. There was an Iona chronicle, but between 724 and 741 there seems to be a separate Pictish chronicle for Oengus's reign which was incorporated. After 741 both Pictish and – even more – Dalriadic entries thin out. The north British entries have been very few throughout, and the last of the entries is at 780. I think now[66] that these north British entries were not made contemporaneously into the Iona chronicle but were entered into the Irish annals from the source used by the *Annales Cambriae* (or from a related manuscript).

The north British chronicle was used as a source for the *Annales Cambriae* at some time after 777. It may even have been drawn up about then from earlier sources. There is nothing in the forms of the names to require a date earlier than this. Kenneth Jackson has very kindly advised me on this point. He says that 'of the great mass of the names I see no reason to suppose that they are not ninth-century'. There are three unusual forms.[67] In *Adomnan*, the -o- points to a source not later than the first quarter of the eighth century, though this could

[65] On St Andrews see Anderson, 'The Celtic Church in Kinrimund' and 'St Andrews before Alexander I'.

[66] For my earlier view, see Hughes, *Early Christian Ireland*, p. 122.

[67] See also above, p. 69, n. 14.

of course have been the *Vita Columbae* itself. The form *Cenioyd* (776) is not of Irish origin, and looks as if it may have come from a Pictish source. One would expect an Old Welsh spelling *Cintigirn(i)* or *Centigirn(i)* for Kentigern, instead of the *Conthigirni* which appears. There are late cases of *th* for *t* in the *Life* of St Cadog and the Book of Llandaf. The spelling of the names does not therefore demand a contemporary chronicle.

There is, moreover, one factor which makes me think that this north British chronicle was not a year-by-year contemporary record, but a scholar's compilation made from scattered notes and memoranda, probably shortly before the writing of the *Historia Brittonum* early in the ninth century. One of the characteristics of a contemporary year-by-year chronicle is that it shows signs of its place of origin. The Iona chronicle definitely does so, with its full record of Iona's affairs. A Bangor chronicle can be reconstructed from the Irish annals with a full list of seventh-century abbots (an unusual phenomenon which can in this case be checked against the seventh-century Antiphonary of Bangor) and quite a lot of detail about the affairs of Dál Fiatach and Dál nAraide, the two kingdoms bordering on Bangor.[68] From the 790s the entries about Armagh become very full and specific. We have seen that from 796 there are entries in the *Annales Cambriae* about St David's and Dyfed. But the north British chronicle shows no clear sign of its origin. I think the answer is that it is a scholar's exercise, put together well after the events.[69] The compiler had fairly full sources for the wars of the English and Britons during the reigns of Edwin, Oswald and Oswy on the Northumbrian side, Cadwallon, Cadwaladr and Penda on the other. After this his sources were not very satisfactory – a few Strathclyde and English kings, a few Pictish battles, three outstanding northern ecclesiastics (Adomnán of Iona, and Bede and his disciple Cuthbert of Monkwearmouth). It was the best he could do from the sources at his disposal.

There are a few entries of *mirabilia* or natural marvels in this section of the *Annales Cambriae*; they are mostly paralleled in the Irish annals, so they may have come from the north British chronicle.[70] These are:

624 Sol obscuratus est.
650 Ortus stellæ.
676 Stella mire <m>agnitudinis uisa est per totum mundum lucens.
684 Terre motus in Eubonia factus est magnus.
689 Pluuia sanguinea facta est in Brittannia, et lac et butirum uersa sunt in sanguinem.
714 Nox lucida fuit sicut dies. . . .
721 Æstas torrida.

[68] On this see Hughes, *Early Christian Ireland*, pp. 119–23.
[69] Cf. Molly Miller's conclusion about the mnemonic character of the late sixth-century entries: 'Commanders', p. 117.
[70] The entries for 650 and 689 seem not to be paralleled in the Irish annals. That for 689 may be found in the F-text of the Anglo-Saxon Chronicle, *s. a.* 685, however, as was pointed out by Phillimore, 'The *Annales Cambriæ*', p. 159, n. 7.

A few Welsh, south British, and Continental entries have been inserted. These are:[71]

613 . . . Et Iacob filii Beli dormitatio.
630 Guidgar uenit et non redit. . . .
645 Percusio Demeticæ regionis quando cenobium Dauid incensum est.
662 Brocmail moritur.
665 . . . Bellum Badonis secundo.
     Morcant moritur.
714 . . . Pipinus maior rex Francorum obiit in Christo.
718 Consecracio Michaelis archangeli æcclesiæ.
722 . . . Et bellum Hehil apud Cornuenses, gueith Gart Mailauc, cat Pencon apud dexterales Brittones: et Brittones uictores fuerunt in istis tribus bellis.
754 Rotri rex Brittonum moritur.
760 Bellum inter Brittones et Saxones, id est gueith Hirford. . . .
775 Fernmail filius Iudhail moritur.

These entries show no signs of localisation[72] and I think they are a scholar's attempt to provide a set of annals after the events, not a contemporary year-by-year chronicle. It is almost impossible to tell how old, and how reliable, were our annalist's sources.

Let us sum up conclusions. The *Annales Cambriae* show signs of specific localisation for the first time at the end of the eighth century, when the entries also become fuller. From then on, I think, a record was kept at St David's until the A-text stops in 954, though some periods are much thinner than others. Welsh chroniclers would appear to have been nothing like as active as Irish ones in the same period. The contemporary chronicle began soon after Wales accepted the Roman Easter. A preliminary section had to be provided. There was a north British chronicle recording the struggle of the English and the Britons, which provided some backbone for this section of the *Annales Cambriae*. This north British chronicle was also used by the Irish annals. Twelve Welsh, English and Continental entries were also inserted. Our compiler had some north British and north Welsh entries for the period before 613, but up to 613 he was mainly copying Irish annals. His interest in history began with a pronouncement about Easter made in 453. These two sections, 445–613 and 613–777, show signs of scholarly construction ultimately from scattered notes. These notes may have been made in the eighth and seventh centuries, but the precise date is uncertain, for even in the early text of the *Annales Cambriae* represented by the Harley manuscript some glosses have crept in.

[71] I think that the entry for 632, 'Strages Sabrine et iugulatio Iudris', must have been in the northern chronicle, as part of the British-English conflict, because it is in the Irish annals.
[72] The reference to St David's in 645 stands alone in this section; one is therefore bound to wonder if it is a retrospective entry.

Bibliography

ALCOCK, Leslie *Arthur's Britain. History and Archaeology, A.D. 367–634* (London 1971)

ALLEN, John Romilly & ANDERSON, J. *The Early Christian Monuments of Scotland* (Edinburgh 1903)

ANDERSON, Alan Orr & ANDERSON, M. O. (edd. & tr.) *Adomnan's Life of Columba* (Edinburgh 1961)

ANDERSON, Alan Orr, *et al.* (facsimile ed.) *The Chronicle of Melrose from the Cottonian Manuscript, Faustina B.IX in the British Museum* (London 1936)

ANDERSON, Marjorie O. 'Columba and other Irish saints in Scotland' in *Historical Studies, V. Papers read before the Sixth Conference of Irish Historians*, ed. J. L. McCracken (London 1965), pp. 26–36

ANDERSON, Marjorie O. *Kings and Kingship in Early Scotland* (Edinburgh 1973)

ANDERSON, Marjorie O. 'St Andrews before Alexander I' in *The Scottish Tradition. Essays in Honour of Ronald Gordon Cant*, ed. G. W. S. Barrow (Edinburgh 1974), pp. 1–13

ANDERSON, Marjorie O. 'The Celtic Church in Kinrimund', *Innes Review* 25 (1974) 67–76

ANDERSON, Marjorie O. 'The Lists of the Kings', *Scottish Historical Review* 28 (1949) 108–18 *and* 29 (1950) 13–22

ANON. (ed.) 'Chronicle of the thirteenth century. MS. Exchequer Domesday', *Archaeologia Cambrensis*, 3rd Series, 8 (1862) 272–83

ARNOLD, Thomas (ed.) *Henrici Archidiaconi Huntendunensis Historia Anglorum. The History of the English, by Henry, Archdeacon of Huntingdon, from A.C. 55 to A.D. 1154, in eight books* (London 1879)

BAINS, Doris *A Supplement to* Notae Latinae (*Abbreviations in Latin MSS. of 850 to 1050 A.D.*) (Cambridge 1936)

BANNERMAN, John W. M. 'A Critical Edition of the Senchus Fer nAlban with an assessment of its historical value' (Unpublished Ph.D dissertation, 2 vols, University of Cambridge, 1964)

BANNERMAN, John W. M. *Studies in the History of Dalriada* (Edinburgh 1974)

BARLEY, M. W. & HANSON, R. P. C. (edd.), *Christianity in Britain 300–700* (Leicester 1968)

BARROW, Geoffrey W. S., *et al.* (edd.) *Regesta Regum Scotturum* (Edinburgh 1960–) [To date, two volumes have appeared: 1960, 1971.]

BARROW, Geoffrey W. S. *The Kingdom of the Scots. Government, Church and Society from the Eleventh to the Fourteenth Century* (London 1973)

BARROW, Geoffrey, W. S. (ed.) *The Scottish Tradition. Essays in Honour of Ronald Gordon Cant* (Edinburgh 1974)

BARTRUM, Peter C. (ed.) *Early Welsh Genealogical Tracts* (Cardiff 1966)

BERNARD, J. H. & ATKINSON, R. (edd. & tr.) *The Irish Liber Hymnorum* (2 vols, London 1898)

BIELER, Ludwig & CARNEY, J. (edd. & tr.) 'The Lambeth Commentary', *Ériu* 23 (1972) 1–55

BINCHY, Daniel A. 'St Patrick's First Synod', *Studia Hibernica* 8 (1968) 49–59

BINCHY, Daniel A. (ed.) *Studies in Early Irish Law* (Dublin 1936)

BISCHOFF, Bernhard 'Turning-points in the history of Latin exegesis in the early middle ages' in *Biblical Studies. The Medieval Irish Contribution*, ed. M. McNamara (Dublin 1976), pp. 73–160

BLISS, W. H., *et al. Calendar of Entries in the Papal Registers relating to Great Britain and Ireland. Papal Letters.* (London 1893–)

BOWEN, Emrys G. *The Settlements of the Celtic Saints in Wales* (2nd edn, Cardiff 1956)

BREWER, J. S., *et al.* (edd.) *Giraldi Cambrensis Opera* (8 vols, London 1861–91)

BROMWICH, Rachel 'Concepts of Arthur', *Studia Celtica* 10/11 (1975/6) 163–81.

BROOKE, Christopher N. L. 'St Peter of Gloucester and St Cadoc of Llancarfan' in *Celt and Saxon. Studies in the Early British Border*, ed. N. K. Chadwick (Cambridge 1963; rev. imp., 1964), pp. 258–322

BROOKE, Christopher N. L. 'The Archbishops of St David's, Llandaff and Caerleon-on-Usk' in *Studies in the Early British Church*, ed. N. K. Chadwick (Cambridge 1958), pp. 201–42.

BROWN, T. J. 'Northumbria and the Book of Kells', *Anglo-Saxon England* 1 (1972) 219–46

BROWN, T. J. (facsimile ed.) *The Stonyhurst Gospel of St John* (Oxford 1969)

BRUCE-MITFORD, R. L. S. 'The art of the Codex Amiatinus', *Journal of the British Archaeological Association*, 3rd Series, 32(1969)1–25

BUCHANAN, George *Rerum Scoticarum Historia* (Edinburgh 1582). A translation by William Bond was published at London in 1722.

BULLOUGH, Donald A. 'Columba, Adomnan and the achievement of Iona', *Scottish Historical Review* 43(1964)111–30 *and* 44(1965)17–33

CARNEY, James *Studies in Irish Literature and History* (Dublin 1955)

CHADWICK, Hector Munro *Early Scotland. The Picts, the Scots & the Welsh of Southern Scotland* (Cambridge 1949)

CHADWICK, Nora K. (ed.) *Celt and Saxon. Studies in the Early British Border* (Cambridge 1963; rev. imp., 1964)

CHADWICK, Nora K. (ed.) *Studies in Early British History* (Cambridge 1954; rev. imp., 1959)

CHADWICK, Nora K. (ed.) *Studies in the Early British Church* (Cambridge 1958)

CHARLES-EDWARDS, Thomas M. [Review of Bannerman, *Studies in the History of Dalriada*], *Studia Hibernica* 15 (1975) 194–6

COLGRAVE, Bertram & MYNORS, R. A. B. (edd. & tr.) *Bede's Ecclesiastical History of the English People* (Oxford 1969)

COLGRAVE, Bertram (ed. & tr.) *The Life of Bishop Wilfrid by Eddius Stephanus* (Cambridge 1927)

COLGRAVE, Bertram (ed. & tr.) *Two Lives of Saint Cuthbert. A Life by an Anonymous Monk of Lindisfarne and Bede's Prose Life* (Cambridge 1940)

COWAN, Ian B. 'The Post-Columban Church', *Records of the Scottish Church History Society* 18 (1972–4) 245–60

COWAN, Ian B. & EASSON, D. E. *Medieval Religious Houses: Scotland, with an appendix on the houses in the Isle of Man.* (2nd edn, London 1976)

CRUDEN, S. 'Excavations at Birsay, Orkney' in *The Fourth Viking Congress, York, August 1961*, ed. Alan Small (Edinburgh 1965), pp. 23–31

DALRYMPLE, James *Collections concerning the Scottish History preceeding the Death of King David the First, in the year 1153* (Edinburgh 1705)

DALTON, John N., *et al.* (edd.) *Ordinale Exon* (4 vols, London 1909–40)

DARLINGTON, Reginald R. *Anglo-Norman Historians* (London [1947])

DAVIES, J. Conway *Episcopal Acts and Cognate Documents relating to Welsh Dioceses, 1066–1272* (2 vols, Cardiff 1946/8)

DAVIES, Wendy *The Llandaff Charters* (Aberystwyth 1979)

DONALDSON, Gordon 'Scottish bishops' sees before the reign of David I', *Proceedings of the Society of Antiquaries of Scotland* 87 (1952/3) 106–17

DONALDSON, Gordon *Scottish Historical Documents* (Edinburgh 1970)

DONALDSON, Gordon & MORPETH, R. S. *Who's Who in Scottish History* (Oxford 1973)

DRUMMOND, William *The History of Scotland, from the year 1423 until the year 1542 . . .* (London 1655)

DUEMMLER, Ernst, *et al.* (edd.) *Poetae Latini Aevi Carolini* (4 vols, Berlin, 1881–1923)

DUFT, Johannes & MEYER, P. *The Irish Portraits in the Abbey Library of St Gall* (Olten 1954)

DUMVILLE, David N. 'Kingship, genealogies and regnal lists' in *Early Medieval Kingship*, edd. P. H. Sawyer & I. N. Wood (Leeds 1977), pp. 72–104

DUMVILLE, David N. '"Nennius" and the *Historia Brittonum*', *Studia Celtica* 10/11 (1975/6) 78–95

DUMVILLE, David N. 'On the north British section of the *Historia Brittonum*', *Welsh History Review* 8 (1976/7) 345–54

DUMVILLE, David N. [Review of Hughes, *The Welsh Latin Chronicles*], *Studia Celtica* 12/13 (1977/8) 461–7.

DUNCAN, Archibald A. M. *Scotland: the Making of the Kingdom* (Edinburgh 1975; rev. imp., 1978)

DURKAN, John & ROSS, A. *Early Scottish Libraries* (Glasgow 1961)

EDWARDS, J. Goronwy [Review of T. Jones (ed.), *Brut y Tywysogyon. Peniarth MS. 20*], *English Historical Review* 57 (1942) 370–5

EMANUEL, Hywel D. 'An analysis of the composition of the "Vita Cadoci"', *National Library of Wales Journal* 7 (1951/2) 217–27

EMANUEL, Hywel D. 'The Latin Life of St Cadoc: a textual and lexico-graphical study' (Unpublished M.A. dissertation, University of Wales, 1950)

EVANS, J. Gwenogvryn & RHYS, J. (edd.) *The Text of the Book of Llan Dâv, reproduced from the Gwysaney manuscript* (Oxford 1893)

FARAL, Edmond (ed.) *La légende arthurienne. Etudes et documents* (3 vols, Paris 1929)

FINLAYSON, C. P. (facsimile ed.) *Celtic Psalter: Edinburgh University Library MS. 56* (Amsterdam 1962)

FLEMING, David Hay *The Reformation in Scotland: Causes, Characteristics, Consequences* (London 1910)

GALBRAITH, Vivian H. (ed.) *The Herefordshire Domesday* (London 1950)

GALBRAITH, Vivian H. (ed.) 'The St Edmundsbury Chronicle, 1296–1301', *English Historical Review* 58 (1943) 51–78

GLEESON, Dermot F. & MAC AIRT, S. (edd.) 'The Annals of Roscrea', *Proceedings of the Royal Irish Academy* 59 C (1957–9) 137–80

GRAHAM, Angus 'Giudi', *Antiquity* 33 (1959) 63–5

GRANSDEN, Antonia (ed. & tr.) *The Chronicle of Bury St Edmunds 1212–1301* (Edinburgh 1964)

GREENE, David & O'CONNOR, F. (edd. & tr.) *A Golden Treasury of Irish Poetry, A.D. 600–1200* (London 1967)

GROSJEAN, Paul 'Les Pictes apostats dans l'Epître de S. Patrice', *Analecta Bollandiana* 76 (1958) 354–78

GROSJEAN, Paul 'Sur quelques exégètes irlandais du VIIᵉ siècle', *Sacris Erudiri* 7 (1955) 67–98

GRISCOM, Acton & JONES, R. E. (edd.) *The Historia Regum Britanniæ of Geoffrey of Monmouth, with contributions to the study of its place in early British history* (New York 1929)

HARRIS, Silas M. 'A Llanbadarn Fawr calendar', *Ceredigion: Journal of the Cardiganshire Antiquarian Society* 2 (1952–5) 18–26

HARRIS, Silas M. (ed.) 'The kalendar of the *Vitae Sanctorum Wallensium*', *Journal of the Historical Society of the Church in Wales* 3 (1953) 3–53

HART, W. H. (ed.) *Historia et Cartularium Monasterii Sancti Petri Gloucestriae* (3 vols, London 1863–7)

HENDERSON, Isabel B. 'A Critical Examination of Some of the Sources for the History of the Picts from A.D. 550 to 850' (Unpublished Ph.D. dissertation, University of Cambridge, 1962)

HENDERSON, Isabel B. 'North Pictland' in *The Dark Ages in the Highlands*, ed. E. Meldrum (Inverness 1971), pp. 37–52

HENDERSON, Isabel B. 'The meaning of the Pictish symbol stones' in *The Dark Ages in the Highlands*, ed. E. Meldrum (Inverness 1971), pp. 53–67

HENDERSON, Isabel B. *The Picts* (London 1967)

HENNESSY, William M. & MacCARTHY, B. (edd. & tr.) *Annala Uladh. Annals of Ulster, otherwise Annala Senait, Annals of Senat; a Chronicle of Irish Affairs from A.D. 431, to A.D. 1540* (4 vols, Dublin 1887–1901)

HENNESSY, William M. (ed. & tr.) *Chronicum Scotorum. A Chronicle of Irish Affairs from the Earliest Times to A.D. 1135, with a supplement, containing the events from 1141 to 1150* (London 1866)

HENRY, Françoise 'An Irish Manuscript in the British Museum (Add. 40618)', *Journal of the Royal Society of Antiquaries of Ireland* 87 (1957) 147–66

HENRY, Françoise *Irish Art during the Viking Invasions (800–1020 A.D.)* (London 1967)

HENRY, Françoise *Irish Art in the Early Christian Period (to 800 A.D.)* (3rd edn, London 1965)

HENRY, Françoise *Irish Art in the Romanesque Period (1020–1170 A.D.)* (London 1970)

HENRY, Françoise 'Remarks on the decoration of three Irish psalters (British Museum, Cotton Vitellius F.XI, St John's College, Cambridge, MS. C.9 (I. 59), Rouen, Bibliothèque municipale, MS. 24 (A.41)', *Proceedings of the Royal Irish Academy* 61 C (1960/1) 23–40

HENSHALL, Audrey S. 'A long cist cemetery at Parkburn sand pit, Lasswade, Midlothian', *Proceedings of the Society of Antiquaries of Scotland* 89 (1955/6) 252–83

HOLINSHED, Raphael *Chronicles of England, Scotland and Ireland* (3 vols, London 1587)

HOSKIER, Herman C. (ed.) *The Text of Codex Usserianus 2 or r² ("Garland of Howth")* (London 1919)

HUGHES, Kathleen *Early Christian Ireland. Introduction to the Sources* (London 1972)

HUGHES, Kathleen *The Church in Early Irish Society* (London 1966)

HUNTER BLAIR, Peter 'The Bernicians and their northern frontier' in *Studies in Early British History*, ed. N. K. Chadwick (Cambridge 1954; rev. imp., 1959), pp. 137–72

HUWS, Daniel 'Gildas Prisei', *National Library of Wales Journal* 17 (1971/2) 314–20

INNES, Thomas *A Critical Essay on the Ancient Inhabitants of the Northern Parts of Britain, or Scotland* (2 vols, London 1729). References are given to the Edinburgh edition of 1879.

JACKSON, Anthony 'Pictish social structure and symbol-stones. An anthropological assessment', *Scottish Studies* 15 (1971) 121–40

JACKSON, Kenneth H. 'Brittonica', *The Journal of Celtic Studies* 1 (1949/50) 69–79

JACKSON, Kenneth H. *Language and History in Early Britain. A Chronological Survey of the Brittonic Languages, First to Twelfth Century A.D.* (Edinburgh 1953)

JACKSON, Kenneth H. 'Once again Arthur's battles', *Modern Philology* 43 (1945/6) 44–57

JACKSON, Kenneth H. 'On the northern British section in Nennius' in *Celt and Saxon. Studies in the Early British Border*, ed. N. K. Chadwick (Cambridge 1963; rev. imp., 1964), pp. 20–62

JACKSON, Kenneth H. (tr.) 'The Duan Albanach', *Scottish Historical Review* 36 (1957) 125–37

JACKSON, Kenneth H. (ed. & tr.) *The Gaelic Notes in the Book of Deer* (Cambridge 1972)

JACKSON, Kenneth H. (tr.) *The Gododdin: the Oldest Scottish Poem* (Edinburgh 1969)

JACKSON, Kenneth H. 'The Pictish language' in *The Problem of the Picts*, ed. F. T. Wainwright (Edinburgh 1955), pp. 129–68

JACKSON, Kenneth H. (ed.) 'The poem *A eolcha Alban uile*', *Celtica* 3 (1956) 149–67

JACKSON, Kenneth H. 'The site of Mount Badon', *The Journal of Celtic Studies* 2 (1953–8) 152–5

JACKSON, Kenneth H. 'The sources for the life of St Kentigern' in *Studies in the Early British Church*, ed. N. K. Chadwick (Cambridge 1958), pp. 273–357

JONES, Thomas (ed. & tr.) *Brenhinedd y Saesson or the Kings of the Saxons. BM Cotton MS. Cleopatra B.v and The Black Book of Basingwerk, NLW MS. 7006* (Cardiff 1971)

JONES, Thomas (tr.) *Brut y Tywysogyon or the Chronicle of the Princes. Peniarth MS. 20 Version* (Cardiff 1952)

JONES, Thomas (ed. & tr.) *Brut y Tywysogyon or the Chronicle of the Princes. Red Book of Hergest Version* (2nd edn, Cardiff 1973)

JONES, Thomas (ed.) *Brut y Tywysogyon. Peniarth MS. 20* (Cardiff 1941)

JONES, Thomas (ed.) '"Cronica de Wallia" and other documents from Exeter Cathedral Library MS. 3514', *Bulletin of the Board of Celtic Studies* 12 (1946–8) 27–44

JONES, Thomas [Review of Wade-Evans, *Vitae Sanctorum Britanniae*], *Transactions of the Honourable Society of Cymmrodorion* (1943/4) 157–65

JONES, Thomas 'The early evolution of the legend of Arthur', *Nottingham Mediaeval Studies* 8 (1964) 3–21

KEELER, Laura 'The *Historia Regum Britanniae* and four mediaeval chroniclers', *Speculum* 21 (1946) 24–37

KEITH, Robert *Historie of the Affairs of Church and State in Scotland, from the beginning of the Reformation to the year 1568* (3 vols, Edinburgh 1844–50). The work was first published at Edinburgh in 1734.

KENDRICK, Thomas D., *et al.* (facsimile ed.) *Evangeliorum Quattuor Codex Lindisfarnensis, Musei Britannici Codex Cottonianus Nero D.IV.* (2 vols, Oltun 1956/60)

KENNEY, James F. *The Sources for the Early History of Ireland: Ecclesiastical* (New York 1929; rev. imp., by Ludwig Bieler, 1966)

KER, Neil R. *Medieval Libraries of Great Britain. A List of Surviving Books* (2nd edn, London 1964)

KER, Neil R. 'Sir John Prise', *The Library*, 5th Series, 10 (1955) 1–24

KIRBY, David P. 'Bede and the Pictish Church', *Innes Review* 24 (1973) 6–25

LAWLOR, H. C.   *Chapters on the Book of Mulling* (Edinburgh 1897)

LAWLOR, H. J. (ed.)   *The Psalter and Martyrology of Ricemarch* (2 vols, London 1914)

LEGGE, M. Dominica   'The inauguration of Alexander III', *Proceedings of the Society of Antiquaries of Scotland* 80 (1945/6) 73–82

LIEBERMANN, Felix (ed.)   *Ungedruckte Anglo-normannische Geschichtsquellen* (Strassburg 1879)

LINDSAY, Wallace M.   *Notae Latinae. An Account of Abbreviation in Latin MSS. of the Early Minuscule Period* (c. 700–850) (Cambridge 1915)

LLOYD, John E.   *A History of Wales from the Earliest Times to the Edwardian Conquest* (3rd edn, 2 vols, London 1939)

LLOYD, John E.   'The Welsh Chronicles', *Proceedings of the British Academy* 14 (1928) 369–91

LLOYD, John E.   'Wales and the coming of the Normans (1039–1093)', *Transactions of the Honourable Society of Cymmrodorion* (1899/1900) 122–79

LOOMIS, Roger S. (ed.),   *Arthurian Literature in the Middle Ages. A Collaborative History* (Oxford 1959)

LOT, Ferdinand (ed.)   *Nennius et l'Historia Brittonum. Étude critique suivie d'une édition des diverses versions de ce texte* (2 vols, Paris 1934)

LOWE, Elias A. (ed.)   *Codices Latini Antiquiores. A Palaeographical Guide to Latin Manuscripts Prior to the Ninth Century, Vol. II, Great Britain and Ireland* (2nd edn, Oxford 1972)

LUARD, Henry R. (ed.)   *Annales Monastici* (5 vols, London 1864–9)

MAC AIRT, Seán (ed. & tr.)   *The Annals of Inisfallen (MS. Rawlinson B. 503)* (Dublin 1951)

MACALISTER, R. A. S. (ed. & tr.)   *Lebor Gabála Érenn. The Book of the Taking of Ireland* (5 vols, London 1938–56)

McCRACKEN, J. L. (ed.)   *Historical Studies, V. Papers read before the Sixth Conference of Irish Historians* (London 1965)

MacDONALD, Aidan   '"Annat" in Scotland: a provisional review', *Scottish Studies* 17 (1973) 135–46

MacDONALD, Robert H.   *The Library of Drummond of Hawthornden* (Edinburgh 1971)

MAC EOIN, Gearóid S.   'On the Irish legend of the origin of the Picts', *Studia Hibernica* 4 (1964) 138–54

McGURK, Patrick   *Latin Gospel Books from A.D. 400 to A.D. 800* (Brussels 1961)

McGURK, Patrick   'The Irish pocket gospel book', *Sacris Erudiri* 8 (1956) 249–70

MacKENZIE, George   *The Antiquity of the Royal Line of Scotland farther cleared and defended* (London 1686)

MacKINNON, Donald   *A Descriptive Catalogue of Gaelic Manuscripts in the Advocates' Library Edinburgh, and elsewhere in Scotland* (Edinburgh 1912)

McNAMARA, Martin (ed.)   *Biblical Studies. The Medieval Irish Contribution* (Dublin 1976) [Proceedings of the Irish Biblical Association, no. 1.]

McNEILL, Peter & NICHOLSON, R.   *An Historical Atlas of Scotland c.400–c.1600* (St Andrews 1975; rev. imp., 1976)

MAC NIOCAILL, Gearóid   *The Medieval Irish Annals* (Dublin 1975)

MacQUEEN, John   *St Nynia. A Study of Literary and Linguistic Evidence* (Edinburgh 1961)

MacQUEEN, Winifred W. (tr.)   'Miracula Nynie Episcopi', *Transactions of the Dumfriesshire and Galloway Natural History and Antiquarian Society*, 3rd Series, 38 (1959/60) 21–57

McROBERTS, David   *Catalogue of Scottish Medieval Liturgical Books and Fragments* (Glasgow 1953)

McROBERTS, David   'Material destruction caused by the Scottish Reformation', *Innes Review* 10 (1959) 126–72

McROBERTS, David   'The ecclesiastical character of the St Ninian's Isle treasure' in *The Fourth Viking Congress, York, August 1961*, ed. Alan Small (Edinburgh 1965), pp. 224–46

McROBERTS, David   'The ecclesiastical significance of the St Ninian's Isle treasure', *Proceedings of the Society of Antiquaries of Scotland* 94 (1960/1) 301–14

MAJOR, John   *Historia Majoris Britanniae, tam Angliae quam Scotiae* (Paris 1521)

MARCHEGAY, Paul   *Chartes anciennes du prieuré de Monmouth en Angleterre* . . . (Les Roches-Baritaud 1879)

MARTIN, Martin   *A Description of the Western Islands of Scotland* (London [1703]). References are given to the edition by D. J. MacLeod (Stirling 1934).

MEEHAN, Denis   [Review of Anderson & Anderson, *Adomnan's Life of Columba*], *Medium Ævum* 31 (1962) 205–7

MELDRUM, E. (ed.)   *The Dark Ages in the Highlands* (Inverness 1971)

MENZIES, Gordon (ed.)   *Who are the Scots?* (London 1971)

MICHELI, Geneviève   *L'enluminure du haut moyen âge et les influences irlandaises* (Brussels 1939)

MEYER, Kuno   'A collation of Rees' *Lives of the Cambro-British Saints*', *Y Cymmrodor* 13 (1900) 76–96

MEYER, Kuno (ed. & tr.)   *Cáin Adamnáin. An Old-Irish Treatise on the Law of Adamnan* (Oxford 1905)

MIGNE, J.-P. (ed.)   *Patrologiae [Latinae] Cursus Completus* . . . (221 vols, Paris 1844–64)

MILLAR, Eric G.   'Les principaux manuscrits à peintures du Lambeth Palace à Londres', *Bulletin de la Société française de reproductions de manuscrits à peintures* 8 (1924) 5–66 *and* 9 (1925) 5–19

MILLER, Molly   'Date-guessing and Dyfed', *Studia Celtica* 12/13 (1977/8) 33–61

MILLER, Molly   'Eanfrith's Pictish son', *Northern History* 14 (1978) 47–66

MILLER, Molly   'Geoffrey's early royal synchronisms', *Bulletin of the Board of Celtic Studies* 28 (1978–80) 373–89

MILLER, Molly   'The commanders at Arthuret', *Transactions of the Cumberland and Westmorland Antiquarian and Archaeological Society*, 2nd Series, 75 (1975) 96–118

MILLER, Molly 'The disputed historical horizon of the Pictish king-lists', *Scottish Historical Review* 58 (1979) 1–34

MURISON, D. D. 'Linguistic relationships in medieval Scotland' in *The Scottish Tradition. Essays in Honour of Ronald Gordon Cant*, ed. G. W. S. Barrow (Edinburgh 1974), pp. 71–83

NASH-WILLIAMS, V. E. *The Early Christian Monuments of Wales* (Cardiff 1950)

O'DONOVAN, John (ed. & tr.) *Annals of the Kingdom of Ireland, by the Four Masters* . . . (2nd edn, 7 vols, Dublin 1856)

O'FLAHERTY, Roderic *Ogygia: seu, Rerum Hibernicarum Chronologia* (London 1685). Reference is made here to the translation by James Hely, 2 vols, Dublin 1793.

O'SULLIVAN, Anne 'The colophon of the Cotton Psalter (Vitellius F.XI)', *Journal of the Royal Society of Antiquaries of Ireland* 96 (1966) 179–83

O'SULLIVAN, William 'The Irish manuscripts in Case H in Trinity College Dublin catalogued by Matthew Young in 1781', *Celtica* 11 (1976) 229–50

PALGRAVE, Francis (ed.) *The Antient Kalendars and Inventories of the Treasury of H.M. Exchequer, together with Other Documents illustrating the History of that Repository* (3 vols, London 1836)

PETRIE, Henry & SHARPE, J. (edd.) *Monumenta Historica Britannica, or Materials for the History of Britain, from the Earliest Period* (London 1848)

PHILLIMORE, Egerton (ed.) 'The *Annales Cambriæ* and Old Welsh Genealogies, from *Harleian MS.* 3859', *Y Cymmrodor* 9 (1888) 141–83

PHILLIMORE, Egerton 'The publication of Welsh historical records', *Y Cymmrodor* 11 (1890–2) 133–75

PINKERTON, John *An Enquiry into the History of Scotland, preceding the Reign of Malcolm III, or the year 1056, including the authentic history of that period* (2nd edn, 2 vols, Edinburgh 1814) [First published at London in 1789]

PLUMMER, Charles (ed. & tr.) *Bethada Náem nÉrenn. Lives of Irish Saints* (2 vols, Oxford 1922)

PLUMMER, Charles (ed.) *Venerabilis Baedae Opera Historica* (2 vols, Oxford, 1896)

PLUMMER, Charles (ed.) *Vitae Sanctorum Hiberniae* (2 vols, Oxford 1910)

PUGH, Thomas B. (ed.) *Glamorgan County History*, III (Cardiff 1971)

RADFORD, C. A. Ralegh *The Early Christian and Norse Settlements at Birsay, Orkney* (Edinburgh 1959)

RADNER, Joan N. (ed. & tr.) *Fragmentary Annals of Ireland* (Dublin 1978)

RAE, Thomas I. 'The political attitudes of William Drummond of Hawthornden' in *The Scottish Tradition. Essays in Honour of Ronald Gordon Cant*, ed. G. W. S. Barrow (Edinburgh 1974), pp. 132–47

REES, William J. (ed. & tr.) *Lives of the Cambro-British Saints, of the fifth and immediate succeeding centuries from ancient Welsh and Latin MSS.* (Llandovery 1853)

RILEY, Henry T. (ed.) *Chronica Monasterii S. Albani . . . A.D. 1259–1307* (London 1865)

RITCHIE, Anna   'Pict and Norseman in northern Scotland', *Scottish Archaeological Forum* 6 (1974) 23–36

ROE, Helen M.   'The orans in Irish christian art', *Journal of the Royal Society of Antiquaries of Ireland* 100 (1970) 212–21

ROTHWELL, H. (ed.)   *The Chronicle of Walter of Guisborough* (London 1957)

RUTHERFORD, Anthony   '*Giudi* revisited', *Bulletin of the Board of Celtic Studies* 26 (1974–6) 440–4

RYAN, John   'The Cáin Adomnáin' in *Studies in Early Irish Law*, ed. D. A. Binchy (Dublin 1936), pp. 269–76

RYMER, Thomas, *et al.* (edd.)   *Foedera, Conventiones, Literae, et Cujuscunque Generis Acta Publica inter Reges Angliae et Alios* . . . (3rd edn, 10 vols, The Hague 1739–45)

SAWYER, Peter H. & WOOD, I. N. (edd.)   *Early Medieval Kingship* (Leeds 1977)

SCHAUMAN, Bella T.   'The Emergence and Progress of Irish Script to the year 700' (Unpublished Ph.D dissertation, 2 vols, University of Toronto, 1974)

SCOTT, John (Lord Scotstarvet)   *The Staggering State of the Scots Statesmen, for one hundred years, viz. from 1550 to 1650* . . . (Edinburgh 1754)

SEYLER, Clarence A.   'The early charters of Swansea and Gower', *Archaeologia Cambrensis*, 7th Series, 4 (1924) 59–79

SIMPSON, W. D.   'The early romanesque tower at Restenneth Priory, Angus', *Antiquaries' Journal* 43 (1963) 269–83

SKENE, William F. (ed.)   *Chronicles of the Picts, Chronicles of the Scots, and Other Early Memorials of Scottish History* (Edinburgh 1867)

SKENE, William F. (ed. & tr.)   *Johannis de Fordun Chronica Gentis Scotorum* (2 vols, Edinburgh 1871/2)

SMALL, Alan (ed.)   *The Fourth Viking Congress, York, August 1961* (Edinburgh 1965)

SMALL, Alan, *et al.*   *St Ninian's Isle and its Treasure* (2 vols, London 1973)

SMITH, J. Beverley   'The "Cronica de Wallia" and the dynasty of Dinefwr. A textual and historical study', *Bulletin of the Board of Celtic Studies* 20 (1962–4) 261–82

SMYTH, Alfred   *Scandinavian York and Dublin. The History and Archaeology of Two Related Viking Kingdoms*, I (Dublin 1975)

SMYTH, Alfred   'The earliest Irish annals: their first contemporary entries, and the earliest centres of recording', *Proceedings of the Royal Irish Academy* 72 C (1972) 1–48

SPOTTISWOODE, John (*alias* SPOTSWOOD)   *The History of the Church of Scotland* . . . *to the End of the Reign of James VI* (London 1655). References are given to the Menston facsimile edition of 1972.

STEVENSON, David   *The Scottish Revolution 1637–44. The Triumph of the Covenanters* (Newton Abbot 1973)

STEVENSON, R. B. K.   'Long cist burials, particularly those at Galson (Lewis) and Gairloch (Wester Ross), with a symbol stone at Gairloch', *Proceedings of the Society of Antiquaries of Scotland* 86 (1951/2) 106–15

STEVENSON, R. B. K. 'Pictish art' in *The Problem of the Picts*, ed. F. T. Wainwright (Edinburgh 1955), pp. 97–128

STEVENSON, William H. (ed.) *Asser's Life of King Alfred* (Oxford 1904; rev. imp., by D. Whitelock, 1959)

STOKES, Whitley (ed. & tr.) 'The Annals of Tigernach', *Revue celtique* 16 (1895) 374–419; 17 (1896) 6–33, 119–263, 337–420; *and* 18 (1897) 9–59, 150–98, 267–303, 390–1

STONES, E. L. G. (ed. & tr.) *Anglo-Scottish Relations 1174–1328: Some Selected Documents* (London 1965; rev. imp., Oxford 1970)

STONES, E. L. G. 'The appeal to history in Anglo-Scottish relations between 1291 and 1401', *Archives* 9 (1969/70) 11–21 *and* 80–3

STONES, E. L. G. & SIMPSON, G. G. (edd.) *Edward I and the Throne of Scotland 1290–1296. An Edition of the Record Sources for the Great Cause* (2 vols, Oxford 1978)

STRACHAN, J. 'The date of the *Amra Choluimb Chille*', *Revue celtique* 17 (1896) 41–4

STUART, John (ed.) *The Book of Deer* (Edinburgh 1869)

TANGL, Michael (ed.) *Die Briefe des heiligen Bonifatius und Lullus* (2nd edn, Berlin 1955)

TATLOCK, John S. P. *The Legendary History of Britain. Geoffrey of Monmouth's Historia Regum Britanniae and its Early Vernacular Versions* (Berkeley, Cal. 1950)

THOMAS, A. Charles 'An early christian cemetery and chapel on Ardwall Isle, Kirkcudbright', *Medieval Archaeology* 11 (1967) 127–88

THOMAS, A. Charles *The Early Christian Archaeology of North Britain* (London 1971)

THOMAS, A. Charles 'The early christian Church' in *Who are the Scots?* ed. G. Menzies (London 1971), pp. 90–102

THOMAS, A. Charles 'The evidence from north Britain' in *Christianity in Britain 300–700*, edd. M. W. Barley & R. P. C. Hanson (Leicester 1968), pp. 93–121

THOMAS, A. Charles 'The interpretation of the Pictish symbols', *Archaeological Journal* 120 (1963) 31–97

THOMSON, Derick S. 'Gaelic learned orders and literati in medieval Scotland', *Scottish Studies* 12 (1968) 57–78

THORPE, Benjamin (ed.) *Florentii Wigorniensis Monachi Chronicon ex Chronicis* . . . (2 vols, London 1848/9)

TODD, James H. 'Remarks on illuminations in some Irish biblical manuscripts' in *Vetusta Monumenta quae ad Rerum Britannicarum Memoriam Conservandam Societas Antiquariorum Londini sumptu suo edenda curavit*, VI (Westminster 1821–83), plates XLIII – XLVI with 16 accompanying pages of discussion (published 1868)

TODD, James H. & HERBERT, A. (edd. & tr.) *Leabhar Breathnach annso sis. The Irish version of the Historia Britonum of Nennius* (Dublin 1848)

TREVOR-ROPER, H. R. *George Buchanan and the Ancient Scottish Constitution* (London 1966)

TREVOR-ROPER, H. R.   *Religion, the Reformation and Social Change, and Other Essays* (2nd edn, London 1972)

VAN HAMEL, Anton G. (ed.)   *Lebor Bretnach. The Irish Version of the Historia Britonum ascribed to Nennius* (Dublin [1932])

WADE-EVANS, A. W.   'Parochiale Wallicanum', *Y Cymmrodor* 22 (1910) 22–124

WADE-EVANS, A. W. (ed. & tr.)   *Vitae Sanctorum Britanniae et Genealogiae* (Cardiff 1944)

WAINWRIGHT, F. T. (ed.)   *The Problem of the Picts* (Edinburgh 1955)

WARREN, F. E.   *The Liturgy and Ritual of the Celtic Church* (Oxford 1881)

WATSON, William J.   *The History of the Celtic Place-names of Scotland* (Edinburgh 1926)

WATT, D. E. R.   *Fasti Ecclesiae Scoticanae Medii Aevi* (Edinburgh 1969)

WEAVER, J. R. H. (ed.)   *The Chronicle of John of Worcester, 1118–1140* (Oxford 1908)

WERCKMEISTER, O. K.   'Three problems of tradition in pre-carolingian figure-style. From Visigothic to Insular illumination', *Proceedings of the Royal Irish Academy* 63 C (1962–4) 167–89

WHITELOCK, Dorothy (tr.)   *English Historical Documents, Volume I, c. 500–1042* (2nd edn, London 1979)

WILLIAMS, Ifor   'A reference to the Nennian Bellum Cocboy', *Bulletin of the Board of Celtic Studies* 3 (1926/7) 59–62

WILLIAMS, Ifor   'Bellum Cantscaul', *Bulletin of the Board of Celtic Studies* 6 (1931–3) 351–4

WILLIAMS, Ifor   'Vocabularium Cornicum', *Bulletin of the Board of Celtic Studies* 11 (1941–4) 1–12

WILLIAMS, AB ITHEL, John (ed.)   *Annales Cambriæ* (London 1860)

WILMART, André (ed.)   *Analecta Reginensia. Extraits des manuscrits latins de la reine Christine conservés au Vatican* (Vatican City 1933)

WORMALD, Francis (ed.)   *English Benedictine Kalendars after 1100* (2 vols, London 1939/46)

WORMALD, Francis   'The calendar of the Augustinian priory of Launceston in Cornwall', *Journal of Theological Studies* 39 (1938) 1–21

Index of Manuscripts

ABERYSTWYTH

National Library of Wales
17110 E (*Book of Llandaf*): 61, 62, 63, 66,
69n, 99
Peniarth 20: 67, 78, 88n

BERN

Burgerbibliothek
671: 24

CAMBRIDGE

Corpus Christi College
93 (*Exeter Martyrology*): 55

St John's College
C.9 (59) (*Southampton Psalter*): 24n, 26,
27n, 32, 33–5, 36

University Library
Ii.6.32 (*Book of Deer*): 1, 14, 15, 16, 22–37
Kk. 5. 16 (*Moore Bede*): 71
Add. 4602 B: 22

DUBLIN

Royal Irish Academy
s. n. (*Cathach of St Columba*): 8, 40
Stowe D.ii.1 (1225) (*Leabhar Ua Maine*):
42
Stowe D.ii.3 (1238), fos 1–11: 35
Stowe D.ii.3 (1238), fos 12–67 (*Stowe
Missal*): 36n

Trinity College
50 (A.4.20) (*Psalter of Rhigyfarch*): 26
52 (*Book of Armagh*): 25
56 (A.4.6) (*Garland of Howth*): 15n, 30–2
57 (A.4.5) (*Book of Durrow*): 27, 33n, 40
58 (A.1.6) (*Book of Kells*): 11, 25, 26, 27,
31, 33

59 (A.4.23) (*Book of Dimma*): 23, 24, 27,
27f., 28, 36
60 (A.1.15) (*Book of Mulling*): 23, 24, 36
60 (A.1.15), fos 95–98: 24
1337 (H.3.18): 25n

DURHAM

Cathedral
A.2.17: 33n

EDINBURGH

National Library of Scotland
Adv. 35.1.7: 6

University Library
56 (D.b.III.8): 2n, 25, 26, 26f., 27

EXETER

Cathedral
3514: 68, 76–9, 84, 85
3518 (*Exeter Martyrology*): 55

FIRENZE

Biblioteca Laurenziana
Amiatino 1 (*Codex Amiatinus*): 26

LICHFIELD

Cathedral
s. n. (*Lichfield Gospels*): 27, 28, 29

LONDON

British Library
Additional 22720: 58
Cotton Domitian A.I: 67, 68, 73–6, 84, 85
Cotton Faustina B.I: 76n
Cotton Titus D.XXII: 56n, 65n
Cotton Vespasian A.XIV: 53–66
Cotton Vespasian E.IV: 76n, 80n, 81

Cotton Vitellius F.XI: 26, 33–5, 36
Harley 1023: 36f.
Harley 1802: 36f.
Harley 3859: 67, 68–73, 73n, 73–4, 84, 85, 86–101
Harley 4628: 20
Royal 6.B.XI: 82n

Lambeth Palace
1229: 25
1370 (*MacDurnan Gospels*): 23, 24, 25, 27, 28, 33, 36

Public Record Office
E.164/1 (K.R. Misc. Books, Series I): 67, 68, 74–83, 84, 85

MILANO

Biblioteca Ambrosiana
C.5 inf. (*Antiphonary of Bangor*): 40, 99

NEW YORK

Pierpont Morgan Library
M.627 (*Drummond Missal*): 2n

OXFORD

Bodleian Library
Auct. F.4.32 (*S.C.* 2176): 25n
Bodley 579 (*S.C.* 2675) (*Leofric Missal*): 64n
Jesus College 10 (*Gloucester kalendar*): 59, 63
Jesus College 111 (*Red Book of Hergest*): 67

Lat. liturg. f.5 (*S.C.* 29744) (*Gospel-Book of St Margaret*): 2n

PARIS

Bibliothèque nationale
latin 4126 (*Poppleton MS.*): 15n, 41
latin 9389 (*Echternach Gospels*): 27, 28

ROUEN

Bibliothèque municipale
A.41 (24) (*Psalter of Saint-Ouen*): 25n, 26, 27

SALISBURY

Cathedral
180: 64n

SANKT GALLEN

Stiftsbibliothek
51: 28
60: 35

SCHAFFHAUSEN

Stadtbibliothek
Gen. 1: 41

STONYHURST

Stonyhurst College
s. n. (*Stonyhurst Gospel*): 35

Index

Aberconway, 78n

Abercorn, 9n, 38, 47

Aberdehoneu, 78, 79

Abergele, 87

Abernethy, 10

*Abloyc/*Abloyt*, 88n

Abraham (Bishop of St David's), 74

Achau Brenhinoedd a Thywysogion Cymru, 88n

Adananus, 8n

Ad Candidam Casam (Whithorn), 49

Adomnán (Abbot of Iona), 1, 8, 9, 13n, 41, 43, 47–9, 49n, 50f., 69n, 72, 95, 96, 97, 99

aduentus Saxonum, 73n

Aed Findliath mac Néill (King), 88

Aedán son of Gabrán (King of Dál Riata), 69n, 90

Ælfric, 55n

Ælfwine (*Ailmine*) son of Oswiu, 95

Ælle (King of Deira), 92

Aeneas, 6

Æthelbald (King of Mercia), 96

Æthelflæd (Queen of Mercia), 88

Æthelred 'the Unready' (King of England), 76

Æthelstan (King of England), 88

Aethicus Ister, 68n

Æthilfrith (King of Northumbria), 44n, 93

Afloeg/Afloedd, 88n

Aid(u)us (St): *see* Maedóc (St)

Ailred of Rievaulx, 6

Ailwin (St), 59, 60

Airchartdan: see Urquhart

Albanact (son of Brutus), 6, 7

Aldbar, 29, 31

Aldfrith (King of Northumbria), 96

Alexander I (King of Scots), 16n

Alexander III (King of Scots), 17n

Alfred (King of Wessex), 88

Alhred (King of Northumbria), 11

alii dicunt formula, 90, 91n

Allan Water, 15

Allonnes, 55

Alpin (King of Picts), 5, 7n, 97f.

Amlaib, 88n

Amra Choluim Chille, 8, 50

Anastasius (Emperor), 73n

Anglesey, 57

Anglo-French influence in Scotland, 15

Anglo-Saxon Chronicle, 99n

Angus (Scotland), 38, 47

Anna (King of East Anglia), 94, 95

Annales Cambriae, 67– 100

annals (Irish): *see* Irish annals

Anstruther, 2

apostata, 50n

Applecross, 45, 51, 98

Arbroath, 49n

Arcadius (Emperor), 73n

Ardchattan, 16

Ardwall Island, 49

Arfderydd (battle of), 70

Argyll, 16

Armagh, 25, 36f., 86, 88, 89, 90, 99

Arran (Earl of), 2

Arrouasians, 16

Arthgal (King of Strathclyde), 96n

Arthur ('King'), 7, 73, 92

Arwystli, 80

Asser of St David's (Bishop of Sherborne), 68n, 87

Atbret Iudeu, 93

Augustine (St, of Hippo), 35, 68n

Augustinian canons, 16, 64n

Awre, 55

Badon (battles of [Mount]), 70, 91f., 94

Balfour (James), 17

Balliol (John), 5, 18

Bangor (Gwynedd), 70, 77n, 91

Bangor (Ireland), 45, 69n, 99

banking-facilities (use of churches for), 12

Bannog, 49, 50n

Barbacianus (St), 55
Barra, 18
Barrovadus, 49
Bartholomew de Cotton, 76n
Battle (Sussex), 76n
Bede (St), 6, 8, 9, 10, 20, 38–52, 71, 72,
    74n, 92n, 93n, 94n, 96, 97, 99
Beli I (King of Strathclyde), 92n
Beli II son of Elffin (King of Strathclyde)
    71n, 92n, 95, 96n
Belin, 92, 94
belt-buckles, 27
Benbecula, 18
Benedict of Gloucester, 60, 61, 63, 65
Benedictine monasticism, 16, 56, 58, 82n
Benén (St), 69n, 90
Bermondsey, 76n
Bernard (Bishop of St David's), 59, 63, 74,
    79
Bernard of Neufmarché (lord of Brecon),
    59
biblical commentary, 25, 40
biblical text (type of), 25f., 31
Birr, 69n, 90
Birsay, 11f.
Blathmac (of Iona), 13
Bleddyn (Bishop of St David's), 74
Boece (Hector), 18, 19
Boisil (of Melrose), 35
books (printed), 2
books (service-), 1, 2, 20, 33
book-satchels, 22, 28, 32, 37
Bower (Walter), 6n
Brabazon (Roger), 4
Bradshaw (Henry), 22n
Brandan (St), 18
Brecc Bennach (the), 49n
Brechin, 16
Brecon (Brecknock), 54, 57n, 58, 59, 76n,
    80
'Brectrid son of Bernith', 96
Brendan of Birr (St), 69n, 90, 91n
Brendan of Clonfert (St), 53n, 58f., 90
Brenhinedd y Saesson, 67, 76, 88n
Bressay, 28
Brian Bóroma (King of Dál Cais), 89
Brigit (St), 40, 69n, 90, 91n
Broichan, 48
brooches, 12
Bruce (Robert): *see* Robert Bruce (King of
    Scots)
Bruide son of Bile (King of Picts), 51
Bruide son of Maelchon (King of Picts),
    9, 10n, 20, 39, 42, 43, 44, 47, 48, 50, 51
Brutus, 6, 7

Brut y Tywysogyion, 67, 77, 78, 79, 80, 83,
    84, 88n
Brycheiniog, 91
Brynach (St), 56n, 57, 58
Buchan, 38
Buchanan (George), 19
Buellt, 80
buildings (ecclesiastical), 2, 3n, 9, 10, 10f.,
    12, 16, 39, 51
Builth, 78
Burton, 76n
Bury St Edmunds (Chronicle of), 4, 76n,
    77, 79, 84n, 85
Bute, 98

Cadafael (*alias* 'Catgabail', King of
    Gwynedd), 93, 94
Cadell (King of Seisyllwg), 68, 87
Cadfan, 73
Cadog (St), 53, 56, 59f., 62, 64, 65, 69n, 99
Cadwaladr, 'son of Cadwallon' (King of
    Gwynedd), 72, 73, 93, 94, 99
Cadwallon (King of Gwynedd), 44n, 70,
    72, 73, 92, 94, 99
Cadwgan (Abbot of Whitland, then
    Bishop of Bangor), 77n
Caerleon, 80, 91n
Cáin Adomnáin, 8n, 69n
Cair Legion: see Chester
Cairnech (St, of Dulane), 57
Calderwood (David), 17
Camber (son of Brutus), 7
Camboglanna, 91
Cambuskenneth, 2
Camlann (battle of), 70, 91
Canterbury, 3
canticles, 33
Ca(n)tscaul: see Heavenfield (battle of)
capitula, 56f., 66
Caradog of Llancarfan, 54, 64n
Caradog (St, of St David's), 58
Carannog (St), 56n, 57, 58
Carantocus (St): *see* Carannog (St)
Cardiff, 82n
Cardigan, 57, 80
Carew (lords of), 79, 85
Carmarthen, 76, 81n, 82, 83
cartularies (monastic): *see* title-deeds
    (monastic)
castellum Credi (battle of), 97
Cedifor son of Gruffydd, 78n
Cellach (Abbot of Iona), 13, 14n
cell-names, 36
cemeteries, 12, 49
Cenél nGabráin, 69n, 90

116

Cenioyd (King of Picts), 69n, 95, 99
Cenrigmonaid: *see* St Andrews
Ceolfrith (Abbot of Jarrow), 9, 38, 39, 45
Ceolwulf (Echaid) son of Cuthwine (King of Northumbria), 96
Cerball (King of Osraige), 88
Ceredig, 73
Ceredig (King of Elmet), 92, 94
Ceredigion, 57, 59, 75n, 81n, 86, 87
Ceri, 80
Charles I (King of Great Britain and Ireland), 19
Chester (battle of), 69, 73n, 90, 91n
chronicles, 1, 3, 4, 5, 6, 7n, 8, 10, 14, 20, 40, 42n, 47, 51n, 67–100
chronological studies, 69n, 73n, 90
church-dedications, 48n, 49, 57, 58, 60, 64
Cian, 49
Ciarán of Clonmacnoise (St), 69n, 90, 91n
Cicero, 68n
Cill Muine: see St Davids
Cinaed mac Alpin, 5, 13, 71n, 88
Cistercians, 16, 77, 78, 79, 80, 81, 82, 83
clas-system, 54, 59
Clonfert, 90
Clonmacnoise, 32, 69n, 88n, 89, 90
Clydesdale, 15
Clydog (St), 53n, 61, 62, 63f.
Clydog son of Cadell (King of Seisyllwg), 68, 87
Cnoc Coirpri (battle of), 98
coarbs, 13
Cocboy: see Oswestry (battle of)
Coel Hen, 70, 91
Colgan (James), 17, 18
Collectio Canonum Hibernensis, 41
Coln Saint Aldwyn, 59
colophons, 22, 23, 25, 33, 37
Columba (St), 1, 8, 9, 10n, 12f., 13n, 14n, 18, 20, 38–52, 69n, 90, 99
Columban Church, 8, 10, 13, 40, 41, 43, 48f., 50f., 51
Columbanus (St), 40n
Colum Cille (St): *see* Columba (St)
Comyn (John), 5
Congal (St), 18
Constantine (King of Picts), 11
Constantine (King of Scots), 13, 14, 96n
conuersi (monastic), 80n
conversion (to christianity), 7, 8, 9, 10, 38–52, 92
Cormac (Bishop of Dunkeld), 15
Cornwall, 72
Coroticus (King of Strathclyde), 9n, 50
Coupar Chronicle, 3n, 6n

Craig (Thomas), 19
Crail, 2
Creich, 98
Crinan (Abbot of Dunkeld), 14
Cromwell (Oliver), 19
Cronica de Wallia, 68, 77–9, 80, 84, 85
crozier (tau-headed): *see* tau-headed crozier
crusades, 75, 81n
Cú Chumine (of Iona), 41
Cuimine (Abbot of Iona), 8
Cummean, 40n
Cumméne fota, 97n
Custennin (St), 64
Cuthbert (St), 8, 35, 38
Cuthbert (Abbot of Monkwearmouth), 72, 96, 97, 99
Cuthman (St), 55
Cwm Hir, 80, 81, 83, 84, 85
Cybi (St), 56n, 57, 58
Cynan, 73
Cynog of Brycheiniog, 70, 91

Dál Cais, 89
Dál Fiatach, 99
Dál nAraide, 99
Dál Riata, 1, 5, 8, 9, 11, 13, 16, 41, 42, 43, 48f., 51, 69n, 89, 90, 96, 97f.
Dalrymple (James), 20
Daniel of Bangor (St), 70, 91
David of Gwynedd, 77, 78n, 81
David (King of Scots, Earl of Huntingdon), 15, 16
David (St), 57, 58, 59, 69n, 90, 90f.
David son of Hywel, 80
De antiquitate Glastoniensis ecclesiae, 54
De Breose family (lords of Gower), 82f., 85
Decuman (St), 58
dedications (ecclesiastical): *see* church-dedications
Deer (Aberdeenshire), 22–37
Denisesburna (battle of): *see* Heavenfield (battle of)
De primo statu Landauensis ecclesiae, 53n, 61
De situ Albanie, 3n
De situ Brecheniauc, 53, 54, 59, 65, 66, 70
Diceto (Ralph de), 17n, 76n
Dissolution of the monasteries, 54
Dixton, 64n
Dochelinus (St), 55, 64
Domesday Book, 67, 74, 81, 82, 83, 85
Donald II (King of Scots), 13n
Dorbbéne (of Iona), 41
Dornoch Firth, 46
Druim Cett, 1

Druim Derg Blathuug (battle of), 98
Drummond (William, of Hawthornden), 17
Drust (King of Picts), 97f.
Drust son of Domnall (King of Picts), 42
Drust son of Erp (legendary King of Picts), 44
Duan Albanach, 1, 7n, 14
Dubricius (St): *see* Dyfrig (St)
Dub-da-leithe (Abbot of Armagh), 13
Dubthach (coarb of St Columba and St Adomnán), 13n
Dulane, 57
Dumbarton, 50n, 96
Dunadd, 98
Dunblane, 16
Duncan I (King of Scots), 14
Dunfermline, 16n
Dúngal, 98
Dúngal son of Selbach, 98
Dunkeld, 10, 13, 14, 15, 16
Dunstable, 76n
Dupplin, 27
Dyfed, 68, 72, 75n, 86, 87, 99
Dyfnwal son of Tewdwr (King of Strathclyde), 96
Dyfnwal son of Tewdwr (King of Strathclyde), 71n, 95, 96n
Dyfrig (St), 53n, 56, 60, 61, 62, 63, 64, 65, 70, 91

Eadfrith son of Edwin, 94
Earn (River), 47
East Anglia, 94
Easter, 10, 39, 69, 72, 73n, 74, 86, 87, 89n, 94, 96, 100
Easter-cycles, 39, 41, 42n, 44, 45, 85, 86n
ecclesiastical buildings: *see* buildings (ecclesiastical)
ecclesiastical organisation, 10, 13f., 15f., 16, 38, 40, 47, 54
ecclesiastical reform (mediaeval), 15
Ecgberht (English *peregrinus*), 72, 96
Ecgfrith (King of Northumbria), 38, 47, 51
Ecgwine (St), 59
Echaid filus Cuidini: see Ceolwulf
eclipses, 99
Edinburgh, 2, 49
Edmund (King of England), 88
Edward I (King of England), 3, 4, 5, 6, 7, 8n, 20, 81, 82, 83
Edwin (King of Northumbria), 70, 72, 92, 94, 95n, 99
Egypt, 6

Eidyn: *see* Edinburgh
Elen, daughter of Llywarch of Dyfed, 68, 87
Elfael, 80
Elfoddw ('Archbishop of Gwynedd'), 69n, 86, 87
Elgin, 15, 28, 30, 37
Elmet, 71, 92, 94
Eneuris (Bishop of St David's), 87
Eoganan (King of Picts), 11
Eowa son of Pybba, 94
Erfyn (Bishop of St David's), 74
Eubonia: *see* Man (Isle of)
Ewias Harold, 63
Exeter, 64n
Exeter Martyrology, 55

Faílbe (Abbot of Iona), 47n
family-name, 43
Feradach son of Selbach, 98
Fergus son of Erc (legendary king of Dál Riata), 18, 19
Ferns, 57
Fife, 15, 47, 50
Firth of Forth, 6, 38, 46n, 47, 50, 51
Fitzwilliam of Carew (William), 85
'Florence' of Worcester: *see* John of Worcester
Florentinus (St), 55, 56, 64
Florentius, 49
Fordun (John of), 3n, 6, 7n, 17n, 18
Fortriu, 13, 47
fosterage, 48
Fothad (Bishop of St Andrews), 15
Fourth General Council, 69n
France, 3, 13
Franciscan libraries, 17
Furness, 83n
Fursey (St), 39

Gabrán son of Domangart, 69n, 90
Gai: see Winwaed (battle of)
Galfridus Stephanus (brother of Bishop Urban of Llandaf), 53n, 61
Galloway, 49n
Gartnait son of Domelch (King of Picts), 44n
Gascony, 75
Gaythelos ('prince of the Greeks'), 6
genealogy, 17n, 68, 85, 86, 88n
Geoffrey of Monmouth, 3n, 6, 7, 54, 61, 63, 66, 73, 74, 76, 84n, 92
Gervase of Canterbury, 76n
Gervase (Abbot of Talley, then Bishop of St David's), 77n

Gildas (St), 69n, 73n, 90
Giraldus Cambrensis, 63, 68n, 74, 87
Giric (King of Scots), 14
Gistlian (St), 58
Glamorgan, 82, 83n, 85
Glannauc (island of), 92, 94
Glasbury, 59
Glasgow, 2, 6, 15, 16, 72n, 91
Glastonbury, 54, 64n, 66
glossaries: *see* Old Cornish Glossary
glosses (Irish), 33n
Gloucester, 54, 58–61, 63f., 65, 66
Godebyr (*Vortiporius*), 73
Gododdin, 49f.
gospel-books, 22–37
Gospel of St John (special role of), 35–6
Gower, 58, 81, 82f., 84, 85
granges (Cistercian), 78
'Great Cause' (The), 4
Great Glen, 36
Gruffydd (Abbot of Cwm Hir), 80
Gruffydd son of Rhys, 78
Guénolé (St), 64
Guidgar, 94
Guoidnerth, 62
Guorchiguil (? Bishop), 87n
Gwent, 86, 88
Gwethenoc, 55, 64n
Gwriad (King of Strathclyde), 95
Gwynedd, 51n, 70, 71, 72, 86, 87, 91, 92, 93
Gwynllyw (St), 59, 60, 65

Haddington, 2
Hadrian's Wall, 91
Hanes Gruffud vab Kenan, 88n
hanging bowls, 12
Harold of Ewias, 63
Hatfield Chase (battle of), 70, 92, 94
Hathulfus de Aura, 55
Hay, 80
Heavenfield (battle of), 70, 92
Hebrides, 18
Henry II (King of England), 81n, 82
Henry III (King of England), 78n, 80
Henry of Huntingdon, 8n
Hentland, 60
Heraclius (Emperor), 73
Hereford, 72
Herewald (Bishop of Llandaf), 82
Hexham, 70n
Hiberno-Scandinavians, 15, 88n
Higden (Ranulf), 6
Hild (Abbess of Whitby), 96
Historia Brittonum, 68, 70–2, 92–5

hoards, 12
Holinshed (Raphael), 19n
Holyrood, 20
Hugh de Sai, 78
Humber (River), 6
Huntingdon (Chronicle of), 5, 6, 7n
Hyfaidd (King of Dyfed), 68, 87
hymns, 40, 41
Hywel Dda, son of Cadell (King of Seisyllwg), 68, 87
Hywel son of Rhys, 78

Iago son of Beli (King of Gwynedd), 88n, 91
Íbar (St), 69n, 90
Idris, 92, 100n
Ifor, 73
Illtud (St), 65
Incarnation-dating, 69n, 73n, 74, 86, 90
Innes (Thomas), 1, 3, 7
Innocent III (Pope), 3
inspeximus, 82
Insular art, 22–37, 47, 52
Inuectiua (spurious) of Cicero and Sallust, 68n
Iona, 1, 3n, 8, 10, 12f., 16, 32n, 38–52, 72, 88, 89, 90, 96, 97, 98
Ireland, 7, 9, 13, 14, 15, 40, 41, 47f., 57, 88n, 98
Ireland's Eye, 15n, 32
Irish annals, 1, 6, 7n, 10, 13, 14n, 40, 42–3, 44, 47, 52, 69–73, 84, 85, 86, 87, 88–91, 92–7, 97f., 99, 100
Irish law, 40, 43, 52
Isabella (Countess of Gloucester), 80
Ishmael (St), 58
Islay, 98
Isidore of Seville (St), 70, 73, 74, 85

James VI (King of Scots), 19
James VII (King of Scots), 19
Jocelyn of Furness, 14n
John (King of England), 75, 76, 77n, 82
John de Breose, 82
John of Caen, 4
John of Hexham, 6
John of Salisbury, 35
John of Tayster, 77
John of Worcester, 76, 77n
Jonathan (Abbot of Abergele), 87
Joseph (Bishop of St David's), 74
Julius Caesar, 74
Justin I (Emperor), 73n
Justin II (Emperor), 73n
Justinian (St), 58

kalendars, 53–66
Kebius (St): *see* Cybi (St)
Kells, 13, 27n
Keneder (St), 59, 60
Kenneth mac Alpin: *see* Cinaed mac Alpin
Kentigern (St), 14n, 69n, 70, 91, 99
Kidwelly, 80
Kieran (St), 58
Kildare, 69n
Kingarth (Bute), 98
king-lists, 1, 3n, 4, 5, 6, 8, 10, 14, 17, 18,
    20, 41–5, 51, 71, 95
kingship, 18f., 44
Kintyre, 69n
Kirkmadrine (Wigtownshire), 49
Kirriemuir (Angus), 28
Knox (John), 18

Lambeth Commentary, 25
Lanarkshire, 15
Lanercost (Chronicle of), 5
Latin, 11, 14n, 16, 25f., 36, 37, 39, 40, 45,
    52
Latinus, 49
Laudent (? a cleric), 87n
Launceston, 64n
Lebor Bretnach, 7n
Lebor Gabála Érenn, 7n
lections, 56n
Leeds, 93n
legendaries, 56, 58
Leinster, 69n, 72, 90, 96
Leo I (Emperor), 74n
Leo I (Pope), 69n, 73n, 74, 86, 89n
Liber Vitae of Lindisfarne, 11
Lindisfarne, 11, 27, 41
Linlithgow, 2
Lismore (Ireland), 32, 40, 69n
Lismore (Scotland), 16
litanies, 64n
liturgical objects (*see also* books
    [service-]), 12, 36n
liturgy, 55f.
Llanbadarn Fawr, 58, 59, 60, 61, 64, 75n
Llancarfan, 54, 59f., 62, 65
Llandaf, 54, 57, 58, 60, 61–4, 65, 66, 69n,
    82, 99
Llandudoch (Dyfed), 57n
Llanelwy, 91
Llangibby, 57
Llangrannog, 57
Llanrwst (battle of), 68n
Llantarnan (Glamorgan), 83n
Llanthony, 25
Llanvadog (Brecknock), 58

Llywarch son of Hyfaidd (King of Dyfed),
    68, 87
Llywelyn (King of Gwynedd), 80, 81
Loch Leven, 14
Loch Ness, 48
Locrine (eldest son of Brutus), 7
London, 4, 81n
long-cist burials, 50
Lorrha, 69n
Lothian, 16, 50
Ludger (St), 55
Lul, 96
Lunberth (Bishop of St David's), 87

Macbeth (Bishop of Ross), 15f.
Macbeth (King of Scots), 14
MacFirbis (Duald), 17
Mackenzie (George), 17, 21
Macrobius, 68n
Madog (St), 57f.
Maedóc (St, of Ferns), 53, 57f., 58f.
Mael Brigte mac Tornáin (coarb of St
    Patricle and St Columba), 13n, 25
Mael Brigte ua Maeluanaig, 36f.
Maelduin (of St Andrews), 15
Maelgwn (King of Gwynedd), 73, 91
Maelgwn son of Maelgwn, 77, 78n, 79
Maelienydd, 80
Maelrubai (St), 45, 51
Magsuen (Bishop of Glasgow), 15
Major (John), 19n
Malcolm II (King of Scots), 14
Malcolm III 'Canmore' (King of
    Scots), 15, 17
Man (Isle of), 69n, 90, 99
Manchán, 40
manuscript-abbreviations, 25, 33
manuscript-decoration, 22–37
manuscripts (general), 1–3, 6, 11, 14, 15,
    16, 16f., 17, 18, 19, 20, 22–37, 40, 41,
    41–3, 53–66, 90
manuscripts (index of specified), 113f.
Mar, 38
Maredudd (King of Dyfed), 68, 72n, 87
Maredudd son of Rhys, 81, 82
Margam, 82, 83n
Margaret (Queen of Scots), 15, 16n
Marshall family, 76, 78, 80
Marshall (Richard, Earl of Pembroke),
    78
Martin (George, of Cameron), 20
Martin (Martin), 18
martyrologies, 55, 56
Mary Stewart (Queen of Scots), 2, 19
Maserfelth: see Oswestry (battle of)

Mathgamain (King of Dál Cais), 89
Matthew Paris, 76n
Mavorius, 49
Mearns (the), 38
Meicen: see Hatfield Chase (battle of)
Melrose, 5, 6, 8
Mercia, 71, 88, 92, 96
Merthyr Clydog, 63
mirabilia, 72, 99
Miracula Nynie Episcopi, 8, 49
missa de infirmis, 35–6
Monasterboice, 27n, 34
monastic rules, 40
Monifieth, 27
Monkwearmouth: *see* Wearmouth
Monmouth (Gwent), 54, 54f., 56, 57, 58,
    61, 64
mons Carno (battle of), 71n, 95, 97
Montgomery, 80
Morauienses, 3n
Moray, 15
Moray Firth, 46
Mordred (son of Loth), 7
Morgan, 94
Morton (Earl of, and Regent), 2, 19n
Moses, 18
Mounth (the), 38, 46
Muiredach (Abbot of Monasterboice),
    27n, 33f.
Munster, 89
Mynyddog Mwynfawr (King of
    Gododdin), 9n, 49

Nairn (James), 20
Nauigatio sancti Brendani abbatis, 53n, 58f.
Neath, 80, 82f., 84, 85
Nechtan (Bishop of Aberdeen), 15
Nechtanesmere (battle of, 685), 9n, 38, 47, 95
Nechton son of Cano (*nepos Uirb*), 43
Nechton son of Derile (King of Picts), 9,
    10, 38, 39, 41, 42, 44, 45, 47, 51, 52, 97f.
Ness (River), 9, 48
Nevern, 57
Newport (Gwent), 60
Newquay, 57n
Nicholas ap Gwrgan (Bishop of Llandaf),
    64
Niduari, 8
Ninian (St), 8, 9, 39, 49, 52
Niuduera regio: see Niduari
Nobis (Bishop of St David's), 68n, 87
nomenclature (Scottish personal), 15f.
Nonnita (St), 58
Norham, 4
Normandy, 75

Norse (*see also* vikings), 11n, 12, 88, 96n
North Britons, 45, 49f., 70–2, 85, 92–7,
    98f.
Northumbria, 9n, 10, 11, 33, 38–52, 70–2,
    73, 86n, 92–7
Nynias: *see* Ninian (St)

obits, 10, 47, 88
O'Clery (Michael), 17, 18
Oengus, son of Fergus (King of Picts), 11,
    95n, 97f.
Offa (King of Mercia), 72n, 88
O'Flaherty (Roderic), 17, 21n
ogom, 46
Óláfr, 13n, 88n
Old Cornish Glossary, 53, 55, 64n, 65, 66
oral literature, 17, 20, 40, 44–5
orans, 32
origin-legend (Pictish), 14
Orkney Islands, 48, 51
Oronsay, 16
Osbald (King of Northumbria), 11
Osfrith son of Edwin, 94
Osney (Oxfordshire), 76n
Osred (King of Northumbria), 96
Oswald (King of Northumbria), 38, 47,
    70, 72, 86n, 92, 94, 95, 99
Oswestry (battle of), 70, 92, 94, 95
Oswine son of Osric (King of Deira), 95
Oswiu (King of Northumbria), 9n, 70, 72,
    92f., 96, 99
Oudoceus (St), 61, 65
Ougen (King of Picts), 71n, 95, 96n
overlordship, 51
Owain son of Gruffydd (lord of S.
    Cardigan), 77, 78, 79
Owain son of Hywel, 68, 86, 87
Owain son of Maredudd, 87

Padarn (St), 56n, 57, 58, 60
Painscastle (*castrum Matildis*), 80
papal administration, 75
paruchiae, 13, 48, 62, 75n
pastoral staff, 59
Paternus (St): *see* Padarn (St)
Patrick (St), 9n, 13n, 18, 40, 48, 50, 69n,
    73n, 90
patronymic, 43
Pehthelm (Bishop of Whithorn), 39
Pembroke, 76, 80
Penda (King of Mercia), 70, 72, 92f., 94,
    95, 99
penitentials, 40
Perth, 2
Peter (St), 10, 39, 51

Peterborough, 5, 76n
Peter de Leia (of St David's), 82
Pharaoh, 6, 7
Pictish language, 49, 69n, 99
Pictland, 5, 8, 9, 10, 11, 13, 33, 38–52, 71, 72, 89, 95, 96, 97f., 99
pilgrimage, 39, 41, 48
Pinkerton (John), 18
Pippin of Heristal, 100
plague, 8, 48f., 88n, 93, 97n
pocket-gospel-books, 22–37
Pontardawe (Glamorgan), 32n
Possessio agrorum sancti Paterni, 58n, 60
Powys, 75n, 86, 87
Premonstratensians, 16, 77n
primacy (ecclesiastical), 62f.
Prise (John), 54
Processus Baldredi contra figmenta regis Anglie, 7
Prosper of Aquitaine, 89n
Psalterium Gallicanum, 33
Psalterium Hebraicum, 25n, 26
psalters, 2n, 24n, 25, 26, 26f., 32, 33–5
pseudo-history, 7, 54, 56, 66
Pybba, 94

Radnor, 57n, 80
Ralph de Diceto: *see* Diceto (Ralph de)
Ralph of Coggeshall, 76n
records (administrative), 2, 3, 4, 8n
Reformation, 1, 2, 3, 18
Reginald (son of Somerled), 16
relics, 13
Restenneth Priory (Angus), 10f., 51
Rhain (King of Dyfed), 87
Rhigyfarch (of Llanbadarn Fawr), 59, 75n
Rhodri son of Hywel, 68, 86
Rhos, 86
Rhoscrowther (Dyfed), 58
Rhun son of Urien, 92
Rhydderch (? Bishop of St David's), 74
Rhys (the Lord), 77, 78, 79, 85
Rhys Gryg (lord of Ystrad Tywi), 78
Rhys son of Gruffydd, 77, 79
Rhys son of Maelgwn, 79
Rhys son of Maredudd (lord of Ystrad Tywi), 78n, 81
Rhys Fychan, son of Rhys Mechyll, 81
Rhys Mechyll, son of Rhys Gryg, 78
Richard (Count of Cornwall), 80
Richard (Count of Pembroke, brother of William Marshall), 80
Rishanger (William), 83
Robert Bruce (King of Scots), 5
Robert (Earl of Gloucester), 61

Roger de Mortimer, 78
Roger of Hoveden, 76
Roger of Wendover, 76n
Rome, 10, 39, 49, 63, 90
Rosemarkie, 16
Ross, 15f.
royal patronage of the Church, 51

Saddell, 16
Sadwrnfyw Hael (Bishop of St David's), 87
St Andrews, 2, 6, 10, 15, 16, 16f., 20, 51f., 98
St Bride's Bay, 58
St David's (Dyfed), 54, 58, 59, 62n, 63, 68, 72–6, 76f., 77n, 78n, 79, 80, 84, 85, 86–100
St Dogmael's, 57
Saint-Florent de Saumur, 55, 56
St Mary's, Monmouth (*see also* Monmouth), 60, 64
St Ninian's Isle, 11, 12, 13
St Peter of Sele (Sussex), 55
St Peter's, Gloucester: *see* Gloucester
Saints' Lives, 6, 17, 18, 40, 41, 53–66
saoi, 13
Sallust, 68n
Saumur, 55
Scone, 2, 5, 16n
Scota (daughter of Pharaoh), 6, 7, 17n
Scotichronicon, 6
Scotland, 1–52, 83, 97–8
Scott (John, Lord Scotstarvet), 19
Scottish Chronicle, 3n
script, 7n, 11, 22–37, 40, 41, 82
scriptoria, 8, 10, 11, 13, 15, 22–37, 40, 41, 44, 45, 55, 57, 64, 65f., 68, 76, 82, 83
secularisation of the Church, 14, 40
secular learned classes, 15
Ségéne (Abbot of Iona), 47n
Seisyllwg, 68, 87
Selbach, 98
Selyf son of Cynan (King of Powys), 90
Senchus Fer nAlban, 1, 14, 40f.
Serlo (Abbot of St Peter's, Gloucester), 59, 60
Seven Sisters (Glamorgan), 32n
Severn (River), 92, 100n
shrines, 12f., 13, 28
Sibbald (Richard), 17
Sibbald (Robert), 20
Sigismund (St), 55
Simul son of Drust, 97
Skye, 97n
Solinus, 68n
Southwark, 76n

Spottiswoode (John), 1, 2, 17, 18
Stephanus (*alias* Galfridus, brother of
   Bishop Urban of Llandaf), 61
Stewart (Lord James), 2
Steyning (Sussex), 55
Stirling, 2, 50n
Strata Florida, 67, 77–80, 83, 84, 85
Strathclyde, 71, 72, 86, 95, 96, 99
Strathearn, 47
Strathmore, 47
Sulien (of Llanbadarn Fawr, Bishop of St
   David's), 74, 75n
symbol-stones (Pictish), 9, 11, 28, 29, 35,
   37, 44f., 45–7, 51
Synod of Birr, 69n
synods, 40
Synodus Episcoporum ('Pa. 1'), 52
Synodus Urbis Legionis, 73n, 91n

Talley (*Tallelecheu*), 77f.
Talorg son of Congus, 98
Talorgan (King of Picts), 71n, 95
Talorgan son of Drostan (King of Atholl,
   Pictish sub-king), 98
Talorgan son of Fergus, 98
Tatheus (St), 56n
tau-headed crozier, 32, 37
Tay (River), 8, 15, 38, 47, 50
Teilo (St), 53n, 61f., 63
Teuderius (St), 55
Tewdwr son of Beli (King of Strathclyde),
   71n, 95, 96n
Tewkesbury, 76n, 80, 82
Theobald (Archbishop of Canterbury),
   60
Thomas (Becket, Archbishop of
   Canterbury), 81n
'three fifties' (division of psalter-text), 33
Tintern, 83
Tírechán, 47f.
Tironensians, 16
title-deeds (monastic), 22, 37, 53, 58, 59,
   60, 61, 62, 63
tonsure, 39
translation (of a saint), 57, 60n
Trent (River), 6
Troy, 6
Trumwine (Bishop of Abercorn), 38
Tryffin son of Rhain (King of Dyfed), 87
Tuadal (of St Andrews), 15
Tuathal (*prímepscop Fortrenn*), 13
Tuathalán (Abbot of St Andrews), 52
Tudy (St), 64
Tweed (River), 6
twelfth-century renaissance, 15

Tynemouth, 5

Udal, 11n
Ulrim, 3n
Urban (Bishop of Llandaf), 61, 63
Urquhart (*Airchartdan*), 48
Ussher (Archbishop James), 17, 32, 33n

Valentinian II (Emperor), 73n
Valle Crucis, 67
Valliscaulian monks, 16
Varrains, 55
Vegetius, 68n
Vergil, 8n
vikings (*see also* Norse), 11, 12, 13, 20, 40
Vitruvius, 68n
Viventius, 49

Walahfrid Strabo, 12f.
Wales, 25, 32, 53–100
Walter of Coventry, 76n
Walter of Guisborough, 4
Ware (James), 17
Waverley, 76n, 81, 83, 84, 85
Wearmouth, 11, 72, 96
Welsh Bicknor (*Bicenouria*), 64n
Welsh Marches, 54, 59, 63f., 66, 78, 80, 85
Wessex, 88
Whitchurch, 60, 64
Whithorn (Wigtownshire), 49
Whitland, 77n, 79, 80, 83, 84, 85
Wilfred (Bishop of St David's), 59, 74
Wilfrid (St), 9n, 38
William I (the Bastard, King of England),
   7
William (Abbot of St Peter's, Gloucester),
   59
William (Archdeacon of Llandaf), 60
William de Breose, 82
William of Malmesbury, 6, 54, 66
William of Newburgh, 76n
William of Saltmarsh (Bishop of
   Llandaf), 82n
William Marshall, 80
William the Lion (King of Scots), 15
Winchcombe, 76n
Winchester, 76n, 81
Winwaed (battle of), 70, 92, 95
Wonnastow (Gwent), 64n
Worcester, 76, 81, 85
Wykes (Thomas), 76n

York, 41
Ystrad Meurig, 77
Ystrad Tywi, 77f., 81, 83